1987

THE LITERATURE OF IMAGES

The Literature of Images

NARRATIVE LANDSCAPE FROM *JULIE* TO *JANE EYRE*

Doris Y. Kadish

Rutgers University Press
New Brunswick and London

"Landscape, Ideology, and Plot in Balzac's *Les Chouans*," *Nineteenth-Century French Studies* 13 no. 1 (Summer-Fall 1984), 43–57.

"The Ambiguous Lily Motif in Balzac's *Le Lys dans la vallée*," *International Fiction Review* 10 no. 1 (1983), 8–14.

"Symbolism of Exile: The Opening Description in *Atala*," *French Review* 55 no. 3 (1982), 358–366.

Library of Congress Cataloging-in-Publication Data

Kadish, Doris Y.

The literature of images.

Bibliography: p.

Includes index.

1. French fiction—History and criticism.
2. Landscape in literature. 3. English fiction—History and criticism. 4. Literature, Comparative—French and English. 5. Literature, Comparative—English and French.

I. Title.

PQ637.L34K3   1986   843'.009   86–3810

ISBN 0–8135–1183–6

British CIP Information Available

For Raymond Woller, my most insightful critic and best friend;
and for my children: Matthew, Rachel, and Eugene

Contents

THE LITERATURE OF IMAGES

I

Reading Landscape

A Pictorial Reading

Almost exactly in the middle of what may well be Honoré de Balzac's most important novel, *Illusions perdues,* there occurs a passage that is of distinct importance to the history of the novel. Balzac's hero, the aspiring writer Lucien de Rubempré, is being initiated into the mercantile practices of the Parisian world of publishing by the cynical journalist and hack writer Lousteau. Here is the lesson Lousteau gives his naïve young confrere on how to dash off a book review:

> And then you explain that nowadays a new literature is growing up that relies on dialogue (the easiest of all literary forms) and descriptions, which dispense with the necessity for thought. You contrast the novels of Voltaire, Diderot, Sterne and Le Sage, so trenchant, so compact, with the modern novel that consists of nothing but descriptions, so dear to Walter Scott. In such a genre there is scope for invention, but for little else. "The novels of Walter Scott are a literary fashion, but not a literary style," you will say. You proceed to fulminate against this lamentable fashion, in which ideas are diluted, and beaten thin, a style easily imitated by anyone, a style in which any writer can win facile success—a fashion that you describe as the "literature of images."[1]

Lousteau is being facetious, at least in part; for a short while later he will advise Lucien to lavish the highest praise on that "literature of images" which he earlier claimed to scorn. But despite the tongue-in-cheek tone, Lousteau's remarks do report an important change that took place in the novel's history and one that Balzac himself did much to advance.

Sometime after Voltaire, and the older "literature of ideas" he exemplifies, there emerged a newer "literature of images" which increasingly contained description, notably the strikingly modern sort called landscape. Landscape was almost completely new when it emerged in the literature of images—as opposed, say, to the portrait, which has a long and established narrative history; later it was followed by such other descriptive forms as the still life and the cityscape. Landscape is of special interest because it was one of the most distinctive descriptive forms to occur in the literature of images. These forms can be referred to as "narrative descrip-

1

tion" when they occur in novels, rather than in poetry; and this term can be defined as a prose passage that dwells at length on the physical properties of the world and interrupts the main plot or the character development of the novel.

Until the literature of images emerged, the main kinds of novels—the picaresque, the epistolary, the *roman-mémoires*—rarely concerned themselves with the appearance of things, their didactic or sentimental focus being more on man than on the world, more on conduct than on atmosphere; novelists shared with thinkers and artists generally the prevailing eighteenth-century conviction that the "proper study of mankind is man." But all that changed. Suddenly novelists seemed to be as interested in nature's moods and forms as poets were, and they proceeded to regale their readers' imaginations with detailed pictorial and geographical descriptions. Readers, for their part, suddenly turned to the novel for the picturesque scenes that the new descriptive novel provided—scenes of gardens, towns viewed from afar, mountain terrains, and rivers.

A concrete example of this new narrative description of nature occurs near the end of another novel by Balzac, *La Peau de chagrin,* when the hero, Raphaël de Valentin, seeks refuge in nature as his death approaches. Raphaël has bound himself, through a strange, diabolical pact made in a moment of despair, to a fate whereby his every desire is fulfilled, but the fulfilling produces a gradual shrinkage of the skin of a wild ass or onager and concomitantly of his life-span. As the end comes near and he retreats to the country, he discovers an odd geographic configuration, which the narrator invites the reader to conjure up in his mind's eye.

The passage begins with a broad panoramic view of a craterlike valley in a mountainous region:

> Imagine an upturned cone, a cone of granite broadly hollowed out, a sort of punch-bowl whose edges were chipped and cracked in fantastic fashion: here were flat slabs of bare rock, smooth of surface, azure-tinted, with the sun's rays playing over them as on a mirror; elsewhere were cliffs gashed with fissures and cracked by ravines which in many places were crowned by groups of stunted trees twisted out of shape by the winds, while underneath hung blocks of lava which sooner or later the action of the rains was certain to bring crashing down.

Next follows about a page more of description in which the crater is viewed from a variety of angles and heights and in which all of its elements are detailed: caverns, vegetation, pools, meadows, rocks, streams, and the like. Finally, toward the end, the higher regions are described:

> At times and turn by turn those tapering needles, those audacious piles, those caverns in mid-air were lit up as the sun moved round to

them or in accordance with the play of the light and were tinged with gold, deep crimson or bright pink, or perhaps took on grey or leaden tints. These summits in fact offered a constantly changing spectacle like the iridescent shimmer on a pigeon's throat. Often . . . a gleaming sunbeam pierced through to the depths of that laughing riot of blossoms and frolicked in the waters of the mountain lake like the streak of gold which steals through the chink of a shutter and invades a Spanish bedroom, sealed for the siesta. When the sun shone directly above the ancient crater which some antediluvian upheaval had filled with water, its rocky walls grew warm, the extinct volcano heated up once more and this rapid rise in temperature fostered germination, quickened vegetation, coloured the flowers and ripened the fruit in this tiny, forgotten corner of the earth.[2]

How does the reader respond to this extended landscape description, which delays and interrupts the plot? For surely the kind of detailed, attentive reading this passage demands is different from that demanded by other narrative components such as dialogue or action scenes. Modern readers, having already gained familiarity with long descriptive passages from the literature of the past two centuries, may fail to appreciate the issue of how to read such passages: their familiarity with description may prevent them from seeing the need to establish an adequate way of reading narrative description.

A common way, from Balzac's day down to the present time, has been to read a descriptive passage by focusing on certain features that the description has in common with a work of visual art—to read it, in short, in the somewhat narrow and superficial way in which many view a painting or photograph. This "pictorial" way of reading has indeed been so common that, despite its inadequacies, it often continues even today to prevail as one of the main ways to read narrative description.

A typical pictorial reading of landscape would focus, for example, on the notions of color and light. Thus the reader of *La Peau de chagrin* would notice that in the first part of the description quoted above the rocks are described as "azure-tinted, with the sun's rays playing over them as on a mirror"; while in the second part, the effects of color and light are even more striking. As the sun moves, the rocks change in hue from gold, crimson, and pink to gray and other dark shades. The overall effect is compared, in a bold and unusual metaphor, to the "iridescent shimmer on a pigeon's throat." And still another uncommon image involves comparing a ray of light penetrating an enclosed room at midday to "a streak of gold which steals through the chink of a shutter and invades a Spanish bedroom, sealed for the siesta." It would be tedious to adduce further examples of what is recognizable by now as the standard discourse of the *explication de texte* (minus the stylistic and grammatical ingredients) as well as the idiom of most landscape criticism down to the middle of the twentieth century.

Although the aesthetic interest of the pictorial effects which such criticism highlights is clearly important, there is also something vaguely unsatisfying about the praise that tends to be lavished on them, as if they were per se the marks of the superior novelist. Admittedly, the literature of images does display a pictorial, imagistic character; any reading that denies this character can be said, prima facie, to be inadequate. The main benefit that accrues from reading pictorially is to encourage a close, attentive reading in which the reader plays an active, picturing role. Such a reading is far more important for landscape description than for other components of narration; for whereas rapid reading may make it possible to cull the chief episodes of the plot, it is inadequate for grasping landscape's detailed pictorial, imagistic effect. And in the absence of that effect, there ultimately is no reading of landscape at all, merely a gap in the text where the reader has failed to grasp or has skipped a certain textual process.

The pictorial reading—as practiced in the *explication de texte* or other similar formalistic exercises—only accounts partially and superficially, however, for the multifarious meanings that landscape can be discovered to possess and produce in the novel. Thus despite the undeniable need to read landscape pictorially, there is an equally urgent need to go beyond a pictorial reading to develop a fuller, enriched, or "completed" reading. I shall identify such a reading as a "relational reading" and, in the next section, shall describe and illustrate three internal relational ways of reading that landscape: first in relation to narrative point of view; second in relation to the novel's other parallel or contrasting descriptive passages; and third in relation to the socio-political outlook that underlies the novel and finds symbolic expression within its pages in conflictual, binarily opposed thematic terms. They are (for reasons considered in the concluding chapter) the only relational ways of reading landscape that make it possible to obtain an enriched and complete reading of the literature of images, as analyses of some exemplary novels will reveal.

There are also external elements that can be linked to narrative descriptions: the pastoral tradition, garden descriptions in eighteenth-century novels, and referential borrowings in novels. These additional ways of viewing landscape lead to a fuller understanding of a relational reading. My discussion of these components shows how landscape developed over time, thereby providing some historical information to give meaning to the practice of narrative description. This chapter concludes with the claim that a relational reading of landscape is a genuinely semiotic reading, though it differs in at least one significant respect from most contemporary semiotic readings of narrative description.

The following chapters will use this reading to illuminate various key novels in the literature of images, works that have been traditionally identified by critics and general readers with nature description in the novel: Jean-Jacques Rousseau's *Julie; ou La Nouvelle Héloïse,* Jacques-Henri Bernardin de Saint-Pierre's *Paul et Virginie,* François-René de Chateaubriand's *Atala,* Mrs. Ann Radcliffe's *The Mysteries of Udolpho,* Mary Wollstonecraft Shelley's *Frankenstein,* Balzac's *Les Chouans* and *Le Lys dans la vallée,* Gustave Flaubert's *Salammbô* and *L'Education sentimentale,* and Charlotte Brontë's *Jane Eyre.* My conclusion presents a theoretical argument for the necessity of the relational reading, based on the semiotic conventions and effects that govern the reading of narrative landscape.

A Relational Reading

To establish firmly the difference between a pictorial and a relational reading, it is necessary to begin with perspective, a fundamental component of an adequate reading of landscape, which needs to be extended beyond its traditional limits in order to provide a more integrated, meaningful reading of landscapes in novels.

In order to consider the workings of perspective, readers typically seek to discover within a landscape a specific vantage point or locus from which the narrative scene, like a pictorial one, is meant to be perceived. In the case of the landscape in *La Peau de chagrin* considered earlier, the vantage point that affords a consistent visual orientation is one from on high, sometimes looking down into the craterlike valley, at other times looking around it, at still other times gazing even higher toward mountain formations: "at the bottom of this bowl," "around this deep basin," "at a certain altitude." From that point in space large shapes in the surrounding topography can be observed: slabs of rock and hanging blocks of lava, a meadow surrounding the crater and a three-acre-wide pool at the bottom of it, streams flowing down the sides of the mountains, caverns in midair, and mountain peaks. Most of the phenomena perceived in this scene are of the large-scale or long-range sorts seen from a distance.

Extending the notion of perspective and relating it to "point of view," taken in a broad sense, provides a more adequate and interesting reading. That broad sense, as defined by a number of modern critics,[3] refers both to the physical vision and to the mental outlook or attitudes of characters who serve as centers of interest in a novel. These critics designate such characters as "focalizers" and attribute to them a privileged role with respect to narration; in other words, they consider that a close tie exists in fiction between the question "Who sees?" and the question "Who speaks?" (a more detailed consideration of this issue is found in chapter 5). These questions imply others concerning where, when, and why the visual or verbal act takes place and to whom it is directed. Since it is typical of narrative landscape to play a crucial role with respect to all of these questions, it is not enough to identify the perspective in a particular passage, for example merely that the view is from on high in *La Peau de chagrin*. It is also necessary to relate that perspective to the larger issue of the novel's total narrative mechanisms of point of view.

Although *La Peau de chagrin* begins with an invisible, unidentified narrator outside the novel, there is nonetheless an important sense in which the reader is "with" Raphaël de Valentin throughout. During roughly one third of the work, while he recounts his past life to Emile, Raphaël himself plays the role of the narrator, thereby reinforcing the equation the reader is likely to make between Raphaël's viewpoint—his thoughts, feelings, actions, and visual perceptions—and the narrator's. But even when the narrator is recounting Raphaël's outlook and vision, Raphaël frequently serves as the center of interest and focalizer of the novel. Accordingly, there is every reason to take Raphaël himself as the implied viewer and describer of the scene under consideration here. And indeed, the text supports such an interpretation. Tormented in mind and body, tragically doomed to a futile and untimely death, Raphaël sees barren rocks that are "chipped and cracked in fantastic fashion," "cliffs gashed with fissures and cracked by ravines," "stunted trees twisted out of shape by the winds," "blocks of lava which sooner or later the action of the rains was certain to bring crashing down." Having just prior to this scene killed a man in a duel and fled from the company of other people, he seeks comfort in nature and thus is predisposed to notice the friendly, happy sunbeam which "pierced through to the depths of that laughing riot of blossoms and frolicked in the waters of the mountain lake." Further examples could be adduced, but already it is apparent that the details perceived in this descriptive passage are not gratuitous instances of pictorialism. On the contrary, they relate meaningfully to the specific point of view of the novel's protagonist.

The second element of the relational reading involves linking a narrative description to other descriptive passages. For *La Peau de chagrin*, the most important observation to be made in this regard is that the description of nature already cited, which occurs near the end, has a parallel descriptive passage near the beginning. There Raphaël obtains the wild ass's skin in an antique shop, the arcane and recondite contents of which are enumerated and described in painstaking detail over several pages. In this description, as in the one at the end, Raphaël is near death and totally cut off from all meaningful human interaction. More, in both cases he "rises above" his condition in the descriptive setting, both physically (ascending the stairs of the antique shop in one case and the mountains in the other) and mentally and emotionally as well (reaching a transcendent, philosophical state in both passages). That one descriptive scene occurs in the city and the other in the country, that one concerns itself with ancient arts and the other with an ancient geological formation, that one embodies Raphaël's will to desire and the other his denial of desire are contrasts that merely sharpen the underlying parallelism of the two descriptive segments of the novel. And there are further similarities and differences that link the description at the end to a variety of others. One especially striking example occurs about one-third of the way into the novel, when Raphaël's view from his garret window of the rooftop gardens of Paris is described; another occurs about two-thirds into the novel in the description of the greenhouse in which he and Pauline dine.

The third element of the relational reading should now be mentioned, for it is still not enough to observe that it is Raphaël who views the landscape from on high in the passage being considered as well as in several parallel and contrasting scenes in *La Peau de chagrin*. In order to arrive at an adequate method for reading narrative landscape, it is necessary to take the further step of considering the social and political features displayed in the description of nature: not just because Balzac and others in the literature of images often dealt explicitly with social and political issues but because of the fact, taken to be axiomatic in this book, that those issues are inherent in all of the forms and functions of literature and most distinctly in the novel. Consider the fact, for example, that the land, the object viewed, is inextricably linked with the issue of the personal and collective possession of property. Now, rarely in the literature of images is the land viewed by its possessor; the view of the country gentleman complacently surveying his property occurs in the prehistory, as it were, of this literature but is not itself a truly evolved form of narrative landscape. On the contrary, the act of viewing in this literature is typically performed by a person who is in some way cut off or alienated from the land: all viewers of landscape are in some sense avatars of that prototypical outsider, Rousseau's Saint-Preux, who will be considered in the next chapter. Indeed it can be argued that alienation is the very bedrock of landscape's existence: thus argues Fredric Jameson, who locates the origin of landscape description in the generalized separation from community ties and traditional social forms that resulted from the rise of capitalism. According to Jameson, what occurs in the process of capitalist reification is that "sight becomes a separate activity in its own right, it acquires new objects that are themselves the products of a process of abstraction and rationalization"; "the visual features of ritual, or those practices of imagery still functional in religious ceremonies, are secularized and reorganized into ends in themselves, in easel painting and new genres like landscape."[4]

Because narrative landscape tends thus to be highly social and political in nature, a relational reading attempts to examine texts with an eye to discovering, through and in their formal, narrative properties, underlying social or economic meanings. Fredric Jameson gives a concise summation of this process of discerning the underlying meanings of forms in his account of the way Claude Lévi-Strauss describes the patterns used in primitive art and culture. As Jameson tells us, "it must be a description already pre-pared and oriented toward transcending the purely formalistic, a movement which is achieved not by abandoning the formal level for something extrinsic to it—such as some inertly social 'content'—but rather immanently, by construing purely formal patterns as a symbolic enactment of the social within the formal and the aesthetic."[5] That it is possible to make such a movement from the formal to the social with respect to narrative landscape—that indeed little has been understood about descriptions of nature in novels without thus transcending their purely aesthetic surface appearance—is one of the basic subthemes that will be developed in this book.

In the passage from *La Peau de chagrin,* the central image of the volcano immediately emerges as an analogue to the violent, disruptive, destructive forces at work both in Raphaël's life and in the society he inhabits at large. These forces can be equated with the excessive, unprincipled, individualistic will to power and possession that, for Balzac, the revolutionary era inaugurated and which the Revolution of 1830 exemplified. The volcano—with its "blocks of lava which sooner or later the action of the rains was certain to bring crashing down"—symbolizes the violent, cataclysmic change that according to Balzac the nefarious forces of individualism were producing in his times. Yet the passage as a whole comes to a close on a positive note, one of rebirth and renewal: the suggestion is that there is a meaning to—a necessary passage through and beyond—the moment of self-destruction and disillusion depicted in the novel. For the "children of the Revolution," as Raphaël and his friends are called, there is hope: not perhaps for the single doomed individual but for the generation as a whole. The promise of growth and positive change held out to that generation can be plainly discerned in the utopian image at the very end of the description in which, as the sun shines down on the ancient crater, "its rocky walls grew warm, the extinct volcano heated up once more and this rapid rise in temperature fostered germination, quickened vegetation, coloured the flowers and ripened the fruit in this tiny, forgotten corner of the earth." *La Peau de chagrin* may be one of Balzac's least socially and historically oriented novels, but it nevertheless does not confine itself to matters purely individual and personal.[6]

Landscape, then, cannot be fully understood or appreciated independently of its relations to narrative point of view, to other parallel or contrasting descriptive passages, and finally to the novel's social and political outlook. If only three relations have been singled out here, it is because

they are necessary for a complete understanding of the novels in the literature of images. Why these three are necessary, and how they are themselves interrelated, will be considered later.

The remaining sections of this chapter elaborate three external elements
that can be used in reading landscape description, elements that pertain to
three overlapping moments in the history of the narrative landscape's formation: the age-old pastoral tradition dating back to Theocritus, Vergil,
and others; garden descriptions in eighteenth-century novels, especially
English novels; and referential elements from the diverse scientific and artistic writings that span the eighteenth century. These elements point
outside the novel and lead the reader outward or backward to the novel's
historical antecedents or to intertextual traditions. Although they do not
provide a complete historical explanation, they do help to illuminate the
way narrative landscape came into being.

The Pastoral Tradition

The pastoral tradition does not provide a "true beginning" for nature description. As Derrida maintains, everything in the world of language is
"always-already-there,"[7] and the narrative landscape is no exception. Telling a story is an act that dates back to prehistoric times, and so, undoubtedly, does the act of using nature scenery in that story. Thus the initial assumptions readers may make, that there existed some inventor or initiator
of the pastoral or of the pastoral's use in the novel, should undoubtedly be
rejected. Such an assumption is neither helpful nor useful.

Moreover, the pastoral does not exist in the novel as a coherent, complete literary system but rather as an arsenal of nature phrases, places,
themes, connotations, and the like. Its signifiers and signifieds, forms and
meanings, which were used consciously and according to strict generic
conventions in the genuine pastoral tradition, now surface, unsystemati-
cally, from the minds and pens of later describers. Pastoral language in
the description of nature in the novel is thus fragmented and but a remnant of a former intertextual tradition. It is a heterogeneous repertoire of
linguistic elements such as that from which, according to Lévi-Strauss,
the primitive mythmaker and the *bricoleur* construct new wholes.[8]

The lexical remnants from the pastoral tradition discernible in the narrative landscape can be characterized by modern standards as both rigidly
conventional and visually imprecise. Over and over again the same fixed
items recur (trees, springs, grass, flowers, fruit, music), invariably accompanied by the same vague epithets (flowery meadows, crystal streams,
shady groves). The indistinct "lovely place" is typical, as are the tautolog-
ical "liquid fountains" to which the eighteenth-century aesthetician Hugh
Blair objected; the pastoral expression clearly does not aim at that regional

and climatic particularization which since Wordsworth readers have come
to expect in a natural scene and which already began to emerge early in the
eighteenth century in James Thomson's *Seasons*. No matter whether the
geographical location described is in the north or south, whether the season is summer or winter or the time of day evening or dawn: the language
will be the same—that same nonparticular, universal poetic diction
which aims to describe, as Pope said, "nature to advantage dressed." The
goal of pastoral language then was not particularization but poetry, not
reality but rhymes and rhythms that would please the reader by their harmonious, their musical, and also their familiar ring: for there is an important sense in which the pastoral tradition is a tradition of repetition rather
than representation, of copying Vergil rather than nature.

Remnants of the pastoral language still appear frequently when nature
description begins to enter the novel in the eighteenth century. An example is provided in Rousseau's *La Nouvelle Héloïse*, a novel perhaps
known primarily for its striking and dramatic alpine scenery. But this
scenery is not without its more conventional components. Indeed the
mountains are often presented in Rousseau's novel in a distinctly pastoral
fashion, as the following description can serve to illustrate: "the small
piece of ground where we were displayed the charms of a cheerful and sylvan refuge; some streams filtered through the rocks and rolled over the
green in crystal rivulets. Some wild fruit trees bent their heads over ours,
the moist and fresh earth was covered with grass and flowers."[9] Elsewhere
such stock pastoral items as pleasant meadows, chirping birds, green
grass, fertile banks, and the like similarly appear. In addition to Rousseau
there is of course Bernardin de Saint-Pierre, whose *Paul et Virginie* is referred to in his own preface as a pastoral. This work too contains the standard conventional vocabulary, despite and alongside its sporadic forays
into the language of exotic flora, fauna, and geography.

From Rousseau to descriptive writers of the nineteenth century, there is
a steady diminution of pastoral language but not a total disappearance.
For example, the novels of Chateaubriand and Balzac to be studied later
still contain the stock bucolic ingredients of waters and shade as well as
such conventional phrases as "delightful country" and "pleasant place."
These intertextual elements derived from the pastoral provide descriptive
writers with a linguistic background, an overall tone—not so much because they consciously choose that background or tone but merely because
it was part of the received tradition of nature description. Meanwhile,
Balzac's vocabulary in the 1830s evinces less pastoralism than Chateaubriand's at the beginning of the nineteenth century, and his in turn less
than Rousseau's and Bernardin's in the eighteenth century. Gradually,
then, the importance of that tradition dating back to Theocritus and

Vergil, that time-honored conventional language of nature, recedes. But it never totally disappears. Throughout the nineteenth century the pastoral lives on in nature descriptions of all stripes, though with the passage of time only as the increasingly dim trace of a language of the past.

Remnants of the pastoral tradition have a specific function in the novel that can best be explained as that of producing a reminder of the literature of past centuries or, to use a term that will be further developed later in this chapter, an "effect" of poetry and art. In producing such an effect, the pastoral remnant bespeaks the existence of an artistic tradition to which author and reader alike are implicitly bound—and by extension, the existence of tradition itself. Using the pastoral lexicon is in other words one way in which ties with the past— specifically, with a common artistic, cultural, and national past—are indirectly established and promoted in the text.

This is perhaps the time to mention, throughout the tradition of the pastoral romance and on through the nineteenth century, the related practice of inserting direct quotations from poetry into prose texts, quotations that function in conjunction with pastoral remnants to produce an effect of poetry and art. This practice has an especially strong hold in the English novel: as early as Richardson and as late as the Brontës, those novels containing narrative landscape also contain—and frequently near or within the landscape itself—lines of verse. In France, the practice gradually diminishes and eventually disappears: whereas *La Nouvelle Héloïse* contains direct quotations from Tasso, Petrarch, and other Italian poets, by the time of Balzac quoting from poetry has ceased to be a standard novelistic practice. Revealingly, with respect to the differences between England and France, when Bernardin's novel, *Paul et Virginie,* crossed the channel, the English translator saw fit—given the filiation with the pastoral emphasized by the author of the preface and within the text itself—to add actual poems to the text, an addition that was presumably thought to be de rigueur in an English version of a novel with such marked pastoral overtones.

An especially distinct and long-lived remnant of the pastoral literature of past centuries in novels is the pleasant place or *locus amoenus.* This privileged, secluded place, where the reflective or artistic mind can find peace, harmony, and repose, recurs throughout the history of literature, assuming such diverse forms as Eden, Elysium, or Arcadia and having such different names as Homer's Garden of Alcinous, Spenser's Bower of Bliss, or Shakespeare's Forest of Arden. Its characteristic ingredients are detailed by Ernst R. Curtius: "It is . . . a beautiful, shaded natural site. Its minimum ingredients comprise a tree (or several trees), a meadow, and a spring or brook. Birdsong and flowers may be added. The most elaborate examples also add a breeze."[10] When some or most of these ingredients occur in a novel—but especially when the very act of calling a place beautiful occurs—there exists a trace of the pastoral tradition. This marker is almost inevitably present in the novels of the literature of images: the description of the mountain refuge in *La Nouvelle Héloïse* quoted earlier is referred to as "a pleasant place," as are so many other landscapes in eighteenth- and nineteenth-century novels. Like other lexical remnants of the pastoral and like poetic quotations, the *locus amoenus* produces an effect of art and a reaffirmation of tradition.

It also has another function, that of announcing a pause in the novel's narrative diachrony or unfolding in time. Indeed, Renato Poggioli notes that throughout literary history the distinctive formal property of the *locus amoenus* was its intrusiveness, its acting to interrupt the main development of a story:

> Its presence in an epic or a chivalric poem, in a romance or a tragicomedy, foretells the unexpected apparition of a bucolic episode, which breaks the main action or pattern, suspending for a while the heroic, romantic, or pathetic mood of the whole. . . . Since the pause normally occurs in an obscure and faraway place, the intermezzo should be termed the "pastoral oasis." Such "oases" appear in the *Aeneid*, the *Commedia*, the *Furioso*, the *Lusiadas, Don Quixote,* and *As You Like It.*[11]

The *locus amoenus* is thus doubly suggestive of tradition. It suggests tradition in a clear-cut way through calling a place beautiful and thus producing a reminder of the poetic language of the past. But it also does so in a less obvious way by interrupting the narrative flow of the text. The interruption—this dwelling on one protracted moment in time—may indirectly suggest to the reader the denial of change that clinging to tradition often represents.

With the thematic remnants found in the literature of images, as with the lexical ones, the pastoral again plays an important role, even though it is one that cannot always be easily pinpointed or formally identified. One of the most important themes concerns the distinctive temporal setting of the pastoral, the past. Ever since Theocritus nostalgically recalled the simple joys of his Sicilian youth in the third century B.C., the backward glance has been an integral part of the pastoral thematics. What the future is for the utopian or the present for the hedonist, the past is for the pastoralist: his basic temporal orientation, a reflection of his quintessentially nonprogressive, conservative, static world view. In conjunction with the backward glance or the theme of real past time is to be found the related theme of the Golden Age, or ideal past time. This is the time, imagined and written about through the centuries, in which simplicity and innocence prevailed, work and pleasure were one, the fruits of the earth always sufficed to man's needs, and the cares and vicissitudes of the modern world were yet to arise.

In the eighteenth and nineteenth centuries, the ideas of the state of nature and primitivism are variations played on the themes of the backward glance and the Golden Age. The variations focus on a civilization that, due to its being "behind the times," bears the distinctive stamp of cultural if not chronological remoteness. Such is the case, for example, in Saint-Pierre's *Paul et Virginie* and Chateaubriand's *Atala,* two novels in which the backward glance, the Golden Age, and cultural primitivism are all active, closely interrelated thematic ingredients. *Paul et Virginie* is a retrospective, nostalgic account of an idyllic existence on the distant island of Mauritius, which nefarious outside forces act to undermine and eventually destroy altogether. *Atala* similarly looks back with nostalgia at the passing of the Natchez tribe and implicitly, at the same time, at the passing of pre-revolutionary France as well. In both novels, moreover, anthropological and chronological primitivism go hand in hand. Chateaubriand's America, like Bernardin's distant island, is more than a cultural backwater; to a significant degree it also represents the temporally transcendent realm of the state of nature and the Golden Age.

The act of looking backward is by definition prescinding oneself from present reality, and thus it is not surprising to discover that the pastoral ingredients in the literature of images reinforce and reflect the overall conservative tenor of this literature. This is not to say that it contains the egregious denial of time and change that characterizes pastoral romances like Honoré d'Urfé's celebrated *L'Astrée,* where aristocrats at play in the country attempt to retreat from all of the economic and social realities of their times. The ideology of the descriptive novel is not synonymous with that found in pastoral romances for the simple reason that it never adheres to the pastoral's thematics in any sustained or systematic way; the pastoral is after all only a remnant in the novel. Not even with the earliest authors in the literature of images, then, are the novels truly set in Arcadia. Significantly, however, Arcadia recurs time and time again in the literature of images: an example is the peasant celebration found in *La Nouvelle Héloïse.* Although Rousseau does not have a genuinely pastoral world view and is not focused exclusively on a conservative past, there is nonetheless a very strong pull, a consistent urge, manifest in his novel—as in the literature of images at large—to eulogize occasionally (if not uniformly) the peaceful, static, pastoral world of the landed gentry and thereby to reaffirm to a significant degree that class's conservative, proprietary values.

Another thematic ingredient of the pastoral is the contrast between city and country, an ingredient so important that it has been taken by some critics as the necessary if not sufficient condition of the genre. For whether or not the contrast is stated, it is always implied: to sing the praises of the simple, innocent, peaceful rural life is by implication to voice criticism of its complex, vice-ridden, disharmonious urban counterpart. Now, the fact of praising the country and criticizing the city is closely linked to the conservative attitude to the past that is a hallmark of the pastoral and an underlying, recurrent theme of the literature of images. In this connection, Raymond Williams maintains that more than just criticism of the city can be inferred from the encomiastic description of the country in pastoral literature. In *The Country and the City,* he argues that by pitting the work-free, innocent country against the greedy, evil city, the pastoral seeks to deny or excuse the economic abuses of the former. "The greed and calculation, so easily isolated and condemned in the city," he states, "run back, quite clearly to the country houses, with the fields and their labourers around them"; and he adds, "There is then no simple contrast between wicked town and innocent country, for what happens in the town is generated by the needs of the dominant rural class."[12] The function of the contrast, according to Williams, is to promote superficial comparisons and prevent real ones.

The narrative landscape inevitably shares in this kind of ideological deception or false consciousness, though to various degrees and in many different ways. The contrast between city and country derived from the pastoral tradition only manifests itself in a direct, easily observable manner in the early years of the literature of images where, for example, Rousseau's Saint-Preux and Bernardin's Virginie are similarly banished from the pastoral haven and made to suffer the corrupting effects of urban life in Paris. In later descriptive novels, although the city–country polarity remains an underlying thematic ingredient, it appears in some modified guise that enables it to serve, ad hoc, a variety of aesthetic and conceptual ends. For example, in Chateaubriand's *Atala* and Balzac's *Les Chouans,* the Golden-Age theme blends with the city–country contrast in the opposition of before and after with respect to historical change: in *Atala* the old patterns of pre-Revolutionary times are pitted against the new community ties that the exile must establish; in *Les Chouans* the relevant opposition is between an atavistic Brittany and a progressive France at large, between an older politics of regional extremism and a newer one of national moderation. The old versus the new is in both cases homologous to the country–city opposition.

In *La Peau de chagrin,* as in other works by Balzac, the pastoral is confined to one portion of the novel. (In *La Peau de chagrin,* it occurs in the last third of the novel; while it is found only in the first half of *Le Lys dans la vallée.*) Already, then, Balzac's novel is far from the traditional pastoral, which develops a uniform tone and thematics throughout the work.

Merely to identify the pastoral components in the last third of *La Peau de chagrin* would be to focus on the use there of conventional, visually imprecise images ("delightfully fresh and smiling landscapes," "cool and shady recesses," "pool of clear water"), ornate style, and profuse natural descriptions. All of these alert the reader to the generic filiation with the pastoral tradition. Especially noteworthy is the situation at the end of the novel in a pastoral enclave or *locus amoenus,* where there exist all of the stock features such as water, shade, the song of birds, along with peace, harmony, and repose: "Here nature was simple and kindly, giving an impression of rusticity both genuine and poetic, blossoming a world away from our contrived idylls, with no reference to the universe of ideas. . . . The warm odours rising from the water, from the flowers and the grottoes which made fragrant this quiet retreat, gave Raphaël a sensation bordering on the voluptuous" (pp. 268–269).

It is not enough, however, merely to enumerate the pastoral components that *La Peau de chagrin,* like most other novels in the literature of images, undeniably displays. It is necessary to note the ways the additional link to the pastoral tradition enhances the internal relational reading. Especially noteworthy with respect to point of view are the opening and closing sentences of the novel, which highlight the negative counterpart, the city of Paris, as a center for artifice and vice: the first sentence reads, "Towards the end of October 1830 a young man entered the Palais-Royal just as the gambling-houses were opening in conformity with the law which protects an essentially taxable passion"; the last lines, referring to the hero Raphaël's frivolous Parisian mistress Foedora, reads, "Last night she was at the Bouffons; this evening she will go to the Opéra. She's to be found everywhere. She is, if you like, Society." Both sentences reveal an unidentified narrative presence that serves to color and condition the reader's attitude to Raphaël and his story. The first sentence alerts the reader, notably, to the novel's critical outlook on Paris and its values.

The external connection to the pastoral tradition also illuminates the internal relational reading of parallel or contrasting descriptions in novels. It is thus to be suspected from the outset that by highlighting the city in the first line of the novel, Balzac is going to develop the traditional opposition between the vice-ridden city and the innocent country at some point, as he in fact does in the last third. Often nineteenth-century describers of the city, not only Balzac but Dickens as well, include landscapes that are important to the overall meaning of their novels. A notable case from Dickens is *Bleak House,* with its opposition between the Chancery in London, exemplifying financial and judicial deception and ruin, and Chesney Wold in the rural region of Lincolnshire, exemplifying the possibility of an escape from the city and a revelation about the truth of the past. It is not surprising, then, that if *La Peau de chagrin* underscores gambling in Paris in its very first sentence, it later makes a place for its pastoral opposite, the innocent country refuge. Since a relational reading seeks to avoid the pitfall of reading landscape apart from its connections with other narrative components, the pastoral reading can be of value by emphasizing the importance of the landscape's relation to descriptions of the city.

The landscape's relation to the novel's social and political outlook can also be illuminated in the light of the pastoral tradition. Readers alerted to that tradition will thus suspect that the mention of a specific and contemporary setting in the first sentence—October 1830 in the English translation, "octobre dernier" in the French original—raises the possibility that the traditional opposition between present and past will be developed. And indeed, when Raphaël flees to the pastoral enclave of Mont-Dore at the end, he is not only seeking to escape from the city, whose vices are variously equated with gambling, Foedora, and Society, but also from the present—notably from its acutely materialistic, mercantile form under that July Monarchy which was instituted three months before the opening of the novel. Of course, no real possibility of escape, either from the city or from the present, is envisioned in *La Peau de chagrin*, which, like most of Balzac's novels, reflects a resolutely pragmatic world view. If the pastoral tradition is illuminating for a relational reading, the reason surely is not that the continued existence of pastoral elements in novels proves the continued existence of the literal pastoral vision or values. The pastoral presence merely serves as a reminder that certain components of novels—words, expressions, places, themes, temporal references—have traditional literary meanings and that those meanings inevitably enter into a landscape's relations with the other narrative components of the novel in which it occurs.

Narrative Garden Descriptions

A second external element that can be related to narrative descriptions is the garden description. Several decades prior to the manifest beginnings of narrative landscape in works such as *La Nouvelle Héloïse,* landscape makes an appearance in larval stage in the lengthy descriptions of gardens, which can be found in a number of important English novels and which have gone all but ignored by historians and critics. Garden descriptions do not vary greatly in the type or features of outdoor scenes depicted; typically they present pleasant views from rural homes, with lawns, trees, slopes, streams, and above all prospects.

When in 1761 Rousseau devotes some fifteen pages to describing Julie's garden in *La Nouvelle Héloïse,* he is following a new English model and not a French tradition. For although there were French romances that contained nature description, those descriptions were mere pastoral touches or short decorative flourishes. The French romance does not provide a model, as does the eighteenth-century English novel, of the extended landscape description in its formative stage. Accordingly, there seems to be little point in rehearsing at length here the various descriptive practices found in seventeenth-century French novels like *L'Astrée, La Princesse de Clèves,* or *Télémaque*—a fascinating topic in its own right, but not one that bears directly or crucially enough on the eighteenth- and nineteenth-century descriptive novel to merit attention in this context. Early French works accord minimal importance to nature description —minimal in the sense both of brevity (usually no more than a line or two) and of infrequency (usually no more than a few descriptive passages in a whole novel). Thus although *La Princesse de Clèves* contains a highly sensitive, symbolic scene in which the duc de Nemour's amorous sentiments are reflected in such natural objects as the weeping willows, this kind of scene occurs only once and is ultimately of only minimal importance in the novel as a whole. Another justification for passing rapidly over the seventeenth-century French novel is the hackneyed, repetitive character of its nature descriptions. Whether the subject is the country of Forez on the banks of the Lignon in *L'Astrée* or Calypso's grotto in *Télémaque,* the same stereotyped style and conventional pastoral language are adopted, with the dearth of descriptive detail making it virtually impossible to distinguish one place from another.

It may seem surprising at first blush to see that the English novel is alone being identified here as a model for the development of the garden description. But there are specific reasons for England's having played such a role. During the eighteenth century, the English were a model of "enlightenment" for French intellectuals with respect to anti-autocratic government, political freedom, science, empirical philosophy, gardening, and culture in general; they also tended to be pathbreakers in developing new literary forms. Samuel Richardson's sentimental novel, Mrs. Radcliffe's Gothic novel, and Sir Walter Scott's historical novel—to say nothing of descriptive poetry and Romanticism generally—arose first in England and only subsequently were adopted and modified to French tastes, doubtless because the political and intellectual atmosphere in England was especially conducive to growth and change.

The same use of short, stereotyped nature descriptions—the total absence of any extended or developed depictions of landscape—persists in France down to Rousseau's time, with primitivism or country life emerging in literary works only as subject for abstract commentary, not for description. Perhaps the most pertinent case in point—the French

novelist before Rousseau who might seem to come closer than others of
those times in focusing attention on nature—is Abbé Prévost. On a number of occasions in his multi-volume *Mémoires d'un homme de qualité* and
Histoire de M. Cleveland, Prévost presents fairly detailed sketches of places,
for example, the approaches to various English cities and small towns.
Still, considering the massive nature of the novels themselves, these
sketches can hardly be taken as very crucial narrative components. In a
similar vein, only minimal significance can be found in the exotic geographical locations evoked in Prévost's novels, for example the wild nature
setting in Louisiana where his celebrated *Manon Lescaut* of 1831 comes to
a close. The naming of the foreign place aside, Prévost actually supplies
little more than the most cursory and conventional notations: all that he
says about New Orleans is that the surrounding countryside was sterile
and sandy; the vegetation limited to a few reeds and leafless trees; and the
city, hidden behind a hill, was visible from the ocean (which incidentally
it is not).

In contrast to the French novel, the English novel prior to 1760 includes a number of works that make a decisive break with the stereotyped
treatment of nature handed down from past centuries. First if not foremost among them undoubtedly is *Robinson Crusoe,* which is often credited
with being the first major novel to be set in a concrete and specific physical environment. True, there is not much actual description of nature in
Defoe's novel. Only about one-third of the way into the story and ten
months after his arrival on the island does Crusoe really look at his surroundings and even then, the "survey of the island" that he undertakes
largely comprises the listing of botanical and geographical terms. It is
nonetheless the case that Crusoe does pause at times to describe places, for
example, that which he will subsequently choose as his Bower:

> At the End of this March I came to an Opening, where the Country
> seem'd to descend to the West, and a little Spring of fresh Water
> which issued out of the Side of the Hill by me, run the other Way,
> that is due East; and the Country appear'd so fresh, so green, so
> flourishing, every-thing being in a constant Verdure, or Flourish of
> *Spring,* that it looked like a planted Garden. [13]

Along with the aesthetics of the garden, Defoe also introduces its econom-
ics, the nascent capitalist notion that the land is real property to be improved and exploited, and that by so doing the landowner is himself enhanced and ennobled. Crusoe makes a revealing statement to the captain
about the Bower: "I told him, this was my Castle, and my Residence; but
that I had a Seat in the Country, as most Princes have, whither I could
retreat upon Occasion" (p. 258). Defoe thus introduces the ideological
underpinnings of the narrative landscape. The land for Crusoe, as for land-

owners as a class from the seventeenth century on, is no longer just an inheritance but an investment. It is no longer the timeless, idyllic *locus amoenus* but a distinctly temporal, historical, and economic phenomenon, the locus for the newly emerging forces of agrarian improvement, development, and change.

Crusoe's Bower—"so green, so flourishing . . . that it looked like a planted Garden"—is followed by numerous other gardens in English novels of the eighteenth century. The most noticeable appearances perhaps occur in the works of Richardson and Henry Fielding, two authors whose widely disparate aesthetic purposes, attitudes, and styles are enormous but whose similarly strong ties with the tradition of romance constitute, all differences aside, the common background against which their novelistic practices stand out most distinctly. Should it seem inappropriate to speak thus of romance in connection with writers commonly regarded as the forefathers of the "realistic novel," it would be well to remember, as Northrop Frye observes in *The Secular Scripture,* that both Richardson and Fielding utilized a long, digressive format that eighteenth-century readers associated with what to them were the familiar formulas and structural patterns of romance. Frye's view that the novel grew up and developed as a "realistic displacement of romance," with few structural features that did not derive more or less directly from the earlier narrative form, is shared by another critic, Henry Knight Miller.[14] Miller sums up the crucial connection between Fielding and Richardson and the romance tradition as follows:

> As Samuel Richardson "translated" into new terms for a specifically middle-class female audience the French salon romance (which he apparently knew only from the English vulgarizations in drama and fiction), Henry Fielding, confronted by the novel fact of *Pamela,* chose an alternative tradition and "translated" into comic terms the masculine chivalric romance, which was in essence a summation of the older romance tradition.

A principal ingredient in this "translation" of traditional forms of romance into modern, eighteenth-century terms was a transformation of the ornamental set piece of description—those elaborate, stylistically embellished descriptions of people, places, and things that had always been an integral part of romance—into the garden description. In the process, there arose new and different features of nature description, not the least of which was the panoramic overview of nature from on high—the French critic Jean Rousset's "vue plongeante," about which I shall have more to say in chapter 6—one of the most recurrent forms in landscape and one of the leitmotifs of descriptive writing for Balzac, Flaubert, and others in the literature of images.

Fielding, for one, was obviously aware of the connection between traditional forms of description in the romance and the garden description, for whenever he stops to describe people or places in detail, he adopts an elaborate, mock-heroic style, as if convention dictates that description be presented in the ornate language of romance. This parodic practice occurs as early as 1742 in the sketchy description of Mr. Wilson's garden in *Joseph Andrews,* and later there occurs an even more striking and developed instance, with the description of Squire Allworthy's estate in *Tom Jones*:

> It was now the middle of May, and the morning was remarkably serene, when Mr. Allworthy walked forth on the terrace, where the dawn opened every minute that lovely prospect we have before described to his eye; and now having sent forth streams of light, which ascended the blue firmament before him, as harbingers preceding his pomp; in the full blaze of his majesty rose the sun, than which one object alone in this lower creation could be more glorious, and that Mr. Allworthy himself present. [15]

Fielding also singles out the view from on high as a salient feature of landscape. The comic title he gives to the chapter in *Tom Jones* containing the description of Squire Allworthy's estate is "The Reader's neck brought into danger by a description." And in the description itself, looking down is a constant theme. The house "stood on the south-east side of a hill, but nearer the bottom than the top of it, so as to be sheltered from the northeast by a grove of old oaks which rose above it in a gradual ascent of near half a mile, and yet high enough to enjoy a most charming prospect of the valley beneath." Then there is a spring "forming a constant cascade of about thirty feet" which "fell into a lake at the foot of the hill, about a quarter of a mile below the house on the south side, and which was seen from every room in the front." Fielding concludes the description by again calling attention in a humorous fashion to the dominant point of view he has been utilizing throughout: "Reader, take care. I have unadvisedly led thee to the top of as high a hill as Mr. Allworthy's, and how to get thee down without breaking thy neck I do not well know."

It is important to emphasize the implicit link between the "vue plongeante" and the ideology of dominance and possession which, according to Raymond Williams, dates back to early times, when "prospects" from castles and fortified villages were the characteristic viewing points of rulers and kings. It was with the likes of such figures of power and authority that the English landlord and country gentleman presumably sought to be identified. According to Williams, Claude and Poussin inspired English gentlemen who went on the Grand Tour to see nature in new ways; they then returned to hire landscapers like Capability Brown, William Kent, or Humphry Repton to create gardens and prospects for their houses. The order thus imposed on the immediate surroundings of the garden reflected that being imposed more generally on the countryside through farming and enclosure. It also reflected the landowner's will to control and command, while at the same time denying that such a will involves human work. Speaking of English landowners of the time, Williams observes that "they succeeded in creating in the land below their windows and terraces . . . a rural landscape emptied of rural labour and of labourers; a sylvan and watery prospect, with a hundred analogies in neo-pastoral painting and poetry, from which the facts of production had been banished."[16]

It is altogether in this spirit of a denial of production and an ideology of dominance and possession that in *Tom Jones,* Fielding presents Squire Allworthy's estate, with its "air of grandeur," "amazing variety," and "admirable taste" symbolically reflecting the superior qualities of the landowner; and the same spirit prevails in Richardson's *Sir Charles Grandison,* written in 1753. Here too the characteristic point of view of the wealthy and powerful gentleman is from on high:

> The orchard, which takes up near three acres of ground, is planted in a peculiar taste. A neat stone bridge in the centre of it is thrown over the river. It is planted in a natural slope, the higher fruit-trees, as pears, in a semi-circular row first; apples at further distances next; cherries, plums, standard apricots, etc., all which in the season of blossoming, one row gradually lower than another, must make a charming variety of blooming sweets to the eye from the top of the rustic villa, which commands the whole.[17]

The same equation also occurs between the attributes of the garden (openness, plenitude, order, artistry) and those of the landowner. The following statement is characteristic: "The gardens, vineyards, etc., are beautifully laid out. The orangery is flourishing—everything indeed is that belongs to Sir Charles Grandison." It is highly significant that the history of the literature of images begins with this egregiously complacent tone, for in various ways an underlying conservatism and compliance with the economic, political, and cultural status quo marks this literature.

Another early novel that develops the garden motif in a noteworthy manner, anticipatory of certain key themes in the literature of images, is Richardson's *Pamela.* Considering the early date of this work—more than a decade before *Sir Charles Grandison*—it is not surprising to discover that Richardson has as yet developed only the rudiments of the garden description, just as Fielding's descriptive technique was not as evolved in 1742 with *Joseph Andrews* as in 1749 with *Tom Jones.* What is noteworthy in *Pamela,* then, is not so much the length as the frequency and importance of its allusions to the garden; it is indeed Pamela's refuge and the locus of all her attempts at both escape and communication with others. The close association that the novel establishes between Pamela and nature in the garden presents another side of that thematics of power and possession observed in *Tom Jones* and *Sir Charles Grandison*. For although the garden belongs not to the servant Pamela but to her master Mr. B—indeed, the garden is where he first exercises his oppressive dominance by trying to seduce her—still, nature's links are not with him but with her; not with the insider but with the outsider. It is the prisoner in the garden, not the owner—the person endowed with spiritual, not material riches—who admires "the turfted Slope of the fine Fish-pond" and notes that the garden in Bedfordshire is larger than the one in Lincolnshire, has "nobler Walks in it," and has "a pretty Canal" as well as a fountain and a cascade.

It is in the light of Pamela's special association with nature that the scene can perhaps best be viewed in which Mr. B, having magnanimously consented to transcend class barriers and to marry his servant, speaks to Pamela in the garden:

> Don't you with Pleasure, my Dear, said he, take in the delightful Fragrance that this sweet Shower has given to these Banks of Flowers. Your *Presence* is so enlivening to me, that I could almost fansy, that what we owe to the *Shower* is owing to *That*: And all Nature, methinks, blooms around me, when I have my *Pamela* by my Side. You are a Poetess, my Dear; and I will give you a few Lines, that I made myself on such an Occasion as this I am speaking of, the Presence of a sweet Companion, and the fresh Verdure, that, after a Shower succeeding a long Draught, shew'd itself throughout all vegetable Nature.[18]

The transmutation of the servant into the lady in the novel is paralleled by that of the outsider into the insider—not into the possessor, for Pamela is not herself the owner or controller of the land here but rather an extension of nature, which her master can take pride in possessing as he does his garden. Later heroes and heroines will go beyond Pamela's essentially passive, submissive relation to nature and seek, through the act of describing the landscape, a psychological, if not real, possession of themselves and the external world around them.

In the decades following Richardson and Fielding, nature description in the English novel gradually moves beyond the narrow confines of the garden to certain less artificially delimited spaces, notably outdoor settings bounded by mountains or bodies of water—in other words, scenes that have the feeling of free, open nature but the physical and visual limits necessary to form a landscape. Thus garden description gradually becomes landscape, as it does with Rousseau in 1761. *La Nouvelle Héloïse* begins with evocations of wild nature in what was at the time the strange and unfamiliar region of Switzerland, even though it later presents an extended description, *à l'anglaise,* of Julie's planted garden. Certain English novelists of the second half of the eighteenth century also present landscapes, perhaps the most noteworthy being Tobias Smollett, the author in 1771 of *Humphry Clinker.* Smollett's novel, like Rousseau's, contains many scenes in which the accent is on an unfamiliar land: Scotland in *Humphry Clinker* constitutes the counterpart of Switzerland in *La Nouvelle Héloïse.* Descriptions of gardens continue to play significant roles in English novels well into the nineteenth century, as for example in Jane Austen's *Mansfield Park,* which dates from 1814. That novel is particularly interesting because of the extent to which it develops, even within the limited framework of the occasional garden description, the opposition that recurs frequently in the literature of images between the landed gentry and their commitment to tradition versus the middle class and their commitment to change.

Returning now to a relational reading of Balzac's *La Peau de chagrin,* it is important to observe that the novel dwells on delimited, gardenlike spaces in nature—spaces surrounding bodies of water or bounded by masses of vegetation—which are the immediate avatars of eighteenth-century gardens, namely, the lake of Bourget and Mont-Dore discussed earlier. There is also the meager city garden that Raphaël perceives when looking down from his Parisian garret window and the indoor garden in the luxurious house he acquires when he becomes rich: "a small conservatory, a kind of salon filled with flowers, opening straight on to the garden" (p. 220).

Balzac's use of the point of view from on high, and the will to power it reflects, are of the utmost importance in considering these descriptions. Raphaël, like many other Balzacian heroes, begins the novel as an impoverished aristocrat and ends up with the wealth that was the prerequisite for gaining a position of dominance and control in his society. He is, then, doubly privileged, originally by his aristocratic name and subsequently by his money. And indeed, Raphaël looks down at nature as a privileged viewer, as an unconscious participant in the ideology of dominance and possession. Thus in the lake of Bourget and Mont-Dore descriptions, he gazes down at a nature that he could have possessed, symbolically in his traditional role as aristocrat or materially in his role as millionaire and which only eludes his control due to the diabolical powers of the wild ass's skin.

In regard to parallel and contrasting descriptions, a noteworthy contrast is apparent between the lake of Bourget and Mont-Dore descriptions on the one hand, in which Raphaël's great wealth fails to procure a control over nature, and the garret-window description on the other, in which Raphaël's poverty paradoxically affords that control. As a poor but healthy and morally pure scholar, Raphaël looks down in that scene at "the flowers

of a hanging garden" and "the sparse and short-lived vegetation in the
gutters, sorry weeds whose colours had been refreshed by the rain and
which the hot sun would change into dry, brown patches of velvet shot
with varying hues" (pp. 107–108). This sparse city garden, emblematic
of Raphaël's poverty, paradoxically constitutes a high point in his relationship with nature because of the freedom, innocence, and inner nobility he possesses at this early stage in his tragic life. Thus he observes,

> In short, the fleeting, poetic effects of the daylight, the melancholy
> of the fog, the sudden sparkle of sunshine, the silence and magic of
> the night, the mystery of dawn, the smoke rising from every chim-
> ney, all the details of that singular landscape, once I had become fa-
> miliar with them, provided me with entertainment. I loved this
> prison of my own choosing. (p. 108)

There, looking down from on high, Raphaël surveys the only space in nature that he is morally worthy of possessing and over which he has complete control.

With respect finally to landscape's relation to the novel's social and political outlook, it is worth mentioning again the description of the
gardenlike conservatory in Raphaël's luxurious Parisian house where "the
mild, pale winter sun . . . filtered through the rare shrubs" (p. 220). The
artificiality of this indoor garden—in French, "une petite serre"—where
flowers bloom in winter is striking. *La Peau de chagrin* suggests that a
comparable artificiality, a fake nature, is all that is left for Raphaël and,
by extension, the other formerly noble members of the generation of
1830 who have made diabolical and degrading pacts with materialistic
forces beyond their individual control. Thus, as with so many other characters and narrators in the literature of images, Raphaël's search to obtain
power and possession parallels and embodies that of his social group, and
narrative landscape serves to reflect that search for possession of self and
the external world.

Referential Borrowings

The rash of writings about nature that date from the eighteenth and nineteenth centuries—writings about subjects as numerous and diverse as
botany, zoology, agriculture, gardening, travel, and painting—furnished
the narrative landscape with a whole group of linguistic elements that I
shall call referential borrowings. They are referential in the sense that they
derive from fields normally considered superior to literature in providing
information or in accurately and objectively depicting the external world.
They are borrowings in the sense that ultimately the novel never adheres
systematically to the practices or standards of those fields. It may try, but

inevitably and properly its efforts are sporadic and subordinate to its own properly narrative, aesthetic dictates.

Identifying these elements as borrowings makes it possible to account for a phenomenon that is familiar to the reader of novels, namely, that certain elements in novels—words, phrases, ordering devices, proper names, even entire passages—are in some way associated or connected with domains outside the narrative; they trigger a response of referentiality. Identifying these elements as borrowings also makes it possible to see them for what they are, namely, formal components of landscape description that combine with other components to produce certain textual effects. The crucial corollary of seeing these elements for what they are is being able to see beyond what they pretend to be, that is, denotative components of a bona fide description of the world that can be verified and relied upon as objective fact. Two sorts of borrowings, a technical or scientific sort on the one hand and an artistic or aesthetic sort on the other, can illuminate and supplement a relational reading.

Technical or scientific borrowings occur in the novel most notably as technical paradigms: narrative description borrows from writings in other fields by using their technical terms in a particular passage or throughout the novel as a whole. Philippe Hamon sheds light on the matter of these paradigms when, following Michael Riffaterre, he designates as a fundamental feature of description the act of reciting a paradigm of words or "descriptive system": for example, the descriptive system of the kernel word "house" is a predictable list of words such as roof, walls, windows, floor, and the like along with the stereotyped phrases or clichés associated with those words.[19] The reader is expected in the mundane case of "house" to know the lexical items in the paradigm; his activity can thus be characterized as recognizing what Hamon calls a "savoir connu," a segment of an established field of knowledge. But whereas regular paradigms like that of "house" are familiar to the reader, the technical sort so popular in the literature of images includes a significant number of items that are "unreadable," that is, incomprehensible without the reader's looking for aid either in a dictionary or within the description itself—that is, through synonyms or through the context. The numerous unreadable botanical species typically found in the literature of images provide an example. For such words, the reader's activity is not so much recognizing a "savoir connu" as coming to realize that there exists what Hamon calls a "savoir nouveau," a field of knowledge that is new and, more importantly, which he does not understand.

In addition to the frequent naming of botanical species in the literature of images, there are innumerable other uses of unfamiliar terms, the uses changing in accordance with the shifting tastes, interests, and economic activities of the times. Early in the nineteenth century, for example, the novel makes frequent use of terms from gardening, as it did in the eighteenth century; later in the nineteenth century, the paradigms tend to derive more from technological fields, such as Emile Zola's use of the vocabulary of coal mining in 1885 in *Germinal*. The effect is the same, however, regardless of the content of the unfamiliar paradigm. The enumeration of botanical species has essentially the same semiotic properties as that of terms from gardening or coal mining. In each case the terms stand out in a novel and produce an obtrusive and gratuitous effect—what Hamon calls an "effet de liste," a display of the describer's lexical mastery. And in each case the reader has the same feeling of unfamiliarity and exclusion from an initiated elite.

Explanations can be given of why novelists or other kinds of describers choose to write for ordinary readers in terms that seem to be appropriate only to the trained specialist, although admittedly they are not explanations that admit of conclusive or even empirically verifiable proof. Michael Riffaterre provides a particularly plausible explanation when he argues that in descriptive poems, technical paradigms are paradoxically intended more to confuse than to enlighten the average reader, the confusion serving the crucial purpose of convincing the reader that science exists and is difficult to master. According to this critic, the unreadable items from technical languages serve "to exclude us from the group of those who speak that language"; their very incomprehensibility "becomes the mimesis of science as a difficultly acquired knowledge and as the privilege of an elite."[20] What Riffaterre says about poetry plainly applies to the novel as well. Excluding the reader from some elite—whether it is a scientific elite or more generally some social, cultural, or political group—is common strategy in the literature of images and one that is often accomplished by emphasizing the mysterious, unknowable language of the Other.

As for the function of the novel's referential borrowings, the modern critic rightly rejects the assumption underlying much traditional criticism that the novelist observes and studies nature the same way the scientist or explorer does and for the same end, accurately recording or "representing" in language the reality of the outside world. These critics assume that the very use of scientific terminology is a gauge of accuracy and an indication that the novelist shares the theoretical, systematic intent of the true scientist. So when he documents the novelist's life, travels, or studies—the fact that Rousseau studied plants or that Chateaubriand traveled to America—he adduces such documentation as proof that representation was the novelist's true intent, which intent he then takes as prima facie evidence of the success of the description as representation. The modern critic, by contrast, argues that the function of narrative description is not to represent reality at all but rather to produce a superficial "effect" of reality, Barthes's now celebrated "effet de réel," the notion upon which Hamon elaborates such variations as his "effet de preuve" and "effet de liste."[21] "Effect" is the key word, serving to emphasize the fact that readers of description are hoodwinked by any manifestation of presumably concrete, referential, denotative language, be it a place-name, scientific word, or historical fact. Hamon observes that readers typically confuse a knowledge of words with a knowledge of the world. Riffaterre points out that readers will derive an indiscriminate sense of referentiality from the very mention of a place-name, even if its referent is wholly unfamiliar; and in a similar vein he notes that "in a paradigm of synonyms, the word with the most aberrant or peculiar shape hyperbolizes the meaning it receives from the context: in a narrative, you fall harder on a *granite* floor than on a *stone* floor, and it would hurt still worse on a *basalt* floor."[22] For example, when Chateaubriand names species of exotic American fauna—the opening description in *Atala* names herons, flamingoes, crocodiles, buffaloes, Virginia doves, caribou, and many others—the reader naturally has the feeling that such zoological phenomena coexist in the particular region described, despite the fact that he probably does not know whether they do or not, nor would his knowing be of much importance to the reading of the novel. He is also likely to feel that Chateaubriand "observed" these creatures firsthand and thus accurately described them, whereas in fact it is common knowledge that the author of *Atala* was capable of such gross errors in naturalistic "reporting" as placing crocodiles in distinctly northern climes.

Related to the use of scientific paradigms is that of artistic ones. Artistic paradigms assume the characteristic forms of referring within a description either to specific painters or to techniques in paintings. A striking example of the use of artistic paradigms occurs in that description near the beginning of Balzac's *La Peau de chagrin* which, as noted earlier, stands as the structural counterpart to the description of the volcanolike geological formation near the end.

> The visitor followed his guide and came to a fourth gallery, where his tired eyes were greeted by, in turn, a number of paintings by Poussin, a sublime statue by Michelangelo, several enchanting landscapes by Claude Lorrain, a Gerard Dow which resembled a page of Sterne, Rembrandts and Murillos, some Velasquez canvases as sombre and vivid as a poem by Lord Byron; then ancient bas-reliefs, goblets in agate, wonderful pieces of onyx! (p. 39)

The very name of the hero of *La Peau de chagrin,* Raphaël de Valentin, would appear to bear a relation to the extensive use of artistic paradigms in the novel, especially since the painter Raphael and his works are actually mentioned on a number of occasions in the text.

The artistic paradigm first gains currency in the English novel, notably in the works of Ann Radcliffe, where the names of Claude Lorrain, Poussin, and Salvator Rosa appear time and again. In a later stage—passing probably from her to Scott to Balzac—it secures a place in the French novel as well. In France, however, artistic paradigms play a more noteworthy role in portraits or descriptions of people than in landscapes or descriptions of nature. Allusions to art also retain a strong English flavor, a fact that Balzac perhaps seeks to emphasize by placing the names of Sterne and Byron alongside those of painters in the passage quoted above. (Elsewhere in *La Peau de chagrin,* he also mentions Shakespeare, Milton, and Richardson.)

The peculiar popularity of the artistic paradigm in England undoubtedly results from a number of closely related cultural causes, the most important of which may have been the practice of the Grand Tour; Christopher Hussey even attributes to this practice the rise of interest in the landscape in England:

> The awakening in England to an appreciation of landscape was a direct result of the Grand Tour fashionable with the aristocracy after the isolation of the country from the rest of Europe during the greater part of the seventeenth century. Not only did the passage of the Alps and the journey through Italy compel some attention being given to scenery, but in Italy the traveller encountered landscape painting. It became fashionable for the aristocracy to pose as connoisseurs, to assemble collections of pictures, and to bring home souvenir pictures of their tour. Simultaneously poets such as Thomson and Dyer devoted their verse to descriptions of scenery, and landowners were busy improving their grounds. Both adopted, as a model of correct composition, the Claudian landscape.[23]

Because the interest in art generally and paintings from or of Italy specifically was so intense among members of the upper classes in eighteenth-century England, it is plausible to assume that when, as readers of novels, they came across a reference to Salvator Rosa or Claude, their tastes were immediately flattered and their attention arrested.

The very notion of a landscape is connected with this interest in painting. Whether one is seeing nature on a trip or reading a description in literature, landscape generally implies the imposition of the pictorial boundaries of a painting. More specifically, the eighteenth-century notion of landscape relied to a very substantial degree on art: in fact, to judge from various English travel accounts and novels of the times, travelers were frequently doing little more in observing nature than classifying certain scenes as instances of Claudian beauty and others as examples of Salvatorial sublime. And if this were not enough, there was always the English traveler's perennial favorite, the Claude-glass—a curved, tinted lens that tinged the landscape with the characteristic colors of Claude's paintings. If we further recall that Claude viewed nature essentially through the "Vergil-glass" of pastoral literature, it becomes increasingly difficult to pinpoint influences and stop the dizzying, seesawing movement from one form of nature treatment to another. Even the very word "landscape," as it is commonly used, is ambiguous, designating sometimes a picture, sometimes a literary description, sometimes an actual geographical scene. An in-depth consideration of the interactions among the various kinds and meanings of landscape would require a more extended development than the present study can provide.

There are other significant considerations for understanding the popularity of artistic paradigms in the novel. The fact that English novels of the eighteenth century, unlike their French counterparts, were rarely illustrated, suggests that perhaps pictorial allusions filled a gap created by the lack of actual pictures within the pages of the book—the same gap, of course, that narrative landscape itself serves more generally to fill. At the time, when the landscape as practiced by Claude or Poussin was so widely emulated and imitated, allusions to that type of painting could probably conjure up in the minds of many readers images that were almost as vivid and precise as if the paintings were reproduced in the novel. Another distinctive feature of English culture that can be mentioned in relation to artistic allusions is England's Christian, Puritan background, which according to Hussey impeded and delayed the kind of appreciation of nature that was a long tradition in, say, China. The austere Puritan culture held the visible world to be sinful and the visual arts to be of questionable moral worth. Owing to the less-developed history of visual imagery in their culture, the English were perhaps more fascinated than the French with painting and artistic depictions of nature, and this fascination quite possibly contributed to the rise of artistic allusions in the English novel. But once these allusions became a standard feature of the descriptive novel at large, they assumed the same form and function regardless of the geographical or national setting of their occurrence.

Allusions to pictorial art in the descriptive novel function much the same way as do the quotations from poetry that derive from the pastoral romance in the literature of images. The artistic allusion, like the poetic quotation, acts to create a superficial impression that the novel partakes of whatever superior qualities (loftiness, profundity, universality, truth) are typically attributed to other, more elevated art forms. This impression is produced regardless of whether it is a question of an "effet de peinture" or an "effet de poésie."

There is another explanation for the widespread practice of referring to paintings within descriptions and undoubtedly for the practice of reading description pictorially. Traditionally the notion of *ut pictura poesis* was used in support of a representational theory of art: since a pictorial work was taken as a more clear-cut instance of imitation than a literary one, to compare the two was to elevate literature as representation to the rank of painting. Roland Barthes in recent times has made the point that allusions to art further representational theory; in *S/Z,* he argues that an effect of art inevitably functions as an effect of reality—that there is some strange logic at work whereby a novel that is able to copy art is taken as ipso facto able to copy the real world.[24]

It is time to examine *La Peau de chagrin* in the light of scientific and artistic paradigms. With respect specifically to landscape's relation to parallel or contrasting descriptions, it is important to note that the novel begins and ends with descriptions strongly marked by referential borrowings, one based on artistic and the other on scientific paradigms. The first centers on the "savoir connu" of art—names of artists and works with which readers probably are familiar—and the second on the "savoir nouveau" of science—terms and concepts from geology and botany with which readers are probably not familiar. Beyond their apparent denotative content, these borrowings serve chiefly to connote "art" and "science" as two alternative forms of transcendence. Significantly, in both descriptions, Raphaël gradually moves upward and achieves a transcendent state which his movement serves to reflect and symbolize. (By transcendence, I mean in this context resolving or surpassing the fundamental problems of the human condition.)

As for landscape's relation to the novel's social and political outlook, it is important to note that Raphaël's transcendent encounters with art and science represent an alternative to social reality, a different, superior reality in which symbolic resolutions to social conflicts are proposed. One example was the utopian image of new vegetation emerging from the ancient crater, as a promise of growth and change. What exactly that growth and change means in specific political terms remains unclear in the book. But, given that the referential borrowings from art are from the art of the past and that the borrowings from science are from the science of the land, that growth and change are undoubtedly conceived of in this novel in the same conservative, reactionary terms to be discovered in the other novels by Balzac to be studied later.

Through the years, and up to the present time, a variety of curious, distinctly nonrelational types of reading have arisen which share with the predominant pictorial type the tendency to separate the narrative landscape from what is taken as being "really" the novel, treating the landscape as one would a poem or photograph that has been inserted into the book one is reading. A recent version, popular in France, has an intriguing newness and complexity to it that masks the shallowness it shares

with its older and simpler counterparts, the shallowness consisting notably in the failure to acknowledge the landscape's crucial connections with
other components of the narration. This recent version originated in the
period of the late 1950s, when theorists of the nascent French New Novel
—Alain Robbe-Grillet, Jean Ricardou, Roland Barthes—denounced
Balzac and others in the literature of images for using description symbolically to equate man and his surroundings. In place of the older Balzacian
description, New-Novel theorists favored such modernist alternatives as
Ricardou's "creative description," a putative exercise in pure form that
promotes the new aesthetic values of fragmentation, discontinuity, and
generalized textuality.[25]

Following the path traced by New-Novel theory, French critics in the
1960s—notably Gérard Genette and again Roland Barthes—added the
authority of the terms and concepts of semiotics to their discussions of
narrative description, but they still practiced a criticism marred by the
flaws of the pictorial reading. Consciously seeking to deemphasize the
symbolic identification of character and setting in the Balzacian
description—which they wrongly assumed to be the sole kind of relationship operative in the literature of images—these critics pressed into the
service of literary history the ancient and until then largely forgotten
genre of *ekphrasis*—a decorative literary set-piece describing a painting or
work of sculpture. After stipulating *ekphrasis* as an ancestor, they then
mistakenly assumed that what is closer to the ancestor in kind is better or
more "authentic" than what is farther removed from it. Such a strategy
underlies Genette's often-quoted discussion of description in his 1969
"Frontières du récit," where he reduces the functions description has had
through history to two, the decorative and the symbolic, and where he
then posits the superiority of Robbe-Grillet's emphasis on the former and
the inferiority of Balzac's emphasis on the latter. Another oversimplification, and another instance of the semiotician's failure to acknowledge the
landscape's relation to other narrative components, occurs in Barthes's
1966 "Introduction à l'analyse structurale des récits," where he contends
that with respect to plot at least, description furnishes merely unessential
"catalyses," as opposed to the syntagmatically crucial "noyaux" of a story.[26]

There is much to be said on the positive side about semiotic theories of
description, even those from the 1950s and 1960s outlined above. Like
the pictorial reading, they have succeeded in identifying and illuminating
the special imagistic, literary language that descriptions display. And
they also have succeeded where earlier pictorial readings such as the *explication de texte* failed in fully acknowledging and articulating description's
properly literary, nonrepresentational nature. They have thus succeeded in
freeing description from its exclusive association with the truth-seeking,
psychologically oriented tradition of a "rise of realism."

   Semiotic theories have changed and evolved since the 1960s. In *S/Z*, for example, Barthes incorporates description into the deeper semantic structure of the novel. He also perhaps implicitly calls into question, by choosing a Balzacian novel as an example for his new method, the validity of that sharp opposition between old-fashioned and modernist description which New-Novel theorists had posited. And certain semiotic theories of description, such as those of Hamon and Riffaterre, have continued over recent decades to provide invaluable insights about description, without which no serious and systematic study of the subject would be possible.

   The method adopted in the present book is not presented, then, as a rejection but as a revision of current semiotic methods. I have relied on those methods, and shall continue to do so in the following chapters, in order to identify the textual and historical materials—the common "always-already-there"—available to novelists in the literature of images, that common repertoire comprising the garden, the "vue plongeante," the technical paradigm, the pastoral remnant, the effect of poetry and art. But there is more to reading description in novels than identifying those elements. Providing that "more" is the goal of the relational reading, it too being a semiotic reading, but one that can perhaps improve on other semiotic readings in doing justice to the unmistakable richness and diversity that landscape in the literature of images invites the reader to discover.

2

Conflicts in Nature:

La Nouvelle Héloïse

Rousseau's Oppositional Thought

Landscape no longer wears the vague colors of the *locus amoenus* or the English garden when, with Jean-Jacques Rousseau, it makes a striking, visible entry into the pages of one of the most influential novels of the eighteenth century, *Julie; ou La Nouvelle Héloïse*. No longer are change and discord eluded, as they were in the stereotyped phrases and traditional topoi of the pastoral. No longer does nature description pass itself off as a neutral, aesthetic remnant of romance, as it did in the eighteenth-century English novel. Landscape with Rousseau is nothing if not riddled with conflict. Whether in the gardens near the country estate of Clarens (the *bosquet* and Julie's Elysée), or in the isolated mountain regions of the Swiss Alps (the Valais and Meillerie), nature in *La Nouvelle Héloïse* is incessantly presented as torn by the characters' divergent desires and opposing principles: giving free rein to individual desire or submitting to the collective will, accepting traditional cultural patterns or creating new ones, living a life of solitude or achieving a meaningful social integration.

That there are multifarious conflicts that arise in *La Nouvelle Héloïse*—social, psychological, political, even metaphysical ones—and that they find their expression in landscape is not surprising in view of Rousseau's tendency to dramatize oppositions in his writing, such as inside versus outside, nature versus culture, good versus bad, and the like. For these dualities form the internal dynamics of Rousseau's peculiar treatment of landscape and provide a convenient vehicle for the expression of conflict, especially social conflict. In this way, Rousseau serves as a model for his successors in the literature of images. The oppositional, conflictual landscape he forges becomes an active ingredient in later writers' very perception of landscape, the first of several grids through which it will become customary for landscape to filter through into the consciousness of writers and readers of the novel.

Rousseau may have developed the conflicts and oppositions that underlie his treatment of landscape intentionally, a view that has some limited validity at the surface level of landscape's relation to character and plot. Even at this level it would be wrong to attribute too much to the author's intent and thereby to imply that Rousseau and others of his time were like self-conscious modern writers who seek actively to innovate and modify existing novelistic practices. But Rousseau perhaps consciously entertained such considerations as where landscape description is to be placed and what effect a particular placement produces, even if he made no explicit comments about them in his prefaces or his correspondence. Even modern authors are not always willing or even able to articulate their formal goals. But such goals unquestionably exist for the modern author, and they undoubtedly did for Rousseau as well.

Another explanation can be found in the writings of French thematic critics who presuppose that writers are driven to express deep-seated conflicts, often dating back to traumatic experiences in early childhood. Such an explanation too has some limited validity: it illuminates the works of individual writers, especially intensely idiosyncratic ones like Rousseau. Perhaps the most important critic in this context is Jean Starobinski, who has written extensively on Rousseau. He suggests that if Rousseau's treatment of external reality is exceptionally conflictual, the reason lies in the exceptionally conflictual conditions of his life—or at least what he perceived those conditions to be. Starobinski identifies the specific conflict that colored Rousseau's experience in terms of "transparency" and "obstacles." "Transparency" refers to the sense of immediacy —the totally direct, open, instantaneous coming together of minds, hearts, and souls—which Rousseau desires and which he seeks in all forms of interpersonal relations, from communication with other individuals to politics. "Obstacles" are the barriers set up by individuals and society that prevent the desired immediacy from taking place. According to Starobinski, Rousseau actually seeks out these obstacles, whether they are real or imaginary. By seeking them out, he confirms his paranoiac sense of denial and deprivation. From this central conflict between transparency and obstacles then follow others, according to Starobinski: between good and evil, nature and society, man and his gods, man and himself, an ideal historical past and a degraded historical present, and so on.[1] Thus there arises an essentially conflictual, oppositional world view.

Where does landscape enter into that world view? The out-of-doors and the countryside plainly emerge in Rousseau's work as privileged places for transparency; they permit if not the desired communication with others at least the next-best thing, communication with oneself. Rousseau's concept of nature thus rejoins, at least superficially, the thematics of the pastoral, as seen in the preceding chapter, in which pastoral literature is always set in some privileged place in the country where special communication with self or others can occur. In La Nouvelle Héloïse, the privileged place or pastoral enclave emerges as a series of increasingly hermetic outside places: Switzerland, rustic and primitive locations like the Valais and

Meillerie, intimate hideaways like the *bosquet* and Elysée. But Rousseau does more than just follow the traditional pastoral thematics. In his privileged places, characters achieve the special transcendent states (immediacy, intimacy, directness, transparency) to which they and Rousseau, according to Starobinski, aspire. One reason for the privileged character of these places in Rousseau's novel—as another thematic critic, Manfred Kusch, perceptively observes—is that they produce a liberation from and transcendence of real time. Kusch demonstrates that all of the otherwise dissimilar landscapes in *La Nouvelle Héloïse* have in common a predominantly vertical structure, which corresponds to a denial of linear, diachronic movement. He then goes on to show that this structure further corresponds at the textual level to that of the hermetically enclosed letters that the epistolary novel comprises.[2]

There are other, more far-reaching ways of explaining Rousseau's oppositional thought, ones that focus less on him as an individual than on the activities of thinking and writing generally. One such explanation is provided by structuralist critics like Lévi-Strauss, for whom basic patterns of correlation and opposition provide the formal structures of all unconscious, symbolic thought. Such critics would focus on the strongly marked binary oppositions that mark the thinking of Rousseau and other eighteenth-century writers: theirs is a moralistic attitude, reducing experience to such dichotomies as self or others, familiar or exotic, inside or outside, and the like. In thought that is dominated thus by opposition, the dichotomies naturally form clusters (self and familiar and inside versus other and exotic and outside). Since these clusters are frequently symbolic and unconscious, they permit the free passage from one element in the cluster to another—for example from the psychological element of self or others to the spatial element of inside or outside. Examining the clusters and the passages among elements within them proves especially illuminating for understanding Rousseau's treatment of landscape.

Especially relevant to an understanding of Rousseau's oppositional thought is Lévi-Strauss's idea that the passage among elements at the deep structural level of symbolic thought reflects an unconscious drive to resolve conflict. Lévi-Strauss notes that the chief function of myth in primitive societies is to provide an expression in an imaginary world of a conflict experienced in the real world, for example, the conflict between the will to survive and the danger of extinction due to seasonal famine. The pairs of contraries concomitant to the conflict—such as survival or extinction, life or death—are transformed and brought into relation symbolically with other contraries—mother or daughter, elder or younger, man or woman, land or water.[3] The "semantic axes" of family, age, sex, and geography, then, are all made relevant to the symbolic expression of conflict. The myth provides mediations and resolutions to the conflict on the symbolic level—for example, by forging strange mythical figures or episodes in which contraries can coexist and combine. The obvious differences between the primitive mythmaker and the eighteenth-century novelist notwithstanding, Lévi-Strauss's explanation of myth sheds light on Rousseau's use of landscape. Landscape is a privileged arena in Rousseau's novel, as telling stories is in primitive societies; in his novel, a largely unconscious search occurs to discover a symbolic mediation to the inside–outside dichotomy. The peculiar, transcendent community in nature that Rousseau depicts in his landscapes (to be considered shortly) constitutes one such mediation.

Another explanation for Rousseau's conflictual use of landscape can be developed from Jacques Derrida's *Of Grammatology* where it is remarked that the notion of outside and inside is for Rousseau and other writers a true ontological imperative. According to Derrida, the logocentric mind, which Rousseau exemplifies, needs to polarize in order to relegate to a subordinate, negative status that which is not self, consciousness, presence, fullness of being and meaning. Derrida places writing and style for novelists of Rousseau's time in the context of such a will to polarize; and Derrida's observation about writing applies with special force to landscape. Like writing generally, the description of nature can be viewed as what Derrida calls the Rousseauian "supplement," material additions to and substitutions for the supposedly full, present ontological entities that the logocentric mind posits but finds lacking in the world. As Derrida observes, Rousseau specifically casts these supplements in the mold of "outsider": "Imitation redoubles presence, adds itself to it by supplementing it. Thus it makes the present pass into its outside"; and Derrida also observes that the outside consistently assumes a negative connotation for novelists like Rousseau: "Whether it adds or substitutes itself, the supplement is 'exterior', outside of the positivity to which it is super-added, alien to that which, in order to be replaced by it, must be other than it. . . . According to Rousseau, the negativity of evil will always have the form of supplementarity."[4]

There is conflict for Rousseau, as Derrida's analyses reveal, in the underlying opposition he perceives between landscape as content on the one hand and landscape description as form on the other. As content—notably concerning open air and plants—nature is a distinctly positive, beneficent, even transcendent component of Rousseau's thought. Derrida notes that for Rousseau "the open air is the element of the voice, the liberty of a breath that nothing breaks into pieces . . . frankness, the absence of evasions, of representative mediations among living spoken words"; and regarding plants he notes in a similar vein that for Rousseau "in Nature, the plant is the most *natural* thing. It is natural life".[5]

Whereas nature as content or signified thus emerges as a positive component of Rousseau's thought, there is reason to believe that nature description as form or signifier has implicitly negative connotations. To be sure, there is no direct basis for concluding that description more than other narrative components is marked by supplementarity for Rousseau; description does not—like harmony in music and color in art, for example—exhibit the chromatic, quantifiable properties that, according to Derrida, predispose those components in Rousseau's mind to excessive stylization. It seems true, however, that the logocentric mind tends to polarize formal components into such dichotomous pairs as melody and harmony or line and color, one of which is always being taken to be more "essential" or closer to the mimetic purpose of the art. With regard to the novel, narration would seem prima facie to be more essential to Rousseau's mind than description. Plainly there exists for him a simple, fundamental core to the novel, to wit, the feelings of two lovers experienced in all their intensity and immediacy. Character, passion, sentiment, and action in the present: together these constitute the central reality, the ideal fullness of being and meaning posited within the pages of *La Nouvelle Héloïse*. Writing, landscape, description of scenes or events in the past are only exercises in language, compensatory practices that arise when true feelings and passion are denied. Especially with the novel's hero and describer of nature, Saint-Preux, it will be seen that the true role of the descriptive activity emerges progressively as a compensatory one.

The Hero in Conflict

Saint-Preux, the viewer of nature and author of nature description in *La Nouvelle Héloïse*, is a strangely new and different character—almost a harbinger of the modern antihero by virtue of the personal, social, and economic weaknesses that are his hallmark. What is perhaps most striking about him is his embodiment of numerous conflicts and contradictions. Although he is weak, he has hidden emotional, moral, and intellectual strengths. He is Julie's teacher and her pupil, one of the most adored and beloved of men as well as one of the loneliest, lowly by birth yet noble of heart and mind, an intellectual and a romantic, a victim of social injustice and a defender of the status quo. No wonder that this intriguing and enigmatic character casts a long shadow in the literature of images and that the myriad viewers and describers of nature in that literature are so frequently reminiscent of a figure whose vision and voice will be seen to render description in *La Nouvelle Héloïse* so profoundly problematic.

It will perhaps be useful to provide a brief summary of the novel's plot and the landscapes it contains. Landscape is first introduced, if not exactly developed, near the beginning of the novel in letters 13 and 14, about a third of the way into part 1, after the basic events and dilemmas of the

love story have been established: Julie d'Etange, member of the landed
Genevese gentry, loves and is loved by her young plebeian tutor Saint-
Preux, knowing full well—as her cousin Claire is quick to remind her
—that the affair will surely incur the severe disapprobation of her father,
currently away from home on business. The intimations of landscape contained in letters 13 and 14 pertain to the *bosquet*, a secluded setting at the
d'Etange country home of Clarens where the lovers embrace, thereby beginning a physical relationship that is consummated shortly thereafter. I
might add that although it is Julie in letter 13 who first alludes to the *bosquet*, it is Saint-Preux who presents a true visual perception of it, notably
involving the effect of the setting sun, in the following letter.

The other events that follow in the first half of the novel are few. Julie's
father returns, and Julie prevails upon Saint-Preux to absent himself for a
time. During his absence, he inhabits first the mountainous region of the
Valais and then the deserted rocky spot of Meillerie across Lake Geneva
from Clarens, both of which he describes in letters to Julie. Friends of the
couple, notably the English aristocrat Lord Edouard Bomston, make some
efforts to convince Julie's implacable father to agree to their marriage, but
to no avail; and Saint-Preux is again exiled, this time to Paris. A number
of minor events are recounted: Claire marries M. d'Orbe, Julie's hopes of
bearing Saint-Preux's child are dashed, Mme. d'Etange dies, the lovers
contract but recover from smallpox. Then Julie submits to the wishes of
her father, renounces Saint-Preux, and marries the middle-aged, aristocratic, dispassionate M. de Wolmar. The first half of the novel ends with
Saint-Preux setting out on a trip around the world.

The second half is even more barren with respect to plot than the first.
Saint-Preux, after a six-year absence, has returned to Clarens, where the
Wolmars and their children now live; the former lovers, whose passion
now is repressed but by no means extinct, are thus in day-to-day contact
again and made to reenact the amorous dreams and desires of the past.
Landscape plays a crucial role in the reenactment: part 4 contains a
lengthy letter addressed to Edouard in which Saint-Preux describes Julie's
garden, the Elysée. This part also contains another letter to Edouard in
which Saint-Preux describes to Edouard a boat trip he took with Julie, on
which they visit the rocky and deserted region of Meillerie described in
part 1. Other than the renewal of Julie and Saint-Preux's love, the second
half of the novel concerns itself with few topics other than the Wolmars'
presumably idyllic existence at Clarens. This existence comes to an abrupt
and tragic end with Julie's untimely death. The novel closes on a note of
uncertainty with respect to the future lives of Saint-Preux and the inhabitants of Clarens.

A conflict is inherent in Saint-Preux's crucial role with respect to landscape. It results from the ambiguous portrayal of the hero, notably the

ambivalent assessment of the value of those very attributes which qualify him to be the chief viewer and describer of nature and the hero of the novel. To begin with the positive side, Saint-Preux plainly is a privileged character for Rousseau; only upon such a character, who is intensely attuned to the perception of nature and pure sensations, could the crucial relation with landscape devolve. For the logic of the novel would have it that it is necessary to be frequently out-of-doors, preferably in new places that one sees with a fresh, especially attentive eye, in order to appreciate nature scenes to the fullest. It is significant to note in this regard that Saint-Preux's roles as focalizer and describer of nature are justified by his being the most widely traveled character in the novel. He is the one who is most likely to be located in distant places and who has through experience presumably acquired an eye for the nuances of the natural world of observable phenomena. Along the same lines, a special psychology is attributed to Saint-Preux. Having been condemned to being always on the outside ("will I not always be in exile from now on?"),[6] Saint-Preux has become accustomed to living only for the present moment and place. He alone among the characters has come to possess that special kind of psychological and physical distance which permits an acute awareness of the surroundings.

It is useful at this juncture to dwell on the inextricable links that exist between writing generally and describing nature in particular, and to observe that along with being the privileged describer of nature, Saint-Preux is also to some extent an authorial surrogate as well. Significantly, it is he who writes the most letters of any single character and who completely dominates the opening letters of the novel. Also significant are the cryptic references to his being a writer: mention is made at one point of a certain Mme. Belon who seems to think, says Saint-Preux, "that I am as completely foolish as my books" (p. 87; p. 106); and at another point, Edouard admonishes the hero, saying, "Do you wish, then, always to be a mere prater like the others and limit yourself to writing good books instead of doing good deeds" (p. 343; p. 525). Indeed critics have not failed to note the personal identification between the author of *La Nouvelle Héloïse* and its hero, an identification that Rousseau himself acknowledged. Along with their both being writers, Saint-Preux is roughly Rousseau's age at the time of writing the novel, and their tastes are virtually identical.[7]

Saint-Preux and Rousseau indeed both appear within the pages of *La Nouvelle Héloïse* in connection with the novel's coherent but aggregate narrative structure. A series of concentric circles provides perhaps the best picture of this structure.[8] At the center is the core inner reality and chief subject of the novel, Julie: her soul, her heart, her faith; in short the moral and spiritual values she embodies. Her home (Clarens), her friend (Claire), and she are together, as Starobinski aptly notes, "the zone of central transparency around which 'a very intimate society' will gradually crystallize."[9] But Julie is far closer to the argument than to the author, to the subject than to the signifier of *La Nouvelle Héloïse*. Immediately beyond her inner circle lies that of the other characters, with Saint-Preux foremost among them. Then there lies the circle of the fictional editor, who appears in the first person in the novel's preface as well as throughout the work in authorial footnotes, of which the 1761 edition contains no less than 165 (more than the novel's 163 letters), with as many as 9 in any one letter. In these footnotes, the editor intervenes to comment on gaps in the text, define terms, identify people, anticipate the plot, agree or disagree with the characters, elaborate, moralize, and the like. The outermost circle, of course, is that of the "real" author, Rousseau, whose name appears on the title page claiming responsibility for collecting and publishing (not writing) the letters that the novel comprises. Saint-Preux, I propose, stands between the clearly external voice of the author and the internal reality of the novel. He is a subtle authorial surrogate who—along with Julie, Claire, and Edouard but much more importantly than those characters —serves as a privileged narrative and descriptive locus within the novel itself. His relation to Julie is homologous to the relation of the writer—at least in Rousseau's logocentric view—to the world of truth and reality he attempts to capture in words.

Yet a strangely systematic devaluation of this character also seems to take place. This devaluation, combined with the privileged role, renders Saint-Preux a curiously conflictual figure in the novel. Consider the matter of his personal identity. Not until part 4 does the appellation Saint-Preux actually appear in the text; and the editor has already acknowledged in a footnote in part 3 that the name, chosen by Claire, is a bogus one. Meanwhile mystery continues to enshroud Saint-Preux's identity to the end of the novel. On one occasion, when he officially releases Julie from her promise to marry only with his consent, he signs his letter "S. G." (p. 327); and on another occasion the editor teases the reader into thinking that perhaps the real name will still be discovered: "It has been said that Saint-Preux was a disguised name. Perhaps the real one was on the address" (p. 674). Then there is the further fact of Saint-Preux's problematic national identity. He is, according to the novel, "wandering, without a family and almost without a country" (p. 61; p. 73). (I might add that almost the same words appear when Chateaubriand attributes a similarly problematic identity to his viewer and describer of nature in *Atala*. Chateaubriand seems by the intertextual echo to validate the association Rousseau makes between the lack of a clear-cut identity and a character's special ability to perceive and describe the out-of-doors.)

There are important social implications for landscape in Saint-Preux's strangely shadowy identity in the novel. All of the novel's 163 letters either feature the name of some character other than Saint-Preux (in French, "De Julie," "A Claire," and so forth) or read simply "Reply" or "Answer." In this curious system of epistolary titles, no letter bears the heading "De Saint-Preux." Now considering that the point of departure and central datum of the love story is Saint-Preux's failure to possess the French sign of nobility, "de," before his name, it seems likely that the lack of *de* before his name in the letters is no mere fluke: the denial of a title in society is purposely made to be echoed in the denial of a title in the text. But there is more. The noble "de" denotes possession of property; the d'Etange name, for example, refers to the land of the barony and château of Etange which Julie's family has inherited and which supports the family and their dependents. Saint-Preux has no such inherited ties with, or rights to, the land. All he has initially are the inner qualities of the aristocrat—as the name Saint-Preux suggests, piety and valor. But through description he can acquire, at least symbolically, the economic rights and powers of the nobility. Through the act of description, he gains an aesthetic connection that stands against his lack of title to the land.

Saint-Preux's lowly social status in *La Nouvelle Héloïse* ultimately provides the true motivation for landscape in the novel. Deprived of possessions, relegated to a marginal position in society as in the world, Saint-Preux turns to writing and landscape through a genuine need to assuage special feelings of loneliness and rejection. Nature description, it is true, is only one sort of writing; but because of the especially intense, even transcendent experience it affords Saint-Preux, it is perhaps offered in the novel as a privileged or even emblematic sort. There is also the fact that it represents a distinctly one-sided kind of communication, a solo act not really inviting a response; it is thus an especially apt reflection of and reaction to Saint-Preux's solitary situation. With respect to Saint-Preux's special need to write, Tony Tanner provides an insightful depiction of this character's status in the novel:

> He epitomizes the man who is forced to deflect and pervert his feelings into writings—hence, among other things, the extraordinarily long and often seemingly semantically depleted letters he writes. They are a kind of onanism, and for him, it is clear, there are many times when what matters is not *what* he is writing but *that* he is writing. It is almost all he is permitted to do by the rules that determine all the relationships in the society in which he lives.[10]

Far more than for other characters in the novel, writing is a compensatory act for Saint-Preux; for unlike other characters who possess a place in a family and society, Saint-Preux is devoid of all else but his pen. Not surprisingly then it is he, more than the others, who is drawn to description, just as it is he who has a proclivity for stylistic embellishment in his writing: for example, his use of Petrarchan fire imagery in the *bosquet* description or, on other occasions, his letters showing signs of what Julie calls "that affected prettiness of style, which, being unnatural in itself, can be natural to no people whatever, but betrays the absurd pretensions of the person who uses it" (p. 238).

It is not enough, however, merely to identify the conflicting nature, both privileged and diminished, of Saint-Preux's status as describer of nature in *La Nouvelle Héloïse*. Description in the novel is not the mere static, aesthetic phenomenon it is often assumed to be. On the contrary, narrative descriptions generally, and landscapes particularly, are nothing if not dynamic. Their distinctive characteristic indeed is that they exhibit an enactment or playing out over time of the conflictual situations from which they arise. The enactment can be discerned in comparing Saint-Preux's role as viewer-describer in part 1 with that which he plays in part 4. In the first part, the descriptions are relatively short and fill his immediate need to prolong and supplement the sensual and sexual intimacy of the love affair. In the epistolary exchange that occurs, Julie, the "descriptee" (the figure in the text to whom the description is directly or implicitly destined) is physically and affectively close to Saint-Preux, the describer: indeed, the closeness is the hallmark of the descriptive act in part 1. Saint-Preux reaches out through description to Julie, and the centripetal force she embodies draws him ever closer into the warm confines of her world, the inside. True, a genuine integration is never accomplished; but the very movement toward the inside reveals his spatial and psychological orientation in the first half of the novel.

There is a noticeable difference in the second half of the novel, where Julie's centripetal force diminishes and the centrifugal force that he himself embodies now prevails. The descriptions in part 4 are long and seem only in some vague sense to satisfy Saint-Preux's needs: it is not at all clear to what psychological end he chooses to dwell for some fifteen pages of the text on the botanical details of the Elysée. These letters are like extended monologues or even carefully composed essays on selected topics. Nor is it clear what effect they have on the "descriptee," Edouard, with whom the describer Saint-Preux has nowhere near the emotional or geographical closeness that he had with Julie in part 1 and to whom he only infrequently refers in these letters. Ultimately the act of describing nature does not succeed in enhancing the intimacy between the two friends. All there is toward the end of the novel is the compensatory act itself of sending a description of nature off to a good but distant friend in a distant land. The nature of this act testifies to Saint-Preux's orientation in the second half of the novel, gradually drifting further into the limbo of the outside world.

The denouement reinforces and restates a centrifugal pattern that is implicit in Saint-Preux's movements and very nature from the start. Significantly, the opening line of the novel and Saint-Preux's very first words are "I must fly from you, Mademoiselle" (p. 25; p. 31), and these words are echoed at the end of the first half, when Saint-Preux leaves on his world trip, saying, "I must climb on board; I must leave" (p. 269; p. 397). Flight, departure, and absence—movement away from the inside—are and always have been this character's ineluctable fate. But it is at the end of the novel that the pattern is most salient. Even before Julie's untimely death brings an end to any hope for a permanent communal existence at Clarens, Saint-Preux has moved outward into the world. Physically he is absent, during both her illness and the final days of her life. Textually he is absent too—a fact that, curiously enough, produces an increased frequency in his being named in the letters of the other characters (e.g., part 5, letter 13 and part 6, letter 3). Whereas in the beginning his voice alone was heard, at the end his voice is no longer audible at all. He has become a mere recipient of letters from the other characters.

Things are significantly different with respect to Julie, who throughout the novel embodies a metaphysical fullness of meaning or presence, at the same time that she serves as the locus on the social plane for the inside that Saint-Preux yearns to penetrate and to which he yearns to belong. It is not surprising that she is not the describer, writer, or stylist; located as she is at the very heart of the family, chosen to embody and enact society's most fundamental moral and religious principles, she is not relegated to the Derridean supplement of language. Even her death has a fullness of meaning that contrasts dramatically with Saint-Preux's mere fading away from the text and into the world at large. For this death is not a mere dissolution: Julie will presumably continue from beyond the grave to dominate morally and emotionally the inner worlds of all those who loved her. For her, death is a sort of transcendence, a realization on the spiritual plane of a complete happiness denied her in reality. In death as in life, she seeks a fullness of meaning in which description has no role to play— a total possession of self and others in "reality," not just in its supplement, language.

Conflict and Community in Nature

The conflictual nature of narrative landscape for Rousseau is strikingly apparent both in the placement of specific landscape passages relative to plot and in the internal development of these passages. Through its placement landscape functions to underscore conflict, notably by emphasizing the division of the novel into two similar but contrasting parts. But underscoring conflict is not the only function of landscape in *La Nouvelle Héloïse*. Landscape also functions as a privileged vehicle for the expression

of symbolic, imaginary resolutions to the problems posited in the novel
—much the way that, according to Lévi-Strauss, myth functions to resolve conflict in primitive societies.

Landscape is introduced, as I have mentioned, near the beginning of
part 1, in letters 13 and 14. Then, also in part 1, there are the descriptions of the Valais and Meillerie in letters 23 and 26. These are the only
descriptions in the first half of the novel. Landscape next occurs in part
4—thus near the beginning of the second half, as in the first half it
occurred near the beginning. Moreover, the description in part 4 of Julie's
Elysée echoes the earlier description of the *bosquet*, inasmuch as both are
located at Clarens—in point of fact on opposite sides of the house. That
Rousseau consciously wishes the later description to recall and be linked
with the earlier one is clear from his including in the Elysée episode a moment in which the now virtuous couple returns, in Wolmar's presence, to
the *bosquet* in order to dispel its amorous charm over their past. The other
principal nature description in part 4, the boat trip in letter 17, also echoes an earlier one inasmuch as Saint-Preux takes Julie to the region of
Meillerie he described in part 1. The return to Meillerie constitutes a nostalgic reliving of the melancholy rapport that Saint-Preux had established
in the earlier description between himself and his wild setting. The first
Meillerie description occurs in winter and expresses a wild despair yet not
devoid of hope; the second occurs in spring and expresses a tender melancholy redolent of a hidden and profound hopelessness that announces the
novel's tragic denouement.

The peculiar, exclusive placement of landscape in parts 1 and 4 of *La
Nouvelle Héloïse* succeeds in furthering a clear-cut division of the novel into
two parts. The division in question is not the formal one (six separate
parts and 163 separate letters) but rather the informal division into two
halves. Although this division, which I refer to as binary narrative structure, is established primarily in the plot, landscape is important in
underscoring the division. The first half of the novel presents Julie and
Saint-Preux's first relationship, the sinful, physical one, whereas the second half recounts their second relationship, the virtuous, platonic one.
The repetition of various secondary events reinforces the binary narrative
structure. Thus Edouard, who in the first half was ready to disregard class
differences for Julie and Saint-Preux's marriage, is in the second half ready
to disregard them for his own. Claire makes the decision to marry in the
first half and, after M. d'Orbe's death, not to marry in the second. Even
the tragic denouement echoes earlier episodes: the near-fatal smallpox that
Julie contracts in the first half is the structural counterpart of her fatal
drowning in the second; and Saint-Preux's departure for his world trip,
which marks the end of part 3, finds its binary echo in Julie's departure
through death at the end of part 6.

Landscape succeeds in contributing to structure because its concrete, visual quality enables it to stand out from the novel's mass of discursive material and effectively mark the beginnings of the text's major parts. The importance of such a structuring device in a long digressive novel like *La Nouvelle Héloïse* cannot be overemphasized. Indeed if Rousseau can lay claim to the distinction of being a novelist—and not just a philosopher or political theorist who happened, with no particular talent or success, to wander into the narrative domain—it is because of his skillful use of such structural devices. Vivienne Mylne aptly notes in this regard that "Rousseau is exceptional among eighteenth-century novelists in his ability to organize a long work as a coherent whole"; and she adds, "This kind of awareness of the crucial stages of a long story, and of the effectiveness of divisions and fresh beginnings, is something one does not find again in the novel until the nineteenth-century novelists, with their third-person narrative, re-establish the use of chapters."[11] One of landscape's chief roles in *La Nouvelle Héloïse* is to produce that sense of "fresh beginnings."

Another feature of the binary narrative structure of Rousseau's novel, and of landscape as an integral part of that structure, is to produce a framework containing antithetical features whereby the reader is encouraged to view the world of the novel in a bipolar or moralistic way. The binary narrative structure acts to give the impression that each part of the novel corresponds to one term of its many fundamental binary oppositions. Strictly speaking this is not the case, since elements of the oppositions exist in both halves. Each part does, however, contain an emphasis on one or another of the various opposed terms. Thus the reader has the general feeling that sinfulness, passion, and revolt mark the first half of the novel and that virtue, reason, and obedience mark the second. The novel seems, more or less, to move from bad to good, from virtue lost to virtue regained. The importance for a lengthy novel such as Rousseau's of thus creating an overall effect of antithesis—of weaving a fundamental sense of opposition into the very structure of the novel—is distinct and undeniable. Antithesis within or between sentences may have a potent contrastive effect in poems; but a novel requires that the antithesis affect major narrative divisions—chapters or whole parts—to produce a coherent contrast of its fundamental meanings.

Binary narrative structure does more, however, than just emphasize conflicts. It also conditions the reader to delve deeper and to discern symbolic resolutions to the conflicts that cannot be resolved at the surface level. As seen earlier, when the primitive mind is confronted with an irreconcilable opposition, it translates that opposition and brings it into relation symbolically with others in which reconciliation and mediation are possible. Thus those mythical and imaginary constructs in which contraries can coexist and combine are created at the deep, symbolic level. Before it can be seen how contraries thus coexist and combine in Rousseau's land-scape, it is necessary to explain why conflict remains unresolved at the surface level in *La Nouvelle Héloïse*.

The chief source of unresolved conflict in Rousseau's novel is Julie's re-jection of Saint-Preux and all that he and the outside represent. Julie's choice to marry Wolmar, the central fact of the plot, dramatizes but does not bridge the gap between her aristocratic father's loyalty to a traditional world of social integration on the one hand and her bourgeois lover's ad-herence to a modern world based on individualistic values on the other. On one side is the cluster of inside, aristocrat, and society; on the opposing side is the cluster of outside, bourgeois, and self. Another source of unresolved conflict is the creation of the presumably ideal society at Clarens. Clarens is supposed to resolve the oppositions that arise in the novel. There the outsider is brought into the inside world, disparate social classes harmoniously intermingle, and the family exists as a mediating structure between self and society. But there is an important sense in which conflict is only masked, not reconciled, at Clarens. Julie's deathbed letter reveals that even she was not happy there, that her own conflict be-tween passion and duty had never been truly resolved. And at the close of the novel there is reason to believe that the ideal community forged at Clarens will not continue to be played out in the years to follow. Clarens was perhaps the personal realization of an ideal for Wolmar, but it did not turn out to be a genuine historical solution to real social problems for any-one else.

The chief reason that Clarens represents only an imperfect resolution to the conflicts posed in the novel is that it is created in the midst of a world of inequality if not downright tyranny, of which within the novel Julie's father is an egregious example (though not in himself the true cause). In-deed, it is his class and class systems at large, far more than he as an indi-vidual, who are the real culprits, as Edouard is quick to point out in speaking to the elderly aristocrat about nobility: "The mortal enemy of laws and freedom, what did it ever produce in most of those countries where it has flourished except the force of tyranny and the oppression of the people? Do you dare to boast, in a republic, of a rank that is destruc-tive to virtue and humanity? Of a rank that boasts of slavery, and in which men blush to be men?" (p. 170). Inequality is thus inherent in the society Rousseau depicts in the novel, as it is for him in society generally.[12] Michèle Duchet notes in this regard,

> Thus each moment of Julie and Saint-Preux's "history" repeats the process of perversion whereby man strays from his intended purpose, gives in to his passions without respect for "natural" order and neces-sarily becomes corrupt in a corrupt society. . . . Depraved and alien-

ated in a society where nothing can legitimatize their passion, they have lost their natural being.[13]

Where inequality exists, the self thus remains alienated. On the surface, new social formations and solutions can be created, but on the deep personal level the integration between self and society—the true sense of communion and community—cannot be achieved.

Jean Starobinski articulates a central opposition in Rousseau's novel when he observes that it comes to a close with a choice: "Between the absolute of the community and the absolute of personal salvation, he opted for the latter. Julie's death signifies that option."[14] In order to resolve the opposition between community and self in a sustained and substantial way, Rousseau would have to spell out proposals for change within the pages of the novel, for example, a program for replacing tyrannical figures such as Julie's father or paternalistic, autocratic ones such as Wolmar with new figures who embody the principles of justice and equality. Neither in the novel nor even in his political writings can Rousseau conceive of change in concrete terms, his reputation in the popular mind as a revolutionary notwithstanding. But what cannot be conceived directly, in terms for example of specific solutions for the society at Clarens, can be conceived in the imaginary world of landscape. In that imaginary world, the ideal community to which the self aspires and from which it is excluded in the real world of inequality, assumes complex and multifaceted symbolic expression.

The way in which a community in nature is achieved in *La Nouvelle Héloïse* involves a curiously consistent pattern—a miniature dramatic enactment of the resolution of the conflict between self and others contained within the landscape itself. For, appearances to the contrary, it is in the very nature of landscape to involve an enactment of some sort, to be dynamic and dramatic. In the descriptions of the Valais and the second description of Meillerie, the enactment takes the form of the text's progression through a series of stages. First, temporal and spatial movement is arrested and a focus on the self is obtained. Next, oppositions are stated and antithetical terms are presented as coexisting and contrasting in nature. Finally, a sense of community is achieved, a state in which differences dissolve and disappear and in which a harmonious interaction occurs among self, nature, and others. That the same pattern can be discerned in two widely distant and different descriptions is not just a coincidence, but rather provides evidence that a consistent urge to resolve basic conflicts constitutes the internal mechanism of these descriptions.

The first stage of the minidrama enacted in the Valais and the second Meillerie descriptions—referred to below as (1) and (2), respectively—can be seen in the following quotations:

(1) On foot, I slowly ascended the mountains along rather rugged
trails, led by a man I had employed as my guide but in whom during
the whole trip I found a friend rather than a hired assistant. I wished
to meditate but I was always distracted by some unexpected sight.
(pp. 64–65; p. 77)

(2) We reached the place after an hour's walk over winding and
cool paths which, ascending imperceptibly between the trees and the
rocks, were not otherwise inconvenient except in their length. Approaching and recognizing my former signs, I was prepared to find
myself ill, but I overcame it, I hid my distress, and we arrived.
(p. 335; p. 518)

The initial emphasis is on a progressive movement in space (ascended,
trails, trip, paths) as well as in time (slowly, an hour's walk, length). This
movement, emblematic of the progressive course of time and history, occurs, significantly, in the company of another person with whom Saint-
Preux has a relationship of inequality: the guide in the first passage is his
social inferior, while Julie, in the second, is his superior. The difference
almost immediately ceases to be important, however. The other person is
soon forgotten and an intensely personal state is soon arrived at whereby
the self loosens its moorings to reality and others and exists only in and
through its subjective, transcendent relationship with nature.

The second stage of the drama entails the statement of oppositions — or
perhaps it would be more accurate to say their overstatement or exaggera-
tion. Such statements of opposition occur elsewhere in Rousseau's descriptions, though rarely in so striking a form:

(1) Sometimes immense rocks hung ruinous over my head. Sometimes high and clamorous waterfalls deluged me with their heavy
mist. Sometimes a perpetual torrent at my side would open an abyss
which my eyes dared not fathom. Sometimes I was lost in the obscurity of a luxurious forest. Sometimes as I emerged from a gorge a
pleasant meadow gladdened my eyes. (p. 65; p. 77)

(2) This solitary place formed a retreat, wild and deserted but full
of those kinds of beauties which please only sensitive souls and appear horrible to the others. A torrent caused by the thawing snows
rolled in a muddy steam twenty feet from us and noisily carried
along dirt, sand, and stones. Behind us a chain of inaccessible crags
separated the flat place where we were from that part of the Alps
called the glaciers, because of the enormous peaks of ice which, incessantly increasing, have covered them since the beginning of the
world. To the right, forests of black firs afforded us a gloomy shade.
A large wood of oak was to the left beyond the torrent, below us that
immense body of water that the lake forms in the midst of the Alps

separated us from the rich shores of the Vaud region, and the peak of the majestic Jura crowned the landscape. (p. 355; p. 518)

The first passage contrasts the immensity of nature with the vulnerability of man and opposes the rocks on high to the chasms below. It also contrasts the observer's distinct perception of sound to his blurred vision; the awesome, frightening abyss and rock formations to the pleasant, cheerful meadow. The second passage reinforces and supplements the oppositions contained in the first. Here, such fundamental spatial oppositions as near and far, high and low, left and right, horizontal and vertical are everywhere at work to organize and give visual, structural coherence to the descriptive act. Both passages come to a close with a strikingly positive image, that of the "pleasant meadow" and that of the "rich shores of the Vaud region." These closing images—which already contain intimations of a community in nature—are striking precisely because of the antithetical context out of which they arise. The rough isolation and sterility of the mountains do not only serve Rousseau as casual components of local color. Rather, the mountains are both setting and symbol for Saint-Preux's withdrawal from society and search for transcendent, subjective meaning. Only through and in contrast to the personal and geographical isolation represented by the mountains does the opposite of that isolation —the social integration represented by pleasant meadows and rich shores—assume its full meaning as a mediating figure in Rousseau's novel.

In the third stage of the drama enacted in Rousseau's landscapes, images of community in nature are developed. The process can perhaps best be observed in the attributes of the "pleasant meadow" in the Valais description:

(1) Next to a cavern there were houses; there were vineyards among landslides and where one would have expected only brambles; delicious fruit was found among rocks, and fields in the midst of precipices . . . nature seemed to take pleasure in acting in opposition to herself, so different did she appear in the same place in different aspects. Toward the east, the flowers of spring; to the south, the fruits of autumn; and northward, the ice of winter. She united all the seasons at the same time, every climate in the same place, different soils on the same land, and formed a harmony unknown anywhere else among the products of the plains and those of the Alps. (p. 77)

Although at first glance sterility and isolation might be expected to characterize Saint-Preux's mountain refuge, productivity and harmony turn out to be its true attributes: this becomes apparent solely on the basis of the symbolic treatment of nature, even before the novel turns, later in the letter, to extolling in explicit economic terms the qualities of the region. The symbolism at work here is of the sort associated earlier with Lévi-Strauss; it entails translating into terms of natural phenomena the oppositions that cannot be resolved in terms of human life. A community is achieved through the harmonious interaction between man and nature that could not be achieved by man in society. Significantly, nature has made itself exceedingly responsive to man's needs and wants, enabling and even favoring agricultural productivity despite the meager resources of the land. The whole process indeed is strikingly harmonious, with hours of the day, seasons, diverse climates and topographical formations all coexisting in a "harmony unknown anywhere else." Responsible for this harmony is the personified presence of "nature," which appears here, like Julie at Clarens, as an active feminine force: it is important to know that the word nature is feminine in gender and is referred to throughout the passage in the original French as *elle* and *la*. But there is an obvious and crucial difference between Julie and nature. Julie encountered real social differences and conflicts at Clarens that ultimately could not be resolved, whereas nature, at least as symbolically conceived in landscape, does not. In the ideal, imaginary world of landscape in which Rousseau resolves social conflict, differences simply dissolve and disappear.

A similar community in nature is achieved in the Meillerie description. In this case, a special spot is singled out, a distinct avatar of the pastoral *locus amoenus*:

> (2) In the middle of these great and superb objects, the small piece of ground where we were displayed the charms of a cheerful and sylvan refuge; some streams filtered through the rocks and rolled over the green in crystal rivulets. Some wild fruit trees bent their heads over ours; the moist and fresh earth was covered with grass and flowers. As I compared such a pleasant place to the things which surrounded it, it seemed that this deserted spot should have been the refuge of two lovers who alone had escaped the general confusion of nature. (p. 335; p. 518)

The rocks that surround this special place in no way preclude the passage of water, necessary to sustain life and permit agricultural productivity: indeed, this "cheerful and sylvan refuge" is a paradigm of such productivity, despite its sterile surroundings. As in myth, landscape here emerges as a structure of mediation. A harmonious interaction among self, nature, and others is indeed strikingly apparent here. Nature, personified, displays its charms; streams are busy at work actively providing the needed irrigation of the soil. The most striking personification, however, is that of the wild fruit trees, which seem lovingly to caress and protect the lovers. Here, Saint-Preux and Julie can find the acceptance, the equality, and the enduring bonds with others that reality has so consistently and tragically denied them. Here, they can stand outside of time and history in the ideal, utopian world of the ancient pastoral. Not only they but also this *locus amoenus* have escaped the "general confusion of nature" mentioned in the last words of the passage.

Several critics have noted this underlying denial of history. Jean Starobinski's comments in this regard are general and far-reaching:

> Rousseau only needs history, however, in order to furnish an explanation of evil. It is the idea of evil that gives the system its historical dimension. Becoming is the movement whereby humanity acquires guilt. Man is not naturally corrupt; he became so. The return to goodness thus coincides with the revolt against history and, specifically, against the existing historical situation. If it is true that Rousseau's thought is revolutionary, one must immediately add that it is so in the name of an eternal human nature, and not in the name of a historical progress.[15]

Another critic who concludes that Rousseau ultimately denies history is Manfred Kusch. In the following passage he discerns the denial specifically in Julie's garden, although elsewhere he has discovered it in the other landscapes as well:

> The garden is a privileged and jealously guarded space in which the elect are able to abandon their consciousness of the progression of time and the process of continuous change. By concentrating awareness on the experience of the present (le coeur, la promenade), man may attain at least the illusion of having returned to the source of humanity. As the stream may be made to produce its own springs, historical man can rediscover an image of his fundamental being in a garden surrounded by history.[16]

The ensuing chapters record the increasing historicism of the literature of images, the growing awareness, if not always direct acknowledgment, within the pages of the novel of the weighty existence of social and political events. Such an acknowledgment is not tantamount, I hasten to add, to a willingness or indeed ability to resolve social conflicts in a direct, positive manner that would find some straightforward, explicit expression in the text. These conflicts will still be deep-seated and their solutions still largely symbolic. Landscape continues, accordingly, to play a mediating role in later novels as it does in Rousseau's. But over time, the conflicts are less and less of the abstract philosophical sort found in Rousseau's writing (self versus others, nature versus culture); more and more they assume the variegated colors and configurations of concrete, contemporary history and politics.

3

Exiled in Exotic Lands:

Paul et Virginie and Atala

European Points of View

This chapter treats two descriptive novelists—Jacques-Henri Bernardin de Saint-Pierre and François-René de Chateaubriand—who have traditionally been grouped together, not only because they embody a common "pre-Romantic" stage in the development of French literary history but perhaps more importantly because they both wrote about the time of the tumultuous, chaotic events of the French Revolution—immediately prior in the case of Bernardin's *Paul et Virginie*, which dates from 1788, and roughly a decade later in that of Chateaubriand's *Atala*, which dates from 1801. Although they share a common historical context, these two celebrated descriptive novels do not display a common political outlook. Bernardin's novel upholds, at least on the surface, a Republican belief in a liberal, egalitarian society; Chateaubriand's implicitly promotes a Monarchistic adherence to a conservative, hierarchical one. Nevertheless, the special nature of the conflicts generated in the Revolutionary period does produce a common treatment of landscape in *Paul et Virginie* and *Atala*.

The conflictual nature of landscape in *Paul et Virginie* and *Atala* can perhaps best be understood in terms of the exotic subject of their landscapes. Superficially, it is true, the exotic subjects seem merely to provide a fresh setting, a decorative effect of local color. These subjects pose, however, certain very basic questions regarding the identities of the viewers of the exotic lands, the reasons for their location in the distant places, and the cultural and political values that affect their visions of exoticism. To answer these questions, it is necessary to acknowledge the subtle and multiple interconnections that exist between the exotic subject of landscape and such specific historical issues as colonialism and the exile and emigration of aristocrats after the French Revolution. The exotic in landscape is of the utmost importance for understanding the conflictual nature of landscape in the evolutionary stage of the literature of images represented by Bernardin and Chateaubriand. Like Rousseau's conflictual landscape based on opposition, theirs based on exoticism are grids for filtering landscape through into the consciousness of the novel's characters and readers. Unlike Rousseau's landscape, however, theirs display a distinct degree of historical specificity, a consistent though largely covert concern with such conflicts as that between a historical past and present, between old and new social and political forms, between traditional European or Christian values on the one hand and the alternative political and cultural model discovered in the exotic place on the other.

Attempting to uncover the conflicts embodied in Bernardin and Chateaubriand's landscapes beneath the superficial layer of local color requires examining the strikingly similar use of point of view in the two novels and its relation to the concept of exoticism. The opening pages of *Paul et Virginie* and *Atala* display virtually the same multiple, embedded narrative structure: this can perhaps be partially explained by the influence on Chateaubriand of Bernardin's novel, which he claimed to have known by heart.[1] The structure consists of an initially unsituated, seemingly omniscient voice, which then is identified as that of a first-person narrator. He is then replaced by another first-person narrator, an old man in both cases, who looks back upon events in his past life and who is thus both narrator of and participant in the story. This structure both hints at and yet contains within fixed limits the specifics of the narrators' identities in the two novels: in both cases the identity, which is so crucial for establishing exoticism, is that of the European outsider; Bernardin's narrator is a colonialist and Chateaubriand's is a political exile. I shall call the embedded narrative structure used in both *Paul et Virginie* and *Atala* a "containment strategy," following Fredric Jameson, and shall define this term as a narrative topic or technique that is truly pregnant with social and political meaning and yet acts paradoxically to control and limit the production of such meaning in the text.[2] It is characteristic of the evolutionary stage to which *Paul et Virginie* and *Atala* belong, when novelists still aspired to express general and universal truths and not merely local and historical ones, that Bernardin and Chateaubriand had consistent recourse to containment strategies.

The first important ingredient in the containment strategy that Bernardin and Chateaubriand deploy entails beginning with an anonymous, omniscient, generalizing type of narrative voice—one that raises yet fails to answer the questions of the narrator's identity and physical or temporal situation. This voice continues throughout several paragraphs of nature description at the beginning of the two novels. Consider their opening sentences: "On the eastern coast of the mountain which rises above Port Louis in the Mauritius, upon a piece of land bearing the marks of former cultivation, are seen the ruins of two small cottages"; "In days gone by, France possessed a vast empire in North America, extending from Labrador to the Floridas and from the shores of the Atlantic to the most remote lakes of Upper Canada."[3] From these sentences alone, it is impossible for the reader to answer with any certainty such questions as who is viewing nature, when the act of perception or description occurs, or even from what vantage point the scene is being viewed—although answers to these questions can be offered once the reader obtains more information about the narrative situation. Initially, then, the containment strategy is to maintain a general tone and thereby to forestall and contain the revelation of the specific conditions of the narrative act, for example, that a European traveler or inhabitant of the colonies is imposing his personal vision on the exotic place.

Several paragraphs into each text, when an "I" appears, it becomes possible to conclude that the provenance of all that has been read so far is a first-person "frame narrator," whose voice will be heard exclusively at the beginning and end. It is a voice that is not heard much but which, by virtue of its important initial and terminal placement, remains primordial in the novel. But even when the presence of this frame narrator has become apparent, a very general narrative tone is still used to forestall revealing the specifics of the narrative situation. This practice is especially salient in *Paul et Virginie* where, unlike *Atala*, until the end of the novel the reader knows virtually nothing about the frame narrator. He seems to be a European who is a transient sojourner on the distant island. In fact, however, all that is sure is that at the beginning he expresses a love for nature and an interest in hearing the principal narrator's tale, and that at the end he claims to have cried in hearing about Paul and Virginie's sad fate. The frame narrator can, of course, have other functions in addition to containment. Vivienne Mylne notes, for example, that this narrator serves to promote a sense of verisimilitude; furnishing details about the act of storytelling was a typical eighteenth-century technique for validating that act.[4]

It is significant that the longest and perhaps most salient description that *Paul et Virginie* contains—the one that occupies the syntagmatically crucial liminal position at the very beginning of the novel—is presented by the frame narrator who, as just noted, has no identifiable social, national, or personal traits. The reader is thus prepared for nature descriptions, and the reflections on social issues contained therein, for which no one assumes direct responsibility. These descriptions are passed off instead as general observations and exotic scenes. Consider for example the following sentence from the second paragraph of the opening description:

> At the entrance of the valley which presents those various objects, the echoes of the mountain incessantly repeat the hollow murmurs of the winds that shake the neighboring forests, and the tumultuous dashing of the waves which break at a distance upon the cliffs; but near the ruined cottages all is calm and still, and the only objects which there meet the eye are rude steep rocks, that rise like a surrounding rampart. (p. 2)

This description contrasts the calm found in the hidden enclave with the stormy, tumultuous conditions that prevail beyond its protective boundaries. Such a contrast constitutes an implicit rejection of the outside world of society—precisely the rejection formulated directly by the principal narrator and characters later in the novel. Here, however, the rejection is indirect. What is in fact a personal and largely social vision of landscape passes itself off as an objective observation of an exotic place.

In the case of *Atala*, matters are somewhat different, although similar generalizing and forestalling tactics apply. At the beginning, the first-person frame narrator barely appears at all; the sole indication of his presence is in the following phrase: "there emerge from the depths of the forest such sounds, and the eyes behold such sights, that it would be futile for me to attempt their description." In contrast, this narrator does not hesitate to call attention to his presence and to furnish information about himself at the end of the novel. There, he speaks of his travels to the exotic places described in the story and the conditions of his having heard the story from the Indian descendants of its chief participants. One of the most notable pieces of information is that he, like the principal narrator, is a political exile. Speaking of the exiled Indians whose hapless fate he evokes in the closing lines, he states: "like you, I wander at the mercy of men, and, less fortunate than you in my exile, I have not brought with me the bones of my fathers!" (p. 82). The important fact of the frame narrator's status as exile colors his perception and description of nature.

Another containment strategy at work in both *Paul et Virginie* and *Atala* involves the view from a boat on the ocean or river. The panorama of the island that is presented at the beginning of *Paul et Virginie* suggests a point of view facing the island and located at some distance from it. This point of view then shifts and seems, in the following sentence, to be looking at the ocean from the island: "On the left rises the mountain, called the Height of Discovery, whence the eye marks the distant sail when it first touches the verge of the horizon, and whence the signal is given when a vessel approaches the island." Even with the shift, however, the emphasis is on the boat–island axis and thus implicitly on the water as a narrative locus. (This sentence also acts to foreshadow Virginie's tragic return to the island at the end of the novel.) In *Atala*, the river serves as the implied narrative locus of the opening paragraph. The panoramic geographical view contained in the first sentence can, for example, be attributed to a traveler on a boat looking at a map. The rest of the opening description could then be said to record what is visible to the narrator from the river, like a camera filming a close-up. Later, significantly, the principal narrator will recount his story seated on a boat looking at the river. There is containment here in that Bernardin and Chateaubriand consistently attribute to the water the very specific social symbolism of historical change and social turmoil; yet at the same time they downplay the specifics of the water as the locus for narration—as if they sought both to grant and to deny the narrator a situation in time and history. There perhaps exists for

Bernardin and Chateaubriand that ambivalence about the water which, according to Jameson, makes the sea generally a privileged place for containment, as with Conrad, for whom it "is a border and a decorative limit, but it is also a highway, out of the world and in it at once."[5]

Subsequent to the opening pages attributable to the frame narrator, both *Paul et Virginie* and *Atala* present the first-person narration of the principal narrator. Again, containment strategies are at work in the text. The chief one consists in attributing a distinct social identity to this narrator while at the same time denying the political implications of that identity. In Bernardin's novel, the "old man" who both recounts the events of Paul and Virginie's lives to the frame narrator and depicts himself as a participant in those events is an inhabitant of the French colonies. The political implications of this identity entail implicitly upholding conservative European values generally and conservative colonialist values specifically. The fact that the upholding of these values is only implicit and was not the conscious intent of Bernardin, a liberal and egalitarian-minded author, must of course not be overlooked, for it undoubtedly explains the political ambivalence evident in *Paul et Virginie* and its landscapes.

It is essential with respect to Bernardin's colonial subject first to distinguish between an individual living in the colonies and the institution of colonialism itself and, second, to recognize the political power that the latter possesses. For according to Albert Memmi and other writers on the subject, it ultimately is the institution, not the personal motives and sentiments of individuals, that counts: "Colonial relations do not stem from individual good will or actions; they exist before his arrival or his birth, and whether he accepts or rejects them matters little. It is they, on the contrary which, like any institution, determine *a priori* his place and that of the colonized and, in the final analysis, their true relationship."[6] Now, Bernardin would have it that colonial relations *do* stem from individual goodwill, notably from that evinced by his benevolent old man, the narrator. Indeed the novel would have it that the old man bears no relation whatsoever to the exploitative, cruel figure of the colonialist; the poverty and humility of the one are repeatedly contrasted with the wealth and social dominance of the other. And it is true that the old man does not exploit anyone, grows just enough food to meet his own modest needs, and has no slaves to assist him.

But direct exploitation is a less important criterion according to Memmi than privilege; and according to that criterion, Bernardin's benevolent old man is in fact a colonialist. To cite a small but revealing detail, in spite of his claims to reject all comforts normally enjoyed by Europeans in the colonies, the old man reveals that for special occasions, high-quality French wines were his standard fare. Memmi denies that there exists that class of neutral colonials to which Bernardin's narrator purports to belong:

A colonial is a European living in a colony but having no privileges, whose living conditions are not higher than those of a colonized person of equivalent economic and social status. By temperament or ethical conviction, a colonial is a benevolent European who does not have the colonizer's attitude toward the colonized. All right! Let us say right away, despite the apparently drastic nature of the statement: a colonial so defined does not exist, for all Europeans in the colonies are privileged.[7]

Even the act of viewing people and nature in the colonies reflects the colonialist's privileged status. In "Black Orpheus" Sartre contends that the white man has for three thousand years enjoyed the privilege of seeing without being seen.[8] This is tantamount to saying that the European's visual powers and privileges are homologous to his economic ones, that to see a foreign culture as different, picturesque, or exotic is at the same time to impose one's values upon it.

Another containment strategy is that of presenting him as both an actual inhabitant of and an outsider to the exotic land. The reason for this strategy is to endow the narrator with two attributes, the requisite familiarity with the land and the necessary education and training to describe it; the "real native" or member of the colonized class would not have, to Bernardin's mind, the second of these attributes. Thus he has recourse to a European observer, but one whose European status he seeks to minimize. The minimizing is a strategy that produces yet limits and controls the social meaning in the novel, as did the strategies of generalizing the narrative tone in the frame and of sidestepping the political ramifications of the old man's association with colonial life.

Still another strategy involves the novel's male protagonist, Paul. Paul is the final link in the chain of embedded voices and points of view used in *Paul et Virginie*. That chain comprises three figures who embody varying degrees of integration into colonial life: the frame narrator is a mere visitor, the principal narrator is an inhabitant, and Paul is an authentic autochthon of the colonies. It is true that Paul is not himself a narrator; but he does have a privileged role with respect to both narration and description, in many of the ways that Saint-Preux was seen to have such a role in the last chapter. Often, the novel indirectly depicts his point of view on nature. It is also true that Paul is not exactly a "true native" inasmuch as his parents were French and he and his mother enjoy the privileged status of Europeans. The containment strategy consists in this case of using Paul to bridge the gap between two cultures by virtue of his being tied to his European heritage on the one hand and his being born in the distant colonies on the other. By establishing a series of points of view with increasingly greater but never total integration into the native culture, Bernardin establishes a cultural continuum rather than a dichotomy between the native and the European, the colonized and the colonizer. The act of viewing the land as an outsider thus becomes a matter of degree and its social and political implications are thereby controlled and contained.

Similar containment strategies affect the treatment of the principal narrator of Chateaubriand's *Atala*. After the opening pages of the novel attributable to the frame narrator, two characters appear on stage: one is Chactas, an elderly Natchez Indian chief, who serves as the principal narrator; the other is René, a young French exile to America living with the Indian tribe, who serves as the principal listener or narratee. The story chronicles Chactas's early years in Spain, his return to his native land, and the ill-starred passion he conceives for Atala, the daughter of a Spanish father and an Indian mother. It is apparent from just these few brief details that the strategy of creating a continuum of native and European voices and points of view applies also to *Atala*. Chactas, the principal narrator, in speaking to René, the principal narratee, sums matters up when he says, "I see in you the civilized man who has become a savage; you see in me the savage whom the Great Spirit has (I know not for what purpose) chosen to civilize" (p. 22). On the continuum, Atala and Chactas together stand nearest to but not totally integrated into the Indian culture, just as René and the frame narrator stand farthest away but not totally removed from it. The latter's knowledge of Indian language and customs is revealed, for example, when at the end of the novel he greets the last fleeing survivors of the Natchez tribe in what Chateaubriand would want us to believe is the authentic Indian way: "Brother, I wish you a blue sky, many roes, a beaver mantle, and hope" (p. 78).

Not only is Chactas placed on a continuum of native and European points of view, there is the further containment strategy of projecting onto him as a native the concerns of the European frame narrator, notably a nostalgic concern for his homeland and the drama of exile and emigration. In this regard, an association arises with the author himself. Chateaubriand's egotism—"I speak eternally of myself"—is well known, and it is thus not surprising to find that all of the narrative participants in *Atala* (the frame narrator, René, Chactas as both narrator and participant in the story, Atala herself) are exiles and as such are avatars of what Chateaubriand himself was. The strategy consists in this case of using the native observer as a double of the European—the frame narrator and the author—in order to sidestep the political ramifications of being either a native or a European. The author can allude to conflicts and even discover symbolic solutions to them without having to address directly the pressing problems of contemporary life.

It is pertinent in this context to mention Pierre Barbéris's contention regarding Chateaubriand's other short novel, *René*. Having studied the various first-person narrators in *René* and in Chateaubriand's other writings, Barbéris discovers that there is no clear-cut distinction for this author between a fictional "I" and a strictly historical one; rather, there is a calculated game of hide-and-seek whereby an authorial presence assumes greater or lesser degrees of responsibility vis-à-vis its statements about history. The reason for this game, Barbéris claims, is the problematic nature of history itself in Chateaubriand's time: "The ambiguity of the modern world will always prevent anyone, be it Chateaubriand or another, from providing clear-cut answers: if clear-cut answers were available, the discourse would be political not literary."[9] What Barbéris says about the game of hide-and-seek and the reasons for the game in *René* applies equally well to *Atala*, where Chactas is merely another fictional "I" responsible in part for the novel's historical and political meaning. Also applicable is Barbéris's demonstration of how with Chateaubriand the novel can be used as a sustained political metaphor. In the case of *René*, the tenor of the metaphor is the aristocrat's return to France under Napoleonic rule. In the case of *Atala*, it is his nostalgia for a pre-Revolutionary monarchical society.

Identifying Chactas's role in the production of historical and political meaning in *Atala* is essential for understanding his role in nature description. Chactas is himself responsible for relatively little actual landscape in the text. The chief descriptions of nature have the frame narrator, not Chactas, as their narrative source. There are only a number of short descriptive passages in Chactas's story, all of which are variations played on the themes introduced by the frame narrator at the beginning of the novel. Moreover, *Atala* exhibits motifs that emphasize Chactas's limited perceptual powers. The most obvious is his blindness. The principal narrator thus can only recollect nature settings; he can no longer actually perceive them. There also is the related motif of the darkness that enshrouds nature when Chactas recounts his story. As with Chactas's limited role generally as describer of nature, so too with these motifs, there is again containment at work. In this case, it consists of using Chactas to further the symbolic meaning that occurs in landscape while at the same time limiting and controlling his participation in this production. By establishing fixed limits within which the principal narrator can function as viewer of nature, history, and society, the novel assures that the European point of view of the frame narrator retains its priority.

The conflicts that arise in *Paul et Virginie* and *Atala*, in short, are attenuated by the very mechanisms used to introduce those conflicts, so that one gets a less historically specific set of conflicts at work in the novel. How and to what extent does landscape play a role in that attenuated expression of social conflict in the two novels? The specifics of nature description in *Paul et Virginie* and *Atala* will show that the exotic landscape is far from being the mere geographical or aesthetic digression that it is often taken to be. It is not an incidental detail but a consubstantial part of the unifying themes and patterns of the novels. Nor is exoticism the socially or politically neutral subject that the readers and perhaps even the authors assumed it to be. Intimations of Bernardin's ideal Republic and of Chateaubriand's ideal Monarchy are everywhere to be found in the diverse and heterogeneous natural phenomena—mountains, trees, rivers, plants—that abound in their descriptions of nature.

In Search of the Republican Ideal

Landscape in *Paul et Virginie* has been frequently discussed, but only at the superficial level of local color. Again and again critics have praised Bernardin for his exotic flora and fauna and for his sensitive renderings of light, season, and mood: indeed they have singled him out not only as one of the forerunners of French Romanticism but even as the creator of the exotic novel in France.[10] But no one to my knowledge has as yet seriously attempted to go beneath the surface and explore the unifying principle of his landscapes or their relation to the overall structure of the plot. Little attention has been given for that matter to the plot at all, the prevalent suspicion seeming to be that Bernardin's narrative practices are, like his political and philosophical outlook, seriously marred by incoherence and conceptual confusion.[11] There is in short an ambivalent critical attitude to Bernardin, which dwells on his paramount contribution to the development of landscape and Romanticism while at the same time virtually ignoring or dismissing his substantial achievement as a novelist.

There is more coherence than meets the eye in *Paul et Virginie*, and this coherence manifests itself in large part through the novel's principal landscapes. Three of these landscapes will be the primary focus of the discussion that follows: the opening description of the island, the description of Paul's garden, and the description of the old man's home in the forest. All three landscapes embody the novel's central conflicts between the old and the new, between traditional European and Christian values on the one hand and the alternative political and cultural model developed in the exotic place on the other. The alternative model is that of an ideal egalitarian, Republican society; early in the novel it appears that establishing such a society has been the most profound aspiration of Paul and Virginie's mothers in coming to the island: "But they found consolation in reflecting that their more fortunate children, far from the cruel prejudices of Europe, would enjoy at once the pleasure of love and the blessings of equality" (p. 13). However, the Republican ideal remains only imperfectly realized in *Paul et Virginie*, even on the imaginary plane of landscape. Bernardin tends to have recourse either to the containment strategy of shifting from the social to the transcendent plane, thereby eluding any sustained development of social models, or else to one of fostering illusions about social interaction, presenting as a new egalitarian alternative what in truth is a reaffirmation of the status quo. These containment strategies establish definite limits for dealing with social and political issues in the novel.

The opening description of the novel begins with an emphasis in the first paragraph on distance, both temporal and spatial. The mention that is made of "the marks of former cultivation" and "the ruins of two small cottages" plainly posits a retrospective point of view from the frame narrator who, subsequent to having heard the story, looks at the landscape as the scene of past events. Spatial distance is suggested generally through the panoramic vision of the island and specifically through references to far-off objects in space: "the distant sail," "the verge of the horizon," "the furthest bounds of the island," "the expanded ocean." Place-names also bespeak temporal and spatial distance. References to "the Bay of the Tomb" and "the Cape of Misfortune" further the sense of a retrospective vision insofar as they foreshadow Virginie's tragic fate. And the name of the port (Port Louis) and the island itself (in French, Ile-de-France) are resonant with the homeland and its king. That oblique allusions should be made in the description of the exotic landscape to the psychological states of remembering and perhaps even longing for the homeland is not surprising. In his analysis of the colonial mentality, Memmi contends that the distant homeland always casts its shadow on what the colonialist sees around him, despite his ostensible rejection of that homeland. "The result," says Memmi, "is that the colonialist is unsure of his true nationality. He navigates between a faraway society which he wants to make his own (but which becomes to a certain degree mythical), and a present society which he rejects and thus keeps in the abstract."[12] Colonialists generally thus evince the same drive to contain and control social and political issues that novelists such as Bernardin and Chateaubriand do in writing about colonies. It is easy to imagine European inhabitants of the distant land—as both authors were—casting their eyes on their immediate surroundings but seeing instead the distant homeland which they continue to remember and whose values they tend unwittingly to reaffirm.

The distinguishing mark of the distant reality beyond the island, significantly, is its chaotic, turbulent nature, which is evoked principally through images of the stormy sea; these images appear at the beginning and end and as a leitmotif during the course of the novel. It is plain that they evoke some kind of negative or disruptive forces in the faraway French society—forces such as social conflict, injustice, upheaval, abrupt change, or perhaps all of these combined, while the spot in which the protagonists live and in which the principal scenes of the novel are set represents a shelter from the disruptive forces of the stormy sea. Paul and

Virginie's enclave is presented in precisely such terms: "Within this inclosure reigns the most profound silence. The waters, the air, all the elements are at peace" (p. 2). As the novel develops, it becomes apparent that the social character of the shelter—its value as pastoral haven, utopia, or ideal Republic—is indeed the central subject.

It would be wrong to overlook the conflictual nature of the opening description in *Paul et Virginie* and take it as a simple rejection of the old (the world of the stormy sea) and affirmation of the new (the shelter as a social structure offering relief): for the shelter is not only affirmed but subtly undermined at the same time in Bernardin's novel. The undermining occurs in a number of ways in the opening description. The most obvious is by the mention of "the ruins of two small cottages." It is thus apparent from the start, even before the social significance of the shelter has been developed, that despite its peacefulness it does not succeed in being a viable place to live and work.

Further evidence of the dual process whereby the value of the shelter is both affirmed and undermined, and thus of the essentially conflictual character of *Paul et Virginie*, is provided in the on-the-spot account of the objects that "meet the eye" as the viewer-describer enters the valley:

> Scarcely does the echo repeat the whispers of the palm-trees spreading their broad leaves, the long points of which are gently agitated by the winds. A soft light illumines the bottom of this deep valley, on which the sun shines only at noon. But even at the break of day the rays of light are thrown on the surrounding rocks; and their sharp peaks, rising about the shadows of the mountain, appear like tints of gold and purple gleaming upon the azure sky. (p. 2)

On the one hand, the shelter plainly is offered here as a social place, a new and different world in which people together can find happiness. On the other hand, the shelter is presented as a transcendent place, a static world in which the individual, cut off from others, can find inner peace: for there is an important sense in which the preceding passage presents not only a glimpse of community but also an epiphany. All of nature seems to be glimpsed here in a moment of silent prayer, with objects in nature pointed upward and bathed in a luminous, otherworldly glow. Moreover, a sense of divine majesty can be discerned, especially in the original French text, where the surrounding rocks and their peaks are designated as the *couronnement* of the enclosure. The regal colors of gold and purple in which the mountains appear further the sense of majesty. The religious images that appear in the text contradict the Republican ideal both because of the hierarchical values they reveal and because of the strictly personal, transcendent experience they suggest, an experience tantamount to refusing to participate in a collective existence with others over time. These religious images thus serve as an indication of the essentially ambiguous attitude the novel exhibits to the Republican ideal, an ideal that it both promotes and fails to realize in landscape.

It is very much to the point at this juncture to mention some of the characteristics of what the historian of religion Mircea Eliade calls "religious space." There exists, Eliade tells us, a certain special area—like Bernardin's enclave—that is qualitatively different and unique in the religious experience of space. This area "allows the world to be constituted, because it reveals the fixed point, the central axis for all future orientation."[13] This is the space at the center of the world. Not only is this space centrally located; it extends upward to the heavens and downward to the depths of the earth and sea. The opening up onto the heavens is especially crucial to assure an opening "by which the gods can descend to earth and man can symbolically ascend to heaven."[14] Thus there is constituted a vertical, cosmic axis of which the sacred pole or pillars are the most frequent symbols, along with the closely related symbol of the mountain. To the religious mind, the existence of this axis assures communication with the sky.

Eliade's religious space has distinct relevance for the enclosure that serves as the setting of *Paul et Virginie*. In the passage being considered here, verticality is strongly emphasized. The vertical axis starts at the bottom of the valley, extends up the side of the mountains, and reaches its terminal point where the mountain peaks and the heavens meet. Eliade notes in this regard that religious space is always "open above—that is, in communication with heaven, the paradoxical point of passage from one mode of being to another."[15] In Bernardin's novel, the temptation is often strong to make the passage to a transcendent mode, to leave behind the social demands of the enclosure and day-to-day existence. This temptation can be discerned from the outset in the verticality and religious character of Paul and Virginie's enclosure.

Two short descriptive passages later in the novel present variations on these religious themes. In one, the moon appears, and the landscape once again glows with a spiritual luminescence. The mountains especially attract light, their peaks producing a glistening, silvery effect. Then the reader learns that the "stars sparkled in the heavens, and were reflected in the bosom of the sea that repeated their trembling images" (pp. 73–74). Implicit in this description is the notion of the cosmic axis extending from the sea below to the heavens above. Another passage describes an ascending movement, reaching up piles of rocks, through difficult paths, toward a "cone of hanging and inaccessible rocks called the Thumb," followed by this detailed scene:

At the foot of that cone is a stretching slope of ground, covered with lofty trees, and so high and steep that it appears like a forest in air, surrounded by tremendous precipices. The clouds, which are attracted round the summit of the Thumb, supply innumerable rivulets, which fall to so great a depth in the valley situated behind that mountain, that from this elevated point we do not hear the sound of their fall. (pp. 79–80)

The transcendence here involves reaching a point where the summit of the mountain and the clouds are one—that point of passage which is a consubstantial part of the religious experience of space. It was seen in chapter 1 that at the end of *La Peau de chagrin*, Balzac's character also experiences a transcendent experience in a special place designated in the text as a "cone"; so too, incidentally, do the protagonists of George Sand's *Indiana*. The cone clearly is a recurrent element of the narrative landscape and an indicator of intertextual influence.

Landscapes in *Paul et Virginie* thus display a dual process whereby nature is endowed with social significance on the one hand and with a conflicting religious, transcendent significance on the other. The result is a refusal to play out over time the existential, historical experience of life with others in society. Such a refusal is a profound and inescapable theme in Bernardin's novel. Although he is not the only character to choose this course, it is the narrator who introduces the religious along with the social in the nature descriptions examined thus far, and he who is torn between the competing forces of society and religion. On the surface, it is true, he has rejected religion: for example he does not go to church as Paul's and Virginie's mothers do. But beneath the surface, religion has not totally loosened its hold. Nor have certain other of the old, European values which he claims to reject but which still color his perceptions and produce conflict when the island is conceived as a new social alternative.

To turn away from landscape per se momentarily, it is apparent that as with religion, so too with social class, *Paul et Virginie* exhibits an essentially conflictual outlook. In this case, the conflict arises from the collision of the narrator's new egalitarian principles with his old European prejudices. Because of these prejudices, Paul and Virginie's enclave is undermined and doomed to failure as an ideal Republic from the start. To understand the nature of these prejudices and the conflicts to which they give rise, it is necessary to provide a brief summary of the information about the main characters supplied in the early pages. Mme. de la Tour, scion of an ancient noble house, has married beneath her social class, and her family has disowned her. The couple emigrates to the colonies where, after M. de la Tour's untimely death, Mme. de la Tour is left alone with an infant girl, Virginie. Fleeing from society, she settles in the deserted, rocky region of the enclosure where she encounters a French peasant woman, Marguerite, similarly alone and occupied with the care of an infant, her son Paul. Class issues have also caused Marguerite's flight from society. Seduced and deceived by a nobleman, she has decided to leave home, "and go, where her fault might be concealed, to some colony distant from that country where she had lost the only portion of a peasant girl—her reputation" (p. 6). The two women band together and, with the help of their neighbor, the "old man" and principal narrator of the novel, they create a presumably egalitarian, communal society in the enclosure.

Even from the start, however, this society is not the perfect model of an ideal Republic that the narrator presents it as being. Many readers have noticed that the community's dependence on Mme. de la Tour's and Marguerite's faithful servants Domingue and Marie belies the author's avowed Republican beliefs. But there are other, more subtle indications as well. In the novel the aristocratic mother is referred to, respectfully, as "Madame," whereas her peasant counterpart is designated, familiarly, by her first name. Likewise, in dividing up the enclosure for the two women, the narrator grants to Mme. de la Tour the upper and to Marguerite the lower part: in many places, France among them, the higher sections of a town typically are inhabited by the upper classes. It is possible even to interpret the names of the two mothers symbolically: Virginie's mother is lofty, like a tower; Paul's is earthy, like a "marguerite" or simple daisy. There is an irony, I might add, connected with the aristocratic name "de la Tour" and its lofty connotation, insofar as the name was not Mme. de la Tour's but that of her nonaristocratic husband. In short, through such subtle reminders, class differences are not forgotten in the new society, its participants' protestations to the contrary notwithstanding.

The principal narrator has a role in the implicit inequality in the enclosure's communal life. There is an important sense in which the inequality can be said to derive from him. It is the narrator who speaks of one mother with respect and the other with familiarity. It is also he who is prone to racist comments, saying that Paul was "indifferent as a Creole with respect to what was passing in the world" (p. 83), or that the natives were speaking in "the usual desultory manner of the indolent Creoles" (p. 119).

More significant than chance remarks like these, however, is the narrator's consistent tendency to delude himself about differences with respect to class and race. Examples are provided in two episodes in which the native and European inhabitants of the island intermingle. In the first, Paul and Virginie are lost in the woods after having tried to help a suffering black slave; grateful natives form a procession to carry the children home. All here is order, gratitude, and harmony, despite the fact that the result of Paul and Virginie's supposed good deed was to return the slave to her master and probably to worsen her fate, if not to seal her doom altogether. The second episode again contains a procession, a likely symbol of the colonialist's desire to impose order and control on the natives' movements; in this case it is the funeral procession for Virginie. What is noteworthy in this procession is the distinct social hierarchy that is followed and which the narrator in no way thinks to question or reject:

> A body of grenadiers led the funeral procession. . . . Eight young la-dies of the principal families of the island, dressed in white, carrying palm branches in their hands, bore the body of their young compan-ion covered with flowers. They were followed by a choir of children chanting hymns. After them came all the principal inhabitants of the island, the administrative staff, followed by the governor and the crowd of the people. [16]

The text would of course have it that the "crowd of the people," the na-tives of the island, are as willing and happy to accept their lowly place in the procession as on the island generally. It would also have it that they are as grieved by Virginie's death as if she were herself a native. In short, *Paul et Virginie* presents a mere illusion of the harmonious intermingling of natives and Europeans, just as it presents an illusion of the equality be-tween social classes. The old man is unable to see the non-Republican ele-ments in the island society. As a result, the novel as a whole cannot transcend its European point of view on the colonies or its hierarchical conception of society.

To return now to the specifics of landscape, the lengthy description of Paul's garden reveals the same conflicting urges toward the new and the old, the egalitarian and the hierarchical observed elsewhere. The tension that underlies this description is apparent from the start: Paul "at twelve years of age, was stronger and more intelligent than Europeans are at fifteen, and had embellished the plantations which Domingue [in French, "le noir Domingue"] had only cultivated" (p. 33). Paul thus emerges from the outset as embodying the conflicting qualities of the native and the European—the innate strength and intelligence of the former versus the aesthetic sensibility of the latter. Now, at first blush the native element in Paul seems to carry the greatest weight, but in many ways Paul can be found to have more of the European. The second sentence of the descrip-tion presents him symbolically in the typical role of exploiter of the is-land's resources: he had gone with Domingue "to the neighboring woods, and rooted up young plants of lemon-trees, oranges, and tamarinds." Sub-sequent sentences further the symbolism of exploitation by presenting Paul's horticultural achievement in terms of the accumulation and display of great wealth. Thus white flowers hang upon his agathis tree "like the crystal pendants of a lustre" and the trunk of the papaw tree "forms a column set round with green melons, surmounted by a capital of large leaves." The image that comes to mind is one of the luxurious, ostentatious home of a wealthy landowner.

Then there is the control and mastery Paul establishes in the garden. The plants obey the cultivator, referred to in the French text as "leur jeune maître," by affording him shade and fruit. And he is careful to keep the entire garden under his close scrutiny: "Those trees were disposed in such a manner that you could command the whole at one view." Indeed Paul cultivating his garden is like the colonialist running his plantation. The text states, significantly, that Paul *subjugated* the plants according to his designs, the notion of subjugation being unfortunately lost in the English translation, which renders the phrase "en assujettissant ces végétaux à son plan" as "in blending these vegetable productions to his own taste." As with people, so too with plants, egalitarian principles simply do not hold sway in the enclosure, although the narrator presumably thinks that they do. Thus it is not surprising to discover that Paul's plants must conform to a hierarchy: "He had placed in the middle of this hollow the plants of the lowest growth: behind grew the shrubs; then trees of an ordinary height; above which rose the venerable lofty trees which bordered the circumference." The result is that hierarchical yet harmonious aggregate which to the narrator's mind is tantamount to an ideal, egalitarian world: "Every plant grew in its proper soil, and every spot seemed decorated by Nature's own hands"; "He had drawn some advantage from the most rugged spots; and had blended, in harmonious variety, smooth walks with the inequalities of the soil, and wild with domestic trees" (p. 35).

In the third and last lengthy landscape in *Paul et Virginie*—the description of the old man's home in the forest—there is again evidence of the tensions between the new and the old, between the principal narrator's will to forge new social alternatives on the one hand and his tendency to fall back upon traditional European values and institutions on the other. This description, like the opening one, displays a containment strategy: no sooner does it raise social issues than it sidesteps them, no sooner does it evoke images of an ideal Republic than it veers off in the direction of a personal transcendent experience. Not surprisingly, the narrator begins the description of his forest retreat by saying that "there is much there that is interesting, especially for a man who, like me, prefers self-communion to looking abroad upon external objects" (p. 96). Even when the principal narrator finds evidence in nature of the social integration necessary for a Republic, it is only his own personal experience ultimately that concerns him. Bernardin perhaps never got past his early obsession with Robinson Crusoe alone on his island; the narrator in his forest retreat is more a solipsistic than a social being.

The description of the narrator's retreat in *Paul et Virginie* initially appears to dwell wholly on the harmonious interaction that exists in his forest home among its vegetal, animal, and human inhabitants. But the interaction is in fact quite limited. With respect to vegetation, the most striking images of interaction concern the vines called lianas: "There intertwine lianas of various foliage, which reach from one tree to another, forming here arcades of flowers and there canopies of verdure." Even here, however, what is important to the narrator is not only the symbolic union of the vines but also the personal benefits he derives from the arcades and canopies they form. Similarly he is pleased that the river and the trees cooperate to provide him with "a long canal shaded by all varieties of foliage" and that the odor from the forest vegetation obligingly perfumes his clothing. As in the vegetal so too in the animal domain, the interaction is of only limited concern to the narrator. He does observe, it is true, that the monkeys coexist happily and display human feelings of affection: "some swinging in the air, suspended by their tails; others leaping from branch to branch with their little ones in their arms." But his greater concern seems to be with the companionship "the domesticated inhabitants of our forests" afford him, just as his concern with the birds that travel from afar to grace his forest retreat is with the color and joyful warbling and chirping sounds they provide.

It is not surprising, in view of the limited kind of interaction that characterizes Bernardin's landscape, that the description comes to an end on a resolutely personal and transcendent note. A striking image of falling water occurs:

> The river which runs rippling over a bed of rocks through the trees, reflects here and there in its limpid waters their venerable masses of verdure and shadow, as well as the sports of their inhabitants; a short distance beyond it is precipitated over ledges of rocks, forming in its fall a sheet of water smooth as glass, and breaking at the bottom into a foaming mass. Innumerable confused sounds issue from these tumultuous waters, which, dispersed by the winds of the forest, sometimes seem near and sometimes far off, and sometimes deafening as the clang of cathedral bells (p. 97).

As in the opening description, the tumultuous movement of water serves here to evoke social upheaval: the water "is precipitated over ledges of rocks" and ends up "breaking at the bottom into a foaming mass." This upheaval is no sooner evoked, however, than it is dismissed; its sounds are "dispersed by the winds of the forest" and then finally transformed into "the clang of cathedral bells."

Whereas the upheaval is dismissed and dispersed in the narrator's retreat, as are serious social problems generally, the inner, transcendent experience of nature is enhanced and intensified. It is pertinent in this context to cite another use of water imagery in the novel: elsewhere the text states that in the solitude of nature, the soul can find "the pure consciousness of herself, of Nature, and of its Author" and that "the muddy water of a torrent which has ravaged the plains, turning aside from its course into some little basin, deposits its slime, resumes its primitive clearness, and, once more pure, reflects within its own banks the verdure of the earth and light of heaven" (p. 93). Similarly in the narrator's forest retreat, there is the reflection in the river's "limpid waters" of the "venerable masses of verdure and shadow." There is clear water, "smooth as glass," an obvious analogue of the clear, pure state of consciousness and transcendence the narrator has achieved in nature. Achieving that individual state is not tantamount, however, to achieving a comparably pure or ideal social state. The narrator of *Paul et Virginie* is apparently too concerned with the one to develop the other, even on an imaginary, symbolic plane.

The transcendent, essentially asocial tendencies seen in landscape are reflected in the similar tendencies that become apparent in the tragic ending of *Paul et Virginie*. Virginie has been prevailed upon to leave the island enclave and go to France, where Mme. de la Tour's rich aunt has tried to force her to accept the false values of a shallow, materialistic world. Due to her persistent refusal to comply, Virginie has been sent back home; but a storm arises at sea and because of her extreme modesty, which prevents her from disrobing in order to save her life, she drowns. Her distraught loved ones cannot endure for long the sorrow incurred by this tragic death; the deaths of Paul, Marguerite, and Mme. de la Tour follow shortly upon Virginie's. But the veneration this death inspires does endure. Faithful to her name, Virginie remains in the memory of her island compatriots as the eternal embodiment of purity, innocence, and virtue. The happiness she was denied in life is granted to her in death, not only in the afterlife but also in her lasting role as a symbol, even a saint, of virtue.

A number of readers and critics of *Paul et Virginie* have underscored the centrality of this religious experience. One of these was Chateaubriand, who in *Le Génie du Christianisme* comments that, taken out of its religious context, Virginie's death would be patently absurd. Chateaubriand observes that "Paul's lover is a 'Christian' virgin; and the dénouement, which would seem ridiculous with a less pure belief, here becomes sublime."[17] Clifton Cherpack also focuses on the essentially religious dénouement of *Paul et Virginie* but goes farther than Chateaubriand by making the vital connection between the end of the novel and the European point of view that is manifest in the novel as a whole. According to Cherpack, Bernardin's point in *Paul et Virginie* is "to show his readers that civilization's prejudices remain ineradicable in transplanted Europeans, however close to nature they may come to live."[18] Cherpack goes on to note that these prejudices are embodied most notably in Mme. de la Tour and the narrator, despite the latter's claim to be an enemy of civilization; in these characters persists a Christian pessimism whereby a terrible price must be paid for living and whereby death and the hereafter are superior to life. This pessimism is what renders ambiguous the characters' world views, their ostensible liberation from Christian or European values notwithstanding. Thus Mme. de la Tour at the same time wants an egalitarian society and yet wants Virginie to acquire the wealth that would assure her a superior place in the island's social and economic hierarchy. And thus the narrator at the same time ostensibly rejects religion yet resorts to Christian arguments about the unworthiness of life and the value of death in trying to console Paul.

Analysis of the denouement of *Paul et Virginie* thus supports what has been seen in the novel's landscapes, the profound and inescapable effect of the European point of view. It is thus not purely by chance that the egalitarian society that the novel at the surface level seeks to promote proves at a deeper level to be unrealized. Despite the apparent willingness to forge new social alternatives, all of the old values remain in place. The notions of "equality" and "Republic" do not assume depth and consistency: either an implicit hierarchy masquerades as the Republican ideal or else a personal and religious transcendence takes the place of a true resolution of social, collective conflicts. The novel, in short, represents a stage at which social and historical conflicts are conceived in a concrete way but resolutions to these conflicts have just begun to be glimpsed on the author's horizon. Two decades later, with Chateaubriand, a far more solid and specific sense emerges of what resolutions to social conflicts represent.

In Search of the Homeland

The fundamental conflict that underlies the exotic landscapes found in Chateaubriand's *Atala* and which furnishes the internal dynamics of this celebrated descriptive novel is, as in Bernardin's novel, a conflict between the old and the new, between traditional European and Christian values on the one hand and the alternative cultural and political systems discovered in the colonies on the other. The conflict is posed in different terms and divergent fashions in the two works, however. Perhaps the most noteworthy difference lies in the greater willingness or ability to concretize solutions to social conflicts that Chateaubriand's novel displays. This specificity is especially salient in the lengthy description with which Chateaubriand begins his novel, which develops the ideal homeland that *Atala* proposes indirectly as a solution to social conflict. Resonance of the ideal homeland can then be discovered later in the novel in other landscapes and major episodes.

The following interpretation of the opening description in *Atala* focuses on one specific symbolic meaning, that of the French aristocrat's exile after the Revolution and his resulting search to resolve conflicts between his past and present and his individual and collective consciousnesses, a meaning illuminated at the end of the novel by the revelation that the narrator is an exile. Exile proves to have as much thematic significance in both parts of the novel's frame; it simply finds a less direct form of expression in that odd, extended, symbolic description of the Mississippi River to be examined now.

The existence of an underlying symbolism of exile at work in *Atala* is manifest from the beginning of the novel, as is a vivid sense of the homeland that has been left behind. The historical fact of France's losing its colonial empire is mentioned in the very first line: "In days gone by, France possessed a vast empire in North America, extending from Labrador to the Floridas and from the shores of the Atlantic to the most remote lakes of Upper Canada" (p. 17). This mention conveys from the outset the exile's feeling of nostalgia and regret and announces the key themes of loss and defeat. It is even possible to detect oblique allusions to the fall and exile of the French monarchy in the second sentence, where such words as "unknown seas" and "Bourbon" are used to describe the principal American rivers: the allusions are stronger in the original French, where one also reads that the St. Lawrence River "se perd à l'est dans le golfe" and the Mississippi "tombe" from north to south to the Gulf of Mexico. Also noteworthy is the initial use of the past tense, which situates events in the past and reflects the exile's preoccupation with history and memory. A retrospective perspective on events is thus posited from the very beginning.

Equally significant is the fact that the past tense in the first paragraph dies away and is suddenly replaced by the present tense in the second; for at the beginning of the novel there is a strong pull toward an immediate and concrete experience of the present—such as an exile might have of creating a new life and rejecting the old, of searching to create a new homeland. The preface to the first edition of the novel states that "*Atala* was written in the desert and in the huts of savages"; and though almost certainly apocryphal, this claim is echoed in the opening description's appearance of an on-the-spot report of natural phenomena—phenomena being perceived concurrently with the written transcription of them. The pull toward immediacy at the beginning of the novel is thus more than just a pull toward a sensually fulfilling present moment. Because of the way in which perception and writing are joined in an attempt to capture present reality fully, there develops a metaphysical sense of presence and fullness of meaning. And indeed, that sense was, according to Jean-Pierre Richard, what Chateaubriand sought in nature in the early years when *Atala* was written: "In the American forest he discovers with wild joy an immediate and sensory presence"; "At one and the same time unified, varied, and radiant, nature can thus be dreamed of as the locus of a sort of ontological triumph."[19]

Already in the first two paragraphs of the novel, then, the peculiar temporal situation of the exile emerges, with its divergent impulses toward recollection and nostalgia on the one hand and immediacy and presence on the other. That the two impulses can coexist in the landscape indicates one of its chief symbolic functions in *Atala*, that of producing an imaginary synthesis of divergent temporal dimensions. In the landscape generally, as in the first two paragraphs, the immediate is rooted in the past and indelibly stamped with history's tragic mark, while at the same time the past is remembered from within an immanence, a sensuously perceived present moment: to quote Richard again, "What is memory if not the ability to leave the present and enter into the past, then to return from the past to the present, but a present now enriched and intensified by the resonance of an anteriority?"[20] By achieving a synthesis of past and present, the exile can recreate in the present moment and place what he possessed and lost in the past, to wit, his home.

In paragraph three, landscape again functions as a symbolic synthesis of past and present and fulfils another symbolic function as well: that of supplying the exile with an imaginary union of self and other. Achieving this union is tantamount to achieving the sense of a home, a place where the self belongs and has ties with his fellow countrymen. Near the beginning of this paragraph, allusions are made to the cataclysmic events of Chateaubriand's time:

> the Meschacebe . . . waters a delightful country, which the inhabitants of the United States call New Eden, while the French have bequeathed to it the gentle name of Louisiana. A thousand other rivers, all tributaries of the Meschacebe . . . enrich it with their silt and fertilize it with their waters. When all these rivers are swollen with the winter floods, when storms have leveled entire sections of the forests, the uprooted trees collect in the streams. Soon the mud cements them, vines bind them together, and finally plants take root everywhere and solidify the remains. Swept along by the foam-crested waves, these masses move down to the Meschacebe. The river takes hold of them and carries them down to the Mexican gulf, where it leaves them on the sandy banks, thus multiplying its mouths. At times it lifts its voice as it passes the hills, and pours its flood waters around the forest colonnades and pyramids of Indian tombs; it is the Nile of the wilderness. But grace is always joined with splendor in scenes of nature. While the middle current is pushing dead trunks of pines and oak trees down to the sea, floating islands of pistia and water lilies, their yellow blosoms rising like little banners, drift upstream along the banks in the two side currents. Green serpents, blue herons, pink flamingoes, and young crocodiles take passage on

these floral vessels, and the entire colony, unfurling in the wind its golden sails, drifts, sunken in sleep, to a landing in some hidden cove of the river. (pp. 17–18)

Allusions to Chateaubriand's time are made through the mention of the floods and storms to which the Mississippi's tributaries are subject; and man's helplessness in the face of these events is suggested through the verbs used to describe the trees being swept along by the river's movements. The trees indeed constitute an especially strong element of Chateaubriand's symbolism; throughout the novel, they represent man, just as the river does time and history. Here, the tragic participants in the drama of the river's tempestuous movements are "the uprooted trees" and the "dead trunks of pines and oak trees" (in French, "les cadavres des pins et des chênes"), the latter being especially evocative of those other victims of social change, the last of the Natchez, seen drying their dead son's body on the branches of a tree in the Epilogue. Another key symbolic factor is apparent in the forest colonnades and pyramids of Indian tombs, which Michael Riffaterre has identified as part of an architectural vocabulary or *thème monumental* that is a stylistic constant in Chateaubriand's writing. Not only a linguistic embellishment, this theme serves to link past and present, to institute the dimension of time in the text. The monument is in Chateaubriand's imaginary world a meeting point of people and periods that reality has separated.[21] It thus reinforces the function of landscape as a structure of temporal mediation and as a means for creating an imaginary sense of the homeland.

Still another area of symbolic expression in paragraph three involves oblique allusions to the common fate of the exiles in the distant land. Early in this paragraph, there is a concentration of verbs ("collect," "cement," "bind," "take root," "solidify") which all suggest an attaching or joining of the uprooted trees, like exiles banding together to share their suffering. And a similar symbolism of coming together and sharing a common fate appears later in the paragraph, where serpents, herons, flamingoes, and crocodiles "take passage" with "the entire colony" and drift off together to a remote place on the river.

Not only does paragraph three contain symbolic allusions to the plight of the exile, it also proposes a mediation between the conflicting pulls of his individual versus his collective sense of identity. Alone, cut off from his roots, the exile longs for a spirit of community which, history having denied him, he projects onto the landscape. This can be seen in the structure of the paragraph. It begins with reference to the "Meschacebe" and the "delightful country, which the inhabitants of the United States call New Eden." The edenic, utopian quality of this part of the description is clear, as Dennis J. Spininger has demonstrated, for example in the presentation of water as a creative, nourishing, fertilizing force.[22] Thus paragraph three begins on the positive note of the individual's original integration with the other in Eden. This positive note, suspended during the episode of the "dead trunks of pines and oak trees," reappears abruptly at the end of the paragraph with the sentence "But grace is always joined with splendor in scenes of nature." Then, a rich, brilliantly colored array of vegetal and animal life appears. And the young crocodiles finding a resting place present an image of peace and community. Spininger views the crocodiles along with the "serpents" mentioned here as discordant elements, indicating that the new Eden of America, unlike the old one of biblical times, is marked by man's duality after the Fall.[23] But although crocodiles and serpents may in themselves have negative connotations, here they appear in the charming, colorful company of "blue herons" and "pink flamingoes," thus in a context of poetic harmony rather than religious discord. With the implied individual's exile thus framed by images at the beginning and end of the paragraph suggesting an imaginary union of self and others, landscape again functions as mediating structure.

The union of self and other is an especially important component of Chateaubriand's landscape in the remainder of the opening description. The drive to achieve this union and to express it symbolically in landscape reflects the search for the homeland. The rest of the description, comprising paragraphs four through seven, contrasts the two sides of the river: first the western side is evoked briefly in paragraph four; then the eastern side, in detail, in five, six, and seven. The contrast that occurs here is somewhat surprising; for were the reader not alerted to the difference between the two sides by the author, he might well focus on their similarity, both being similarly primitive and richly inhabited by plant and animal life. But Chateaubriand is careful to accentuate the antithetical nature of the scene: "The two banks of the Meschacebe present the most extraordinary picture." Then at the beginning of paragraphs five and seven, he dwells on opposition: "Such is the scene on the western bank; but it changes on the opposite side, and the two shores form an admirable contrast"; "While in the savannahs beyond the river everything is permeated with silence and calm, here, on the contrary, everything stirs and murmurs."

There are a number of different explanations for Chateaubriand's emphasis on antithesis at the beginning of *Atala*. One is the aesthetic need to provide a linguistic framework for description. As Thomas C. Walker notes, "it makes it easier for the reader to visualize the whole of this very long description."[24] Another is the novel's moral, philosophical purpose; for it is characteristic of antithesis to present a bipolar situation that demands taking sides and thus making an evaluative or moral choice. Emphasis on antithesis in the opening description thus conditions the reader to respond to such crucial antithetical concepts as the opposition between primitive and civilized society which Chactas, as noted earlier, articulates in saying to René, "I see in you the civilized man who has become a savage; you see in me the savage whom the Great Spirit has (I know not for what purpose) chosen to civilize" (p. 22).

It is, however, the symbolic rather than the linguistic or moral value of Chateaubriand's use of antithesis that is of interest here. By establishing an opposition between the two banks of the river, the text can subsequently resolve the opposition through the mediating structure of the landscape. The mediation is prefigured in paragraph four in the brief description of the western bank:

> On the western shore, savannahs spread out as far as the eye can see, and their verdant swells, receding in the distance, seem to rise into the blue of the sky where they fade from view. In these endless prairies herds of three or four thousand wild buffaloes wander about aimlessly. Occasionally a bison heavy with years breasts the waves and finds repose among the high grasses of some island in the Meschacebe. By his brow crowned with twin crescents, by his ancient, muddy beard, he might be taken for the god of the river, casting a satisfied eye over the grandeur of his waters and the wild abundance of his shores. (p. 18)

There is a striking quality of absence on this bank in contrast to the other, a contrast that Chateaubriand invites the reader to make. An absence of distinct temporal or spatial limits is apparent in expressions such as "as far as the eye can see," "receding in the distance," "fade from view," "endless," "wander about aimlessly." Natural phenomena exist here, but with little direction or design. Distinct species of trees and plants are also absent in the vague, timeless "savannahs," "verdant swells," "prairies," and "high grasses." Indeed, the plant life on the western bank, with its indistinct colors and dissolving contours, has an impressionistic, out-of-focus quality to it. Also lacking are ties and attachments of the mediating sort noted earlier with regard to trees and crocodiles. The savage herds of buffalo wander aimlessly side by side. The single bison, as alone and remote as a god, solipsistically enjoys his dominion, unmindful of other living creatures. The western bank lacks both differentiation and socially mediating structures.

In contrast with the western, the eastern bank is marked by the distinctness of its plant and animal life. Indeed, as many as fourteen botanical species and nine zoological ones appear in paragraphs five and six. There is also a highly developed, almost human interaction among animals, who are seen eating, playing, bathing, strolling, working, and

even—with "feeble moanings, muffled bellowings and gentle cooings"
—making love.

A similar spirit of communion and community can be discerned in the
presentation of plant life in paragraph five.

> Overhanging the streams, grouped together on rocks and mountains
> and scattered in the valleys, trees of every shape, of every hue and
> every odor, grow side by side and tangle together as they tower up to
> heights which weary the eye. Wild vines, bignonias and colcynths,
> twine around the foot of these trees, scale the boughs and crawl out
> to the tips of the branches, swinging from the maple to the tulip tree
> and from the tulip tree to the hollyhock, forming a thousand bowers,
> a thousand vaults and a thousand porticoes. Many times, as they
> stray from tree to tree, these vines throw floral arches [in French,
> "des ponts de fleurs"] across the arms of rivers. From the heart
> of these clumps the magnolia raises its motionless cone; capped
> with great white blossoms, it commands the entire forest, with no
> other rival than the palm tree, which gently waves its verdant fans
> beside it.

The notion of attaching or coming together, applied earlier to the uprooted trees, emerges progressively in this paragraph. First, towering
trees "grow side by side and tangle together" (in French, "se mêlent,
croissent ensemble"). Then, changing registers from the high to the low,
the text applies the same notion to flowering bushes and vines, which intermingle with one another, cover the trees' branches, form vegetal links
from tree to tree, and even unite trees on opposite sides of the river's small
tributaries. The final image in this description of the eastern bank is of a
magnolia tree, and it contrasts sharply with the closing image of the bison
in the description of the western bank. There, the lone bison dominated
the scene; here, the magnolia emerges "from the heart of these clumps."
There, the bison ruled alone; here, the magnolia exercises its reign
crowned with white roses and accompanied by "the palm tree, which
gently waves its verdant fans beside it."

Now it is possible to look beyond the opening description and ask
whether in the novel as a whole there exists an enduring sense of community and homeland that was achieved in the privileged moment of landscape at the start. That this question must receive a negative answer is
apparent from even a cursory consideration of the text. Indians and Europeans alike in *Atala* are for various reasons denied a stable, permanent
homeland. Three descriptive loci are of particular interest in this regard.
Chactas describes two, the forest and Father Aubry's mission; the frame
narrator, at the very end of the novel, describes the third, Niagara Falls.
That there is a positive image of social interaction at the beginning but a

failure to achieve such interaction elsewhere in the novel suggests that in *Atala* there is an ambivalence similar to that discerned earlier in *Paul et Virginie*. There the ambivalence centers on the Republican ideal. Here it centers on the value and viability of both Indian social institutions and colonial, Christian ones.

The forest, as depicted in Chactas's tale, is a place marked by duality and conflict, an image of both the constructive and destructive sides of traditional Indian society. From the beginning of his tale and throughout the first major part of it entitled "The Hunters," Chactas evokes the forest as the natural home of the Indian, the sole place where he can achieve the independence and closeness to nature that are so basic to the native character. Thus Chactas says that while exiled in Spain, he would remain "motionless for hours contemplating the summit of distant forests" (p. 231). To be Indian, for him, is to live the life of the forest. But upon returning to America and entering the forest, Chactas immediately loses his way. Enemy tribes capture him, imprison him, and condemn him to die a violent, savage death. The forest then emerges as both a symbol of life and death, of community and prison, of a construction as well as a destruction of social ties. Herein lies Chactas's quandary. To return to the forest, his home as an Indian, is to affirm his native traditions and his bonds with nature and society. But to return to the forest, the locus of savage customs and practices, is also to encounter danger and eventual destruction. And indeed, Indian society as portrayed in *Atala* is doomed, destroyed not only by the civilized Europeans from without but perhaps more importantly by the uncivilized natives from within.

The conflictual nature of the forest as a symbol of both the constructive and destructive sides of Chactas's Indian homeland is manifest in the numerous images and descriptive passages connected with the forest that *Atala* contains. Frequently there is a distinct resonance of the positive creation of community ties that was articulated in the opening description. Especially striking in this regard are images in which vegetal, human, and animal forms combine or intertwine, such as the following: "As a fawn seems to cling to the flowers of the pink lianas, grasping them with its fine tongue on the steep mountain bank, so I remained suspended on the lips of my beloved" (p. 27); "Almost all the trees in Florida, particularly the cedar and the live oak, are covered with a white moss hanging from the branches down to the ground . . . a swarm of butterflies, bright insects, hummingbirds, green parakeets, and blue jays attaches itself to these mosses and produces the effect of a white wool tapestry" (p. 39). But at the same time, combining or intertwining nature objects often have a menacing, dangerous effect: "With difficulty we pressed ahead under an archway of greenbrier, among vines and indigo plants, bean stalks and crawling lianas, which entangled our feet like nets" (p. 44). In short, the forest for Chactas is a homeland, but not one in which he can live in an ideal state of safety and harmony.

The same conflictual nature which the description of the forest displays in the first major part of Chactas's story, "The Hunters," can be discerned in the description of Father Aubry's mission in the second major part, "The Tillers." At first glance, the mission provides a totally positive social model, an ideal synthesis of native and European culture brought about through the civilizing effect of Christianity. And indeed, Chactas presents the mission as an ideal institution: "I marveled at the triumph of Christianity over primitive culture. I could see the Indian growing civilized through the voice of religion. I was witnessing the primal wedding of man and the earth, with man delivering to the earth the heritage of his sweat, and the earth, in return, undertaking to bear faithfully man's harvests, his sons and his ashes" (p. 55). But alongside the positive effect that Christianity has upon Indian culture there are negative ones. It is in the name of Christianity and civilization that the European inhabitants of America chase the Indians from their ancestral homes. And it is Aubry's negative counterpart, a less enlightened missionary priest, who is responsible for the inhuman vow of chastity Atala took as a child, which motivates her suicide when she falls in love with Chactas. Not surprisingly, in view of the ambivalent portrayal of the Christian influence on Indian culture in *Atala*, the new home created by Aubry as a safe, harmonious enclave within the forest is doomed to destruction, as was the island enclave in *Paul et Virginie*.

As with the forest, so too with Aubry's mission, images of nature dramatize the conflictual presentation of social institutions in *Atala*. Perhaps the most striking nature image presented in the description of the mission is that of a "natural bridge" extending from one mountain to another:

> Going on, we reached the entrance to a valley, where I beheld a wonderful creation—a natural bridge, like the one in Virginia, of which you may of heard. My son, men, especially those of your country, frequently imitate Nature, and their copies are always pretty. It is not so with Nature when she seems to imitate the works of men, while actually offering them models. At such times she hurls bridges from the summit of one mountain to the summit of the next, suspends roads in the clouds, spreads rivers for canals, carves mountains for columns, and for pools she hollows out seas (p. 52).

The mission as a paradigm of the creation of community ties is echoed here in nature as it was at the beginning of the novel. But in the existential world of time and history, the ties established in nature do not endure as they do in the symbolic world. Later in the novel the natural bridge reappears in contexts that clearly connote death and destruction. First of all, it is the place Atala is buried. Then it turns out that many years later, Chactas returns to find that the enemy Cherokee tribe has completely destroyed the mission and that wild forest vegetation has engulfed the mediating structure of the natural bridge: "He came to the place where the mission had been, but he could scarcely recognize it. The lake had overflowed its shores, and the savannah had turned into a swamp. The natural bridge had collapsed burying Atala's grave" (p. 81).

The third and final descriptive locus in *Atala*, Niagara Falls, exhibits conflict and dramatizes the impossibility of establishing a real and enduring homeland outside the imaginary, symbolic realm. The accent in this description, as opposed to the opening one, is on danger, violence, and upheaval. There is a "mighty roar" as the water rushes down to the engulfing depths below; "as it reaches the falls, it is not so much a river as a sea whose torrents surge into the gaping mouth of a chasm" (p. 78). It is true that even in the midst of the wild and tumultuous setting of the waterfalls, certain natural phenomena emerge that suggest life, harmony, community, and other attributes of the social ideals posited in the novel as a whole. But here these phenomena emerge as tragically fragile, ephemeral, and menaced by the destructive forces of history and time. An island "juts out, hollow underneath, and hanging with all its trees over the chaos of the waves"; rainbows, "arch and intersect over the abyss" (pp. 78, 79). The vegetal and animal inhabitants of the opening scene reappear, but this time either as ghosts of their former joyous selves or as creatures dangerously poised over an abyss: "The scene is ornate with pine and wild walnut trees and rocks carved out in weird shapes. Eagles, drawn by air currents, spiral down into the depths of the chasm, and wolverines dangle by their supple tails from the ends of low-hanging branches, snatching the shattered corpses of elk and bear out of the abyss" (p. 79). The ending of *Atala* thus echoes that of *Paul et Virginie*. Both novels close with the death of the heroine and with an evocation of tumultuous waters, symbolic of the uncontrollable forces of social upheaval. The message in both cases is clear: the ideal which was sought after and momentarily achieved in the exotic place will not endure. A cloud of ambivalence ultimately enshrouds all of the alternatives proposed in the novel.

It is not surprising that a note of uncertainty and even pessimism is thus sounded at the end of both novels. Nor is it surprising that Bernardin and Chateaubriand could do no more than articulate conflict and glimpse moments of change symbolically in literature. In their times, with their conceptual and material resources, new alternatives were not easily discovered. Nor were old ones easily forgotten. Both authors went to exotic places, like the narrators with whom they have much in common, to discover new ways and reject old ones. But a cloud of imminent disaster or recent tragedy continually hung over the new place. They arrived in the exotic land in much the same way that, in *Atala*, Aubry imagines the Indian arriving in Europe at the time of the Revolution:

> what would you have thought had you witnessed the evils of society,
> had your ears been assailed, as you set foot on Europe's shores, by the
> long cry of woe rising out of that ancient land. The hut dweller and
> the palace lord both suffer alike, and all lament together in this
> world. Queens have been seen weeping like simple women, and men
> have stood aghast at the volume of tears in the eyes of kings! (pp.
> 64–65)

The difficulties in forgetting the tragic events of the Revolution persisted well into the nineteenth century, as did the unwillingness to let go of the past, of traditional values, of the homeland as it used to be.

4

Women and Nature:

The Mysteries of Udolpho and *Frankenstein*

Nature in Opposition

Ann Radcliffe and Mary Wollstonecraft Shelley both gave literary expression to the problematic role of women in the society of their times. Basic to that expression is an oppositional structure that functions similarly in the two novels considered in this chapter, Radcliffe's *Mysteries of Udolpho* and Shelley's *Frankenstein*. Opposing elements in nature are associated with clusters of socio-political traits embodied in opposing male and female characters in the novel. However, through the introduction of other characters who describe nature or through the special use of landscape at certain key places in the novel, mediations to these oppositions are made possible. The oppositional structures in Radcliffe and Shelley's novels thus exemplify on the one hand the confinement within the thought of their times experienced by these writers and their main characters, and on the other the liberation they envisioned through certain special characters and uses of landscape, a liberation that allowed them to develop alternative ways of thinking about women and nature. (For a French example that embodies the same oppositional structure and promise of liberation, it is worth mentioning Mme. de Staël's *Corinne,* a work that merits further study along the lines to be followed here.)

The oppositional structure in works like *The Mysteries of Udolpho* and *Frankenstein* rests on a fundamental opposition between menacing mountains on the one hand and comforting valleys or fields on the other. That opposition parallels the popular eighteenth-century polarity between sublime and beautiful nature. Harking back to Longinus, Edmund Burke and other eighteenth-century thinkers spoke of the opposition between two contrary types of landscape. The sublime kind—which inspires awe, horror, and mystery—is characterized by such traits as vast depth or height, rugged surfaces, and darkness; it includes objects in nature that are grand and majestic. The beautiful kind—which inspires love—is found in smallness and smoothness, as in leaves, slopes, and streams; it includes objects in nature that are colorful and cheerful.[1]

The associations of the sublime and the beautiful go beyond the physical level of mountains and valleys to a nonphysical level, especially to a

81

"social" level—to the novel's political and economic concerns. At the social level, the physical seme of menacing mountains, for example, will be
seen to be linked in both *The Mysteries of Udolpho* and *Frankenstein* with
such varied nonphysical semes as power and masculinity, whereas the
opposing seme of comforting valleys or fields is linked in both works with
such nonphysical semes as domesticity and femininity. The opposing
semes will also be seen to be linked with an opposition between upper and
lower social classes.

In such highly oppositional writing as Radcliffe's and Shelley's, it
proves helpful to turn to a somewhat more systematic semantic method
than that applied to earlier writers like Rousseau. Such a method is provided by the structuralist A. J. Greimas in his attempts to discover "the
whole semantic universe" of an author's work.[2] Greimas's method has the
merit of forcing the critic to evaluate and reflect upon the notion of opposition itself: of encouraging him to ask the metacritical question of what
constitutes a meaningful or interesting opposition. This Greimas does
through the development and application of his "semiotic square," which
illustrates the difference between two kinds of oppositions. The more interesting kind—and what in common usage "opposition" is generally
taken to mean—is the opposition between contraries (e.g., black versus
white). The other kind is the opposition between a seme and its contradictory (e.g., black versus not-black). With contraries, the opposition is a
positive one, not merely an empty logical one based on negation. Through
the contrary, semantic meaning is provided in the sense that positive
qualities of each contrary must be singled out and proposed as distinctive.
Thus the opposition between white and black involves two distinct semes,
whereas that between black and not-black only involves one, the "not" being a logical rather than a semantic addition.

Now, it is in its application that Greimas's "semiotic square" proves
most valuable. One such application, a Marxist kind, is proposed by
Fredric Jameson when he remarks that studies such as Greimas's are valuable because they "can be reappropriated for a historicizing and dialectical
criticism," which enables critics to assess the extent and significance of
oppositional patterns of thought and the intellectual or ideological closure
they represent. According to Jameson, Greimas's method provides "a vital
instrument for exploring the semantic and ideological intricacies of the
text . . . because it maps the limits of a specific ideological consciousness
and marks the conceptual points beyond which that consciousness cannot
go, and between which it is condemned to oscillate."[3]

In order to apply Greimas's method to map the limits of a writer's "ideological consciousness," I shall follow Jameson in applying it to opposing
characters. Such an application involves singling out four characters who
are closely connected with the novel's two opposing semes[4] (here, female

and male) and to their contradictories (not-female and not-male). A particular character may, through association with the first seme in an opposition, embody a nonphysical quality correlated with it, such as feminine virtue. The main question then becomes to determine which other character, among all of the characters who embody not-feminine virtue, has through association with the second, contrary seme a positive moral quality that stands in clear opposition as a contrary to the first seme. A secondary question is to determine which two other characters most clearly negate or contradict the positive qualities of the main opposing characters: identifying these characters fills out and completes the picture of the novel's semantic system. Identifying these characters in the work of writers like Radcliffe and Shelley makes it possible to reach an understanding of the bases on which opposing roles for women and men are assigned.

Since nature descriptions echo the oppositions involved, they help to identify the kinds of semes involved in the oppositions. Indeed, they are often the best, if not the only, ways to make identifications that are not directly or explicitly supplied in the text. An example from *The Mysteries of Udolpho* concerns Montoni. Although he has positive features in virtue of which he stands as the contrary to the main character Emily, those features are only developed indirectly: for example, through description of sublime, majestic mountain scenes with which he is associated. Thus it is in landscape rather than in character depiction per se that Radcliffe elaborates a male role that is strong and distinctive enough to compete interestingly with Emily's female role.

Next it is necessary to consider the ways characters can act to resolve oppositions. How to move outside of the oppositional structure established by characters and landscapes is one of the chief problems presented in Radcliffe and Shelley's novels. A useful step in uncovering what ways the novels propose to do this is to single out two special characters, aside from the four characters mentioned earlier, as providing new and alternative ways to envision traditional oppositions. Jameson calls these two special characters the neutral and the complex characters.[5] The neutral character involves a neutralization of the initial opposition at a broad, general level at which, for example, a character is both not-masculine and not-feminine. It is by such a dual negation of features in one single character that an escape from the initial opposition is obtained as, for example, an androgynous character who is both not-masculine and not-feminine escapes the male–female polarity. The examples of Valancourt in *The Mysteries of Udolpho* and the Monster in *Frankenstein* will be examined later as illustrations of the notion of the neutral character. These are secondary characters in whom distinctive features tend to be diffused or dissolved. Both of these examples are drawn from characters who do not actively embody positive semantic qualities but seem instead to achieve some limited and passive kind of neutralization of difference. They nonetheless offer one instance of a resolution of the novel's oppositional structure.

The complex character involves an active selection, from all of the possible not-male and not-female qualities, of those specific ones which escape the opposition posed by the contraries. The question, in other words, would be, what specific kinds of not-maleness and not-femaleness are compatible so as to escape the opposition between male and female as it is presented in the novel's central opposition, an opposition based on such features as powerful versus domestic. Here Jameson cites the example of such a common mediatory figure as the trickster, whose complex personal characteristics and unusual actions allow him to combine the required traits.[6] For the role of the complex character, both Radcliffe and Shelley propose characters who are female narrative participants and who are boldly conceived as transcending traditional roles for women.

With respect to both the complex character and the neutral one, special responses to nature enable the writers to resolve oppositions. In Radcliffe and Shelley's novels, characters who display such distinctive responses to nature then emerge as playing distinctive sexual or social roles. And it is in this regard that the placement of landscape descriptions assumes distinct importance. For whether different narrators and describers of nature appear on the scene, as is the case in *Frankenstein,* or different characters and situations affect the main narrator's and describer's relationship with nature, as is the case in *The Mysteries of Udolpho,* the fact remains that certain key positions in Radcliffe's and Shelley's novels facilitate the development of alternative views of women and nature. Those key positions tend, as in many novels in the literature of images, to be either in the exact middle or in the syntagmatically crucial narrative frame of the novel. In those places the novel can most saliently display solutions to the social conflicts it raises. The ways landscape functions to permit the elaboration of the role of the complex character will be spelled out later in the analyses of Emily in *The Mysteries of Udolpho* and of the narrative duo formed by the frame narrator Walton and his narratee, Mrs. Saville, in *Frankenstein.* In both cases, characters succeed in viewing nature in a distinctive way which enables them in some measure to refute and escape the fixed oppositional structure of the semiotic square.

Point of view, a topic not raised by Jameson, is also necessary for an application of the Greimasian model to a study of narrative landscape. For both *The Mysteries of Udolpho* and *Frankenstein,* the semantic square originates from and is dominated by the point of view of the novel's chief narrator or describer of nature: Emily in Radcliffe's novel and Frankenstein in Shelley's. Since almost everything in the novel is seen or recounted by them, the chief problem becomes how to move outside an oppositional structure that they impose on the novel.

This problem is resolved differently in the two novels. In *Frankenstein,* several secondary narrators exist who make it possible to measure the excessive rigidity of the main narrator's oppositional outlook and to propose alternative ways to view nature and human relationships. They, not Frankenstein as narrator, are the neutral and complex characters. In *The Mysteries of Udolpho,* however, Emily is presented ambiguously as the embodiment of the problem and its solution. As a character, she occupies a place in the oppositional structure. But as the implied narrator and describer of nature, she stands above and apart from a structure that arises from her own rigidly oppositional outlook and attempts to serve as a complex character. Not surprisingly, definite limits to her ability to resolve conflicts are apparent in the novel.

As the "semantic and ideological intricacies" of the novels by Radcliffe and Shelley are explored and exposed, it will become apparent that there are indeed barriers that the late eighteenth- and early nineteenth-century writers can only begin to cross. Thus they are to some extent condemned to oscillate, as Jameson says, between the fixed points of a rigidly oppositional structure. With Radcliffe in particular, the inability to envision social change marks her novel, like many others in the literature of images, with the stamp of conservativism. But at the same time, small but highly significant breaks with that oppositional structure are envisioned by both of these early writers. Because landscape plays an active role not only in the expression of the rigid outlook but also in the production of the small but significant breaks, its treatment by women writers like Radcliffe and Shelley is of distinct historical and literary interest.

Beautiful and Sublime Nature

When midway through Ann Radcliffe's *The Mysteries of Udolpho* the eponymous castle finally looms up before the reader's eye—"silent, lonely and sublime . . . sovereign of the scene"[7]—the semantic associations it evokes of maleness, mountains, and the all-powerful Italian villain Montoni have already been well established in the text. Common to the castle, to the mountains in which it is set, and to its Italian and male proprietor, are a cluster of traits that both repel and attract Radcliffe's female protagonist and describer of nature, Emily St. Aubert. Those traits include strength, power, vigor, dynamism, a ruggedly handsome appeal, a propensity for upheaval and change, an appeal to the mind, and an inspiration to artistic imagination.

Before we examine the oppositional structure of which Montoni's male traits are an essential part, it would be useful to summarize the plot. *The Mysteries of Udolpho* begins in southern France at the chateau La Vallée, where M. St. Aubert, his wife, and his daughter Emily lead a peaceful, pastoral existence, which is soon interrupted by Madame's death. M. St. Aubert, advised to restore his failing health and spirits by traveling through the Pyrenees and the Languedoc region, undertakes this journey accompanied by Emily. During the trip, she meets and falls in love with Valancourt. The couple's hopes for happiness are, however, soon dashed by the death of Emily's father, leaving her under the supervision of her foolish and materialistic paternal aunt, Mme. Cheron. Before dying, her father reveals intense emotions of love connected with the late Marchioness de Villeroi; the reason for such emotion remains a mystery until the end of the novel. The aunt marries an unscrupulous, land-hungry Italian, Montoni. He forbids Emily's marriage with Valancourt and takes her and her aunt off to Italy, first to Venice where he attempts to force her to marry Count Morano and then to Udolpho, Montoni's deserted castle in the Apennine Mountains, originally the property of Signora Laurentini, who many years prior to the events recounted in the novel rejected Montoni and then mysteriously disappeared. There, upon his wife's refusal to sign over her property to him, Montoni imprisons her in a tower, where she finally dies of fear and neglect. He then directs his attentions to Emily, who finds help from a young Frenchman, DuPont, also imprisoned in Udolpho. Together, with the servants Annette and Ludovico, they escape Udolpho and leave Italy by boat, only to be caught in a storm and shipwrecked on the French coast. Help is at hand this time from the Count de Villefort who, with his wife, son, and his daughter Blanche, welcome them to his chateau, formerly the home of the Marchioness de Villeroi. There, Valancourt finally arrives on the scene. At first Emily rejects him because of his gambling and alleged carousing while in Paris, but when she learns the mitigating circumstances of his Parisian adventure, she agrees to marry him. She also learns that the Marchioness de Villeroi was her father's sister and was poisoned by the jealous Signora Laurentini who, dying and repentant, at the end of the novel leaves part of her estate to Emily. The final outcome is that Montoni is imprisoned and dies, while Emily and Valancourt live happily ever after at La Vallée.

Despite the length of Radcliffe's novel and its complexity of adventure, a definite structural coherence can be discovered that owes much to the specific opposition between valleys and mountains, which corresponds to the more general eighteenth-century opposition between the beautiful and the sublime. Also relevant in this regard is the geographical opposition in the novel between France and Italy. For if it is true that the descriptions of the two countries mention both valleys and mountains, it is also true that a far greater emphasis is placed on the former in connection with France and the latter in connection with Italy.

The main opposition between valleys and beautiful nature on the one hand and mountains and sublime nature on the other is announced in the very first paragraph of the novel. The reader first sees "the pastoral land-scapes of Guienne and Gascony, stretching along the river, gay with luxu-riant woods and vines, and plantations of olives." The soft-sounding place-names—Guienne, Gascony, and in the same paragraph Garonne and Languedoc—reinforce the soft and gentle features of nature of the beautiful sort. Then, immediately following, the reader discovers "the majestic Pyrenées, whose summits, veiled in clouds, or exhibiting awful forms, seen, and lost again, as the partial vapours rolled along, were some times barren, and gleamed through the blue tinge of air, and sometimes frowned with forests of gloomy pine, that swept downward to their base." The lofty tone and poetic syntax of this sentence in turn reinforce the striking and dominant qualities of nature of the sublime sort. The two sorts of nature then appear together: "These tremendous precipices were contrasted by the soft green of the pastures and woods that hung upon their skirts; among whose flocks, and herds, and simple cottages, the eye, after having scaled the cliffs above, delighted to repose" (p. 1).

Subsequently, on literally hundreds of occasions, the same oppositions will recur, produced by opposing adjectives found in this passage such as pleasant, pastoral, gay, luxuriant, soft, and simple, on the one hand; and majestic, awful, barren, gloomy, and tremendous, on the other. The fem-inine qualities of the valley and beautiful nature are apparent elsewhere in the novel in such adjectives as fertile, blushing, soft, sweet, or gentle; the contrasting male qualities of the mountains and sublime nature can be discovered in such opposing adjectives as dark, vast, wild, impetuous, and bold. Coleridge suggested that these recurrent oppositions were an ar-tistic failure, objecting that Radcliffe's descriptions display "too much sameness; the pine and the larch trees wave, and full moon pours its lustre through almost every chapter."[8] But that sameness promotes and rein-forces Emily's point of view in relation to nature: it marks all the nature scenes with her characteristic oppositional vision, thereby minimizing the differences between Emily and other narrators or describers of nature in the novel. (*The Mysteries of Udolpho* is ostensibly presented by an invisible authorial figure who stands behind Emily in her implicit role as the voice that speaks and eye that sees nature in the novel. And to compound mat-ters regarding the narrative center, the novel at times departs from its nor-mally exclusive focus on Emily's movements: near the end, notably, her narrative double Blanche de Villefort occupies center stage. I might add regarding Blanche's role as Emily's double that Blanche has the same fa-milial and romantic emotions as did Emily, along with the identical sensi-tivity to nature; she even lives through the same terrifying experiences, when captured by "banditti," that Emily did at the hands of Montoni.) But neither the invisible authorial figure nor any other character seriously challenges Emily's control over nature description in the novel. They add nothing that is not in complete conformity with the distinctive point of view she imposes in the novel.

A secondary opposition between the moon and the sun is also developed, which correlates closely with the primary one between valleys and mountains and calls special attention to the opposition between female and male traits. In a typical passage, the moonlit landscape is described as "shadowy and soft" with "the nearer river reflecting the moon, and trembling to her rays" (p. 152). Both "soft" and "trembling" are used throughout the novel to suggest the feminine gender of the moon, along with the actual pronoun "she" and the repeated mention of the moon's "veils" as the protective screen hiding the femininity of the evening landscape.

Now, in contrast, the opposing semantic features of sunlight have a special fascination in Emily's eyes and thus are dwelled on in greater detail and depth in landscapes. Indeed, one of the chief functions of landscape in Radcliffe's novel is to make it possible to understand and appreciate the fascination that sunlight and the related concept of the sublime hold for Emily. Consider, for example, the following description of Emily's approach to the Udolpho castle in which the sun is referred to, revealingly, as "he" and endowed with precisely those masculine and dynamic properties which Emily perceives as a sharp opposition and even a threat to the soft, gentle, beautiful nature to which she is accustomed:

> The sun had just sunk below the top of the mountains she was descending, whose long shadow stretched athwart the valley, but his sloping rays, shooting through an opening of the cliffs, touched with a yellow gleam the summits of the forest, that hung upon the opposite steeps, and streamed in full splendour upon the towers and battlements of a castle, that spread its extensive ramparts along the brow of a precipice above (p. 226).

A number of features of this characteristic passage are worth noting. There is the close association between the sun and the mountains at the very beginning, as well as the dynamic and even violent movement of the sun's rays, "shooting through an opening of the cliffs." Along similar lines, there is a clear association with power and military armaments in this passage, an association that is not unusual in the novel: the sight of gleaming swords capturing the sun's rays is mentioned on a number of occasions. Also noteworthy are the repetitions of words beginning with the letter "s" alone or in combination with other letters; together those repetitions produce an arresting poetic effect that supports the sense of the sun's dynamic effect.

Social and political levels of meaning also attach to physical clusters described in Radcliffe's novel. The most salient such opposition can be identified as that between the values of the upper-middle-class landed gentry on the one hand and those of an emerging materialistic lower class on the other. The gentry show concern for others, for simple aesthetic pleasures, for peace and tranquility, and for the preservation of the status quo. The lower-class values are individual will, material gain, violent change, and social mobility. The importance of landscape to the opposing class structure in Radcliffe's novel cannot be overrated: for in the battle between the two conflicting sets of values the land itself is at stake; it is the single most important thing that separates the older, established class from its newer, disenfranchised counterpart. Indeed, the catalyst of events in *The Mysteries of Udolpho* is the attempts by nouveau-riche villains like Montoni to acquire land, which rightfully belongs to such members of the landed gentry as the St. Auberts.

Another opposition of political significance in *The Mysteries of Udolpho* is the opposition between France and England. One of the typical eighteenth-century containment strategies to which Radcliffe has recourse involves a transposition of the contemporary polarity between England and France into one between France and Italy. In other words, the association noted earlier between France and valleys or beautiful nature is really an association with England, or at least as it existed during some idealized Golden Age of social stability; and likewise, the association between Italy and sublime nature is tantamount to an association with France, along with those "French," subversive elements in English society which threatened the social stability desired by the upper classes. The novel contains numerous statements that, though explicitly about Italy, seem especially appropriate to the political situation in the France of Radcliffe's time, for example: "The prospect of going to Italy was still rendered darker, when she considered the tumultuous situation in that country, then torn by civil commotion, . . . and even every castle liable to the attack of an invader" (p. 145). It was France more than Italy that was associated in the popular and literary mind with such "sublime" notions as violent upheaval and change; dark, dangerous deeds; and rugged, wildly individualistic characters. And, as Mary Poovey notes, in Radcliffe's time political critics like Burke typically focused on abuses abroad as an indirect means of expressing concerns about English society, notably about the increasing social unrest and mob riots that occurred in England in the 1780s. A common cautionary tale was provided in this regard by the French Revolution.[9]

It is now time to look at the characters in *The Mysteries of Udolpho* and examine the ways that landscape makes it possible to assign to them representative roles in the novel's oppositional structure and the ways that assigning those roles, in addition to clarifying the extended meaning in the text, allows the establishment of resolutions to conflicts. Emily and her double Lady Blanche de Villefort are emblematic of valleys—with all of that term's related physical, geographical, and political semes. The name of Emily's French residence, La Vallée, supports the close association of the female protagonist (and implicitly her double) with the key nature element of valleys. Those two characters have such qualities developed and defined in descriptions of valleys and beautiful nature scenes as softness, gentleness, richness, and a propensity for happiness and peace. And most obvious perhaps among their many attributes is the sine qua non of the beautiful person in Radcliffe's world, a love for nature and an almost constant preoccupation with viewing it. Montoni is clearly the character who represents mountains and the sublime: even his name suggests the word mountain to the English-speaking reader. (To the Italian ear, it of course similarly suggests the word *monte*, with its singular augmentative ending *-one* and its plural, *-oni*.) Montoni is handsome, romantic, strong, dynamic, dangerous, rough, and materialistic. Emily and Blanche are of the landowning class, whereas he is an upstart and an outsider, relentlessly committed to social upheaval and illegitimate economic control. It is one of the chief functions of landscape, as noted earlier, to provide a means for developing and elaborating upon his complex character.

The contradictories of the main opposition between the Emily-Blanche duo and Montoni can best be identified among members of the same sex. Once again, landscape helps to identify these characters. Thus Mme. Cheron and the Countess de Villefort can be identified as playing identical negating roles vis-à-vis Emily and Blanche. Not only are the two older women vulgar and weak whereas the younger women are noble and strong; most saliently, Mme. Cheron and the Countess de Villefort both display an insensitivity to nature. And there are other minor characters who display the same characteristics, for example, Mme. Quesnel, the wife of Emily's maternal uncle. Indeed, the novel suggests that whereas there are few people who are strong like Blanche, Emily, and Montoni, there are many who are weak and vulgar like Mme. Cheron and these other female characters.

Montoni's contradictory is the nature-loving M. St. Aubert, whose death near the beginning of Emily's adventures highlights his weakness, through his inability to support and protect his daughter. So too, while he is still alive, does his distinctive relationship with nature, in which a myriad of natural phenomena—steep roads, isolated settings, darkness, ominous sounds—evoke his weakness and vulnerability. In addition, St. Aubert constantly appears as weakened through grief, financial losses, and physical decline. The notion of maleness also sheds light on the difference between St. Aubert, Montoni's contradictory, and Blanche, Montoni's contrary: for although St. Aubert may have many of the young girl's positive moral qualities, he is a man and thus has perforce lived in the world and been exposed to its vices. He cannot then possess the innocence and pure conscience that Emily and Blanche alone possess. In the oppositional world of *The Mysteries of Udolpho,* women possess positive moral qualities that can be found in no male characters, not even St. Aubert and his aristocratic double, the Count de Villefort.

St. Aubert is also Montoni's contradictory on the familial plane. Critics have noted the familial drama that occurs in *The Mysteries of Udolpho* in which, as in childhood nightmares, the "good father" disappears and is replaced by his evil counterpart.[10] Because St. Aubert dies and leaves Emily without protection, the false father usurps his place, just as Napoleon did in France once the paternalistic figure of the king disappeared. The only way social stability could be preserved in the novel would be for the father to be present to contradict and eliminate the power of figures like Montoni.

Whereas it is useful to examine the major opposing semes and their corresponding characters as providing an account of the semantics of *The Mysteries of Udolpho,* it is also useful, following Jameson, to study the characters who, through their special relationships with nature, most successfully provide resolutions to the novel's conflicts. Those characters are Valancourt as the neutral character and Emily as the complex one. Since their roles in this capacity depend largely on the novel's narrative structure and placement of landscape, it would be well to note the three-part division of *The Mysteries of Udolpho*: there is an introductory section, which takes place in France at La Vallée; then the major portion, which occurs in Italy in the "Montoni" region; and the final section, which takes place in France, with a return to La Vallée at the end. One function of this three-part structure in Radcliffe's novel, as was seen earlier regarding Rousseau's novel, is to give form and coherence to an otherwise long and disjointed narration. Radcliffe especially resembles Rousseau in deriving a stronger effect of pattern and structure from informal divisions based on landscape than on formal divisions based on books, parts, or chapters. Thus, although formally *The Mysteries of Udolpho* is divided into two parts, its true thematic division is into three sections according to geographical location.

More specifically relevant to the roles of the neutral and complex characters is the fact that resolutions are appropriate in the last part because, although the characters have changed only superficially, their circumstances and their ways of appreciating nature have changed. Thus nature in the last part of the novel seems to be different and special for Valancourt, who can at the end fully appreciate its qualities. The importance in this regard of Valancourt's fall from innocence, which the reader learns of near the end of the novel, cannot be overemphasized. It is only because Valancourt has gained personal familiarity with both the virtuous life and the materialistic life that he can neutralize the two: he emerges at the end as an experienced but worthy young man who has retained the capacity for virtue and for a firm, irrevocable rejection of the lures of the materialistic world. That capacity is evident in his new and special relationship with nature. At the end, he is truly, as his name implies, both beautiful like the valley and sublime like the French court (*Valancourt*). With Valancourt, however, the accent remains largely on neutralizing the negative, on how he avoids the negative traits of various flawed characters. As Poovey notes, by "dramatizing the socialization of passion" in a good character like Valancourt, "Radcliffe simultaneously constructs a model of how excess can be contained and attempts to negate those disturbing suggestions Montoni aroused."[11]

If it is the role of the neutral character merely to negate, it is the role of the complex character actively to propose and embody new alternatives to the chief opposing terms. This is the role that devolves upon Emily. The fact that she plays that role at all and meets with some limited success in playing it is of undeniable importance to the development of feminist thought in the eighteenth and early nineteenth centuries: Emily may not be a modern feminist hero, but she has gone far beyond Richardson's Pamela, Rousseau's Julie, Bernardin's Virginie, or Chateaubriand's Atala. As a describer of landscape and owner of the land, Emily actively escapes the traditional male–female opposition, whereas those other female characters were condemned for the most part to lives as victims of societal or parental authority. But at the same time, there are definite limits to Emily's achievements in this regard.

With Emily, as with Valancourt, landscape plays a special role in the last section of the novel which furthers the development of the proposed alternatives to social conflicts. Most relevant concerning Emily's function as the complex character is simply the existence of Blanche de Villefort as her narrative double and fellow nature lover and describer: for when Blanche assumes an active role as a character certain differences that set Emily apart as a major narrative figure can best be seen. Whereas Blanche sees nature with the youthful eye of a person secluded in a convent and cut off from the outside world, Emily sees nature with the greater depth that sorrow, loss, nostalgia, and experience alone make possible. Emily's new and mature relationship with landscape, as with the land itself, are what the final section of the novel highlights.

Two different ways in which Emily attempts to act as the complex figure of resolution in *The Mysteries of Udolpho* can be identified, one of which clearly succeeds while the other is more problematic. The successful way involves landscape itself and Emily's role not only as the principal viewer of nature but also an actual writer of landscapes: in the text, she is repeatedly presented as composing poems about nature or performing other artistic activities. As a writer, she actively combines the beautiful and the sublime. I might add that although Emily is not really presented as a writer at the end of the novel, there is an important sense in which the maturity she acquires there suggests a link between her two identities, first as a character and describer and later as the figure who stands behind that character, the novel's implied "author." It is also important to note that as a woman writer and describer of nature, Emily actively combines on the one hand the appeal to virtue, associated in the novel with the beautiful and with woman's superior moral qualities, and on the other hand the appeal to the imagination, associated in the novel with the sublime and with man's superior intellectual qualities. It is interesting to note in this regard that of the dozens of poets whose works are quoted in Radcliffe's novel, the three who appear the most frequently are Thomson, Shakespeare, and Emily herself. Thus she rises to the level of the highest art, a typically masculine achievement, while retaining a prototypically woman's sensitivity to nature.

Regarding the importance of Emily as a writer of landscape, it is also worth noting, following critic Daniel Cottom, that for Radcliffe, landscape is far more than a frivolous aesthetic activity:

> her descriptions of landscape are not simple descriptions of nature. They are conceived of as attempts to draw natural scenes and the mind that perceives them out of deadening linguistic conventions. In effect, then, Radcliffe's labor in describing landscape in these novels is a moral exercise akin to that struggle to rescue virtue from vice so insistently portrayed on the dramatic level of her narratives. [12]

On the moral plane too, then, Emily emerges as a complex figure through her role as a viewer and composer of landscape. Her landscapes, like the author's, are symbolic resolutions of the conflict between Emily's own virtue and the vice embodied in a character like Montoni.

The second, more problematic way in which Emily attempts to serve as the complex figure in *The Mysteries of Udolpho* becomes apparent by her having control over the land as its legitimate owner. At the end of the novel, Emily has acquired or regained control over the property that belonged to all three members of the paternal line, M. St. Aubert, Mme. Cheron, and the Marchioness de Villeroi. She thus acquires the power and control of the man or the father—both her real father St. Aubert and the false father and usurper of Mme. Cheron's land, Montoni. She also implicitly resolves the conflict of social class connected with ownership of property. Between hereditary, aristocratic possession of the land on the one side and strictly monetary, lower- and middle-class acquisition of the land on the other, Emily presents a symbolic, literary resolution. She is clearly not completely aristocratic: her father "was a descendant from the younger branch of an illustrious family" (p. 2) but did not himself possess a title of nobility (as is similarly the case with Valancourt); when Montoni tries to get Emily to marry Count Morano he states, "Here is the offer of an alliance, which would do honour to any family; yours, you will recollect, is not noble" (p. 198). Neither, however, is she completely nonaristocratic: she is the legitimate and hereditary owner of the lands she ultimately controls. In short, she is the ideal middle-class figure of compromise. Because Emily is not noble, upper-middle-class readers could perhaps identify with her more fully; yet at the same time her moral nobility endows her fully with the desirable traits that readers associated with the aristocracy.

What is problematic in this compromise is whether the maturity Emily acquires with age and the social resolutions she proposes regarding ownership of the land and social class are not merely superficial, a mere covering up of problems rather than a serious attempt to solve them. It is worth noting the one way in which Emily fails to arrive at solutions that are as profound or far-reaching as the solutions discovered by heroines portrayed by later women writers, such as Shelley's Safie and Brontë's Jane Eyre. Emily is resistant to change; most critics agree that Emily and Radcliffe are unquestionably committed to the status quo. Speaking of the conflict posed by *The Mysteries of Udolpho* between the familiar, orderly world of Emily's youth and the foreign, chaotic world of Udolpho, one critic notes, "Emily does not grow any wiser; in the end she is merely rescued from the world of Udolpho and brought back to ordered society. There is no more relatedness between her experiences at Udolpho and La Vallée than there is between a nightmare and an awakening in the light of day."[13] And other critics support the idea that conflicts go unresolved in Radcliffe's world by noting that the world of the Gothic novel generally is a conservative, conformist one that precludes modification of any sort: "Characters and events repeat from one generation to the next, enabling the reader to deny changes in time."[14] Emily's name, curiously enough, suggests change and growth: "Aubert," from the French *aube*, suggests the "dawn" of something new; "Emily," in the context of eighteenth-century literature, suggests Rousseau's "Emile" or ideal student of nature. But questions remain unanswered at the close of Radcliffe's novel: What new day is dawning and what studies will Emily undertake? Those were questions for which there undoubtedly were no answers visible to a woman of Radcliffe's time and social class.

The notions of resistance to change and the inability to envision the future are especially significant with respect to the figure of Montoni and his close association in the novel with social upheaval. Significantly, all that Italy represents or is identified with in *The Mysteries of Udolpho* either dies or disappears altogether: Montoni, Mme. Cheron, Count Morano, Signora Laurentini, even the Quesnels, who choose Italy as their permanent residence. Thus upheaval and change are banished, rather than incorporated into some meaningful social or political solution. Thus also, although the novel closes with the final image of Emily in control at La Vallée with Valancourt, it also closes with the sense that Emily will never be completely able to come to grips with the threatening specter of the sublime Montoni.

Two Sides of Frankenstein and Nature

Mary Wollstonecraft Shelley's 1818 novel *Frankenstein* deals with many of the same social and political problems as *The Mysteries of Udolpho,* perhaps most notably the problems that arise when the benevolent, humanizing influence exerted by such female figures as Emily St. Aubert and Frankenstein's bride Elizabeth is menaced by such threatening figures in modern society as Montoni and the mad scientist Frankenstein.

In Radcliffe's novel, a woman is the chief viewer and describer of nature; and although Montoni's threat is never completely dispelled, the novel achieves a resolution of sorts to the opposition between Emily and Montoni by assigning to her, as a woman, control of both landscape and the land at the end. A similar resolution emerges in Shelley's novel. Frankenstein, a man, is in this case the chief narrative source of landscape; and, as with Montoni, the threat of his pernicious influence lingers at the close of the novel. A resolution of sorts is achieved, nonetheless, between the male values embodied by Frankenstein and the female values embodied by his wife Elizabeth and other female characters. And that resolution, like the one proposed in *The Mysteries of Udolpho,* involves women in the narrative act whereby landscape is described and ties with the land are maintained.

A brief summary of Frankenstein's often-told story will help to identify the chief narrative participants and their relationships with landscape. The novel begins with a series of letters written by the novel's first nature describer, the English explorer Robert Walton, to his sister Margaret Saville in London. Nearing his destination, the North Pole, Walton writes to describe first his glimpse of a monstrous creature and then his rescue of a Swiss scientist, Victor Frankenstein, who proceeds to tell Walton his story. Frankenstein, the novel's main narrator and describer of nature, relates how as a young man his plans to marry his cousin Elizabeth were thwarted by his scientific ambitions, which led him to discover the principles of life and to create a monster. Horrified by his success, he spurned the monster, who in revenge first murdered his creator's brother, making an innocent friend of the family, Justine Moritz, seem to bear the guilt; then murdered Frankenstein's dear friend Clerval; and finally, on the night of their marriage, murdered Frankenstein's bride, Elizabeth. Frankenstein also tells how at one point he met with the monster and heard his sad tale. That tale constitutes an embedded narration and makes

the monster a third describer of nature, along with Walton and Frankenstein. The monster's tale centers on his affection for a family of exiled
French aristocrats, the DeLaceys, whom he observes from a distance while
hiding in the forest. It is when that family sees his hideous form and brutally chases him away that he turns his murderous attentions to his creator. The novel draws to a close with Frankenstein dying, after having
chased the monster toward the North Pole and unsuccessfully attempted
to gain revenge for the murders committed against his loved ones. At the
very end, the frame narrator Walton himself encounters the monster after
setting his course southward to England, having abandoned at least for
the time the kind of grandiose scientific pursuits that occasioned Frankenstein's tragic fate.

To understand the oppositional outlook that characterizes Frankenstein's story, it is necessary to consider again the central opposition between mountains and valleys, which, as in Radcliffe's novel, corresponds
closely to the opposition between sublime and beautiful nature. The
mountains are introduced near the beginning of the novel through
Walton's description of the sublime setting of the North Pole: only later
will the opposing term of beautiful nature be introduced through Frankenstein's description of gentle lakes and sunny, green settings. The occasion for the initial description of sublime nature is that Walton has arrived
at a point in his northward journey at which he is enveloped in thick fog
on a sea of ice. As the fog lifts, he writes, "we beheld, stretched out in
every direction, vast and irregular mountains and plains of ice, which
seemed to have no end."[15] In this context the first glimpse of the fleeing
monster is presented: "a being which had the shape of a man, but apparently of gigantic stature, sat in the sledge, and guided the dogs. We
watched the rapid progress of the traveller with our telescopes, until he
was lost among the distant inequalities of the ice" (p. 18).

The sublime, polar nature scenes that mark the beginning of *Frankenstein* find their thematic contrary in chapter 5, when Frankenstein
describes the beautiful natural surroundings of Ingoldstadt, the city in
which he created the monster: "A serene sky and verdant fields filled me
with ecstacy. The present season was indeed divine; the flowers of spring
bloomed in the hedges, while those of summer were already in bud" (p.
65). Later in the novel, similar evocations of beautiful nature recur. The
most striking, perhaps, is the following, which represents one of the few
fleeting moments of happiness that the newly married Frankenstein and
Elizabeth are able to experience: "The wind, which had hitherto carried us
along with amazing rapidity, sunk at sunset to a light breeze; the soft air
just ruffled the water, and caused a pleasant motion among the trees as we
approached the shore, from which it wafted the most delightful scent of
flowers and hay" (p. 191).

Although in most of the novel's landscapes, as presented by the main narrator Frankenstein or by his scientific admirer Walton, sublime and beautiful nature tend to combine to some extent, they nevertheless accentuate one or the other. The dichotomy between the two sorts of landscapes thus reinforces an oppositional outlook, which Frankenstein himself serves to promote and accentuate and which Walton only echoes in the opening letters, once Frankenstein and the monster appear on the scene. The novel's two most extended landscapes, both of which occur in the month of August, provide examples. The first occurs about a third of the way into the novel, at the beginning of part 2 of the narration Frankenstein makes to Walton; the other occupies a parallel position about a third of the way from the end, at the beginning of part 3 of that narration. By accentuating sublime nature in the first and beautiful nature in the second, Shelley establishes the same oppositional effect through landscape in *Frankenstein* as did Radcliffe in *The Mysteries of Udolpho*.

The first of these August scenes described by Frankenstein presents him in the company of his family and friends, attempting to find comfort in nature from the guilt of having created and abandoned the monster. The group's destination is the valley of Chamounix, where initially the sublime and the beautiful are found in harmonious combination. In ascending, however, the viewers progressively leave behind all vestiges of beautiful, living nature: "we saw no more ruined castles and fertile fields. Immense glaciers approached the road; we heard the rumbling thunder of the falling avelânche, and marked the smoke of its passage" (p. 90).

It is significant that Frankenstein soon continues the trip alone, for what he discovers as he travels onward and upward is a nature as stripped of human presence as he himself has become. Thus he notes, for example, the trees that, after the winter avalanche, "lie broken and strewed on the ground; some entirely destroyed, others bent, leaning upon the jutting rocks of the mountain, or transversely upon other trees" (p. 92). Finally, at the top of his ascent, he finds nothing more than glaciers, fields of ice and "Mont Blanc, in awful majesty," which he describes as follows: "I remained in a recess of the rock, gazing on this wonderful and stupendous scene. The sea, or rather the vast river of ice, wound among its dependent mountains, whose aerial summits hung over its recesses. The icy and glittering peaks shone in the sunlight over the clouds" (p. 93). In this setting, and at this moment, the monster emerges and demands that Frankenstein listen to his tale.

The second August scene presents Frankenstein in the company of his friend Clerval, again attempting to find comfort in nature, this time from the guilt of having promised to create a mate for the monster. Instead of an ascent, this scene enacts a descent, as the two friends travel down the Rhine River. Initially, as in the first scene, the harmonious blend of the sublime and the beautiful is discovered: "This part of the Rhine, indeed, presents a singularly variegated landscape. In one spot you view rugged hills, ruined castles overlooking tremendous precipices, with the dark Rhine rushing beneath; and, on the sudden turn of a promontory, flourishing vineyards, with green sloping banks, and a meandering river, and populous towns, occupy the scene" (p. 152). Gradually, however, the accent is placed clearly on the beautiful, the superiority of which is spelled out by Clerval: "Oh, surely the spirit that inhabits and guards this place has a soul more in harmony with man, than those who pile the glacier, or retire to the inaccessible peaks of the mountains of our own country" (p. 153).

It is important at this point to record the association between sublime nature and what is presented as a typically masculine search for truth, a search that—especially at the start of the novel, with Walton—is above all a search in and about nature. The basis for the association between the sublime and the masculine search for truth presumably is that such a search elevates a man's soul and mind, as mountains elevate his eyes or his steps. And indeed, in his search to discover truth, Frankenstein is presented, symbolically, as following a northward path in his travels: from Geneva to Ingoldstadt to England and Scotland and eventually to the North Pole. Now, that upward movement is also presented, revealingly, as a penetration of a clearly feminine presence in nature; and thus the sexual dimension of the sublime and beautiful opposition is introduced. As Frankenstein's teacher, Professor Waldman states about modern scientists: "They penetrate into the recesses of nature, and shew how she works in her hiding places. They ascend into the heavens. . . . They have acquired new and almost unlimited powers; they can command the thunders of heaven, mimic the earthquake, and even mock the invisible world with its own shadows" (p. 42). As this quotation reveals, the sexual dimension is introduced along with a political one, since power over feminine nature is what is at issue here. If scientists who "penetrate into the recesses of nature" and "ascend into the heavens" are closely linked with such sublime natural phenomena as Mont Blanc or the North Pole, they are also connected here and elsewhere with the acquisition of "new and almost unlimited powers." It is not surprising that the creator of the monster is named Victor, for he is indeed the winner in the contest that the novel posits as taking place in the modern world to control and dominate both nature and women. Nor is it surprising that he is named Frankenstein, a name that identifies his sublime penetration and control of nature as "frank," in the sense of intellectually open and genuine, and "stony" (from the German Stein), in the sense of dispassionate and unfeeling. It is also worth noting in this regard that Stein appears in many German place-names with the sense of "cliff" or "mountain."

It is also important that the novel's physical opposition between sublime mountains and beautiful valleys be seen in relation to the matter of social class. The opposition of classes in *Frankenstein* has an immediate association with landscape inasmuch as the lofty, sublime figures associated with mountains are members of the upper class, whereas the lower, beautiful figures associated with valleys are members of the lower class. The first sentence of Frankenstein's narration focuses, significantly, on his social superiority and his family's political power: "I am by birth a Genevese; and my family is one of the most distinguished of that republic. My ancestors had been for many years counsellors and syndics" (p. 27).

Now, at first glance the egalitarianism implied by "republic" appears to contradict the social superiority that Frankenstein is so quick to stress. But this apparent contradiction assumes special meaning if it is viewed in the light of the revolutionary politics in France at the end of the eighteenth century: it is significant that Walton's letters are dated 17— and that the aristocratic French family the monster discovers in the forest is in exile from French tyranny. And it is also significant as Lee Sterrenburg persuasively argues, that Frankenstein creates the monster in the same city, Ingoldstadt, that was rumored to have been the secret source of the French Revolution.[16] If the connection is made with such revolutionary political phenomena in France as the Reign of Terror, it is possible to envision a blend of Republicanism and power that would reach the awful heights of the sublime and would possess "new and almost unlimited powers." Seen from this political perspective the first syllable of Frankenstein's name could be said to connote "French," through the historical association with the Franks or simply through phonetic similarities in French, English, and German. Frankenstein would then be the "French stone," the hard and powerful force that, like Radcliffe's Montoni, has a prototypically foreign nature.

To turn to the semantic opposite of mountains, sublime nature, and masculine power in *Frankenstein* is to turn to valleys, beautiful nature, and the feminine domestic and humanitarian values that descriptions of beautiful nature serve to develop and identify. In those descriptions, as passages quoted above have indicated, an emphasis is repeatedly placed on the notions of life, productivity, and community; those passages contain such characteristic elements as "flowers in bud," "the delightful scent of flowers and hay," "fertile fields," "flowering vineyards," and "populous towns." All of these are in turn closely connected with such values of domestic life as warmth, love, nurture—in short with that concern for others which scientific inquiry is shown to preclude. It is interesting to observe in this regard that Frankenstein's warm and loving friend Clerval rejects science when he arrives at the university and prefers the study of language and literature, especially of authors identified as orientalists; for, as the narrator Frankenstein observes, "When you read their writings, life appears to consist in a warm sun and garden of roses, — in the smiles and frowns of a fair enemy, and the fire that consumes your own heart. How different from the manly and heroical poetry of Greece and Rome" (p. 64). As this passage illustrates, there is a clear association between beautiful nature and the qualities of warmth and love that women and gentle, compassionate men like Clerval value. It is not surprising, then, to discover that all of the beautiful nature scenes Frankenstein describes are ones he visits in the company of either Elizabeth or Clerval. As the latter's name suggests, he has the moral "clarity" that Shelley, like Radcliffe, associates with the beautiful and valleys.

Valleys and beautiful nature of course have political implications, just as mountains and sublime nature do. In contrast with the "new and unlimited powers" possessed by sublime scientists and other male upper-class figures, such traditional moral strengths as fortitude and benevolence are possessed by members of the lower classes like Justine Moritz and the other female characters in the novel, all of whom are in a similar state of economic subservience. Significantly, Frankenstein's mother Caroline and his future wife Elizabeth both enter the family of Frankenstein's father Alphonse as abandoned children and thus similarly assume their domestic role in a position of economic inferiority and dependence. Common to characters such as Justine and the various domestic women depicted in the novel is not only an *absence* of power, which would be a merely negative attribute, but rather a contrary *presence* of positive concern for others and commitment to community values. Landscape serves to concretize and develop this presence in the novel.

In short, *Frankenstein* opposes two contrasting types of landscape and, concomitantly, two contrasting types of social beings. There are those female persons who are beautiful and strong like the mother (in French, *beau* and *fort*) and just in the sense of morally right and sincere like the servant; they occupy a position of economic inferiority but do so with dignity and hope for the future. And there are those male persons who are sublime and strong like the French stone, Frankenstein. But the strength or virtue of a woman such as Elizabeth, celebrated and elevated to the level of a true resolution in Radcliffe's novel, is presented as old-fashioned and ineffectual in the futuristic world of *Frankenstein*. Whatever alternatives there may be, providing a resolution to the sexual and political struggles for power, must be found elsewhere than at the level of the main opposition between mountains, sublime nature, and Frankenstein on the one hand and valleys, beautiful nature, and Elizabeth on the other. At that level, the characters stand squarely within Frankenstein's own narration and are embodiments of his own irremediably oppositional outlook.

The contradictories of the main opposition between Frankenstein and

Elizabeth can best be identified, as they were for *The Mysteries of Udolpho,* among members of the same sex; and landscape helps to identify these characters. Clerval plainly emerges in this regard as contradicting Frankenstein's character. Like Frankenstein, Clerval is a man, but a man in whom all of the problematic sides of the male character are negated: he is neither selfish, nor insensitive to beautiful nature, nor obsessed with personal fame and glory.

There is one feature of nature description in *Frankenstein* that makes it possible to understand Clerval's important relation to Frankenstein's character: the recurrent emphasis on what can be referred to as the "dark side of the mountain" motif. This motif is introduced near the beginning of Frankenstein's narration when he recounts a thunderstorm that "advanced from behind the mountains of Jura" and which results in an old and beautiful oak being reduced to "a blasted stump" (p. 35). Subsequently, storms and other threatening phenomena are always associated with the Jura side of the mountains surrounding Lake Geneva. Especially striking in this regard are two parallel passages that similarly emphasize the dark and bright sides of mountains, notably the contrasting appearances of the Juras and the Alps. The first description occurs immediately after the monster has killed his first victim, Frankenstein's brother William; the second, immediately before he claims his last victim, Elizabeth:

(1) I discovered more distinctly the black sides of Jura, and the bright sides of Mont Blanc; I wept like a child: "Dear mountains! my own beautiful lake! how do you welcome your wanderer?" (p. 70)

(2) we saw Mont Salêve, the pleasant banks of Montalêgre, and at a distance, surmounting all, the beautiful Mont Blânc; . . . sometimes coasting the opposite banks, we saw the mighty Jura opposing its dark side to the ambition that would quit its native country. (p. 190)

Unquestionably, the dark-side-of-the-mountain motif serves to reinforce the oppositional character generally of Frankenstein's narration. More specifically, it serves to introduce an oppositional character within the sublime and thus to stress Frankenstein's own two-sided nature, the bright side of which is represented by Clerval. Just as there are two sides to the sublime mountains, so are there two sides to men like Frankenstein, and by implication to all men: there is in fact talk elsewhere in the novel of the "dark side of human nature" (p. 60). Because Clerval is a man, and in his own fashion a sublime man too, he can serve as Frankenstein's "better half," so to speak—that is, his counterpart and contradictory within the internally divided concept of the sublime. But the better half in Frankenstein is of course doomed, as is Clerval.

The role of Elizabeth's contradictory may be assigned to Safie, the young Turkish girl whom the monster discovers in the forest sharing the exile imposed on the DeLaceys. Safie is thus situated outside of Frankenstein's narration and within the monster's, with the possibility thus presenting itself of an escape from Frankenstein's oppositional world view. Safie displays the positive intellectual qualities that are largely absent from the other female characters, notably from the eternally resigned, all-suffering Elizabeth. Safie is a student of language and literature, like Clerval, and gives evidence of a lively curiosity and intelligence: her name even suggests knowledge, as Knoepflmacher observes.[17] More importantly, she is a foreigner and a rebel. The authoritarian treatment by a forbidding father, which affects virtually all of the characters in the novel, is something that she will not condone. Following the lessons given to her by her enslaved mother, Safie defies her father and chooses her own fate.

But if Safie thus negates the passivity and resignation present in female characters like Elizabeth, she also plays an extremely minor role in the novel. She is sketched briefly in the monster's narration and is not even mentioned elsewhere. Not surprisingly, then, she bears no manifest or distinctive relationship to nature. Because Safie's narrative status is so marginal, she can be said to offer only a glimpse of a solution to the novel's major sexual and political conflicts.

The neutral and complex characters remain to be considered here, both of whom differ from Safie in having real and substantial narrative importance in Shelley's novel: indeed, both are narrators whose voices complement Frankenstein's and whose relationships with nature differ in significant ways from his. Although both are male characters, they nevertheless are male in ways that differ from Frankenstein's and which suggest possible resolutions to the power struggle enacted in the novel.

The first character who escapes the initial opposition between mountains and sublime nature versus valleys and beautiful nature is the monster. As the naïve and unsocialized narrator of his own story, he seems capable of moving beyond the fixed oppositional structure that marks Frankenstein's narration generally and his description of nature in particular. Living completely outside of a society marked by divisiveness and difference, the monster would seem to be the perfect neutral, synthetic figure who could, in and of himself, eliminate conflicts of gender and of social class.

At the beginning of his narration, the monster lives in a state reminiscent of the Garden of Eden or pastoral Golden Age. In that early state, he shares with both Safie and Clerval an essentially androgynous nature in which domestic and intellectual interests combine, irrespective of gender. With Safie, the novel presents a female embodiment of wisdom, nobility, and courage: she is indeed, as Peter Dale Scott observes, "an androgynously balanced corrective to Rousseau's docile, domestic, and affectionate

Sophie, a figure reproved by Mary Wollstonecraft."[18] And with Clerval, the novel proposes a male embodiment of such qualities as benevolence, compassion, and concern for others, again without regard for the typically feminine connotations of these qualities.

Not surprisingly, then, what is most striking about the androgynous monster's relationship with nature is its undifferentiated sensual quality, the absence of divisive oppositional structures like the sublime and the beautiful or male and female. He has a privileged relationship with nature in which what is concrete and practical alone has importance: the forest provides shade; the river offers relief from thirst; birds produce pleasant sounds. When he saw the sun for the first time, the monster remembers, "a gentle light stole over the heavens, and gave me a sensation of pleasure. I started up, and beheld a radiant form rise from among the trees" (p. 98). What is most important in the monster's narration is his own ability to assert the importance of natural phenomena, which the female and other androgynous figures in the novel lack. Therefore, although the accent is on beautiful nature in his descriptions, it is an accent placed, significantly, by a male describer: "It surprised me, that what before was desert and gloomy should now bloom with the most beautiful flowers and verdure. My senses were gratified and refreshed by a thousand scents of delight, and a thousand sights of beauty" (p. 111). Elsewhere, in a similar vein, he says, "In the meanwhile also the black ground was covered with herbage, and the green banks interspersed with innumerable flowers, sweet to the scent and the eyes, stars of pale radiance among the moonlight woods; the sun became warmer, the nights clear and balmy; and my nocturnal rambles were an extreme pleasure to me" (pp. 113–114).

If the monster ultimately fails to provide a meaningful way out of the oppositional structure in *Frankenstein,* it is because he must remain outside society to neutralize its differences. Once he enters society, the ideal, undifferentiated pastoral state and its concomitant sensitivity to nature are lost forever. Unlike the inhabitants of the Garden of Eden, the monster must leave the ideal state through no fault of his own; but the fact remains that he must leave. He can no more live outside society and history than can the DeLacey family live forever in exile in the pastoral enclave of the forest.

The monster's Fall is not without political implications. It is, significantly, a family of French aristocrats who ultimately chase the monster away and condemn him to his postlapsarian condition of misery. Daniel Cottom argues that once these aristocrats are confronted with the real and historical conditions of their existence—that the monster has been the kindly, invisible spirit providing their food and firewood at night— they respond like typical oppressors of the lower classes. As he observes, "When labor becomes subjectivity—as the monster tries to introduce himself to the DeLaceys—it must be rejected and one must flee from it."[19] Only outside the consciousness of self, of history, and of real economic conditions, then, can the monster provide a synthesis of society's oppositional structures, whether they are the sublime and beautiful, man and woman, or in this case the rich and the poor.

Walton, the other character in *Frankenstein* who narrates his own story and who thus resembles the monster in having an independent narrative status, embodies a more successful resolution. A complex figure of resolution, he actively combines the positive features in the main opposing characters, Frankenstein and Elizabeth. Like Frankenstein, on the one hand, he aspires to the sublime, as his descriptions of the polar region at the beginning of the novel indicate. But like Elizabeth, on the other, he embodies feminine, humanitarian virtue. As opposed to Frankenstein, who in penetrating the mysteries of nature eventually causes the misery or death of virtually everyone he loves, Walton harms no one by his attempts to discover the North Pole; he even agrees to abandon the project when his sailors fear for their safety. Moreover, as appears at the beginning of the novel, his greatest need and desire is for a companion, for a sense of domesticity and community.

It is thus not surprising that initially Walton, like the monster, has a privileged, almost idyllic relationship with nature. In his relationship, difference does exist, but it is transcended in the name of utopian ideals. Thus even in the far North in the month of December, he can write, "I feel a cold northern breeze play upon my cheeks, which braces my nerves, and fills me with delight" and says, in a letter to his sister,

> I try in vain to be persuaded that the pole is the seat of frost and desolation; it ever presents itself to my imagination as the region of beauty and delight. There, Margaret, the sun is for ever constantly visible for more than half the year; its broad disk just skirting the horizon, and diffusing a perpetual splendour. There . . . snow and frost are banished; and sailing over a calm sea, we may be wafted to a land surpassing in wonders and in beauty every region hitherto discovered on the habitable globe. . . . What may not be expected in a country of eternal light ruled by different laws and in which numerous circumstances enforce a belief that the aspect of nature differs essentially from anything of which we have any experience? (pp. 9–10)

Although the utopian quality of this description disappears when Walton meets Frankenstein—a meeting that constitutes as it were *his* fall from grace—there is also evidence in the novel that Walton ultimately recaptures his special relationship with nature and emerges as the implied figure of resolution at the end of the novel. This evidence is based on his roles as an Englishman, a writer, and a brother.

Because Walton's English nationality is merely alluded to in the frame, specifically English social problems can be sidestepped and downplayed; returning home to England at the end of the novel can thus be conceived as a solution of sorts. As will be recalled, in *Paul et Virginie* and *Atala,* the real problems of colonialism and political exile were similarly resolved by being contained within fixed limits. Moreover, as in *The Mysteries of Udolpho,* real social problems are treated indirectly through the use of a foreign setting, in this case the French-speaking republic of Geneva. The political threat of the "French stone"—of mountains, monsters, or Montoni—is thus contained as a foreign phenomenon and dismissed from the concerns that the Englishman Walton will have upon returning to England.

Walton also serves as a figure of synthesis and resolution because he is a writer. Even before becoming an explorer, he was a poet, and, as he comments, "for one year lived in a Paradise of my own creation" (p. 11). Perhaps it is to this paradise that he returns at the conclusion of the novel. Noting the mild season and southward direction of his ship's travels at the end, Peter McInerney speaks of "a metaphorical sequence of growth after spiritual death in the wintry north to rebirth and increasing maturity in the warm south."[20] McInerney also argues, on the basis of such anachronisms in the text as references to Coleridge and Byron in letters dated to 17—, that Walton is writing the novel in retrospect, when he can truly understand Frankenstein's story and overcome its divisive structure.

Another way, finally, in which Walton synthesizes conflicting characters and issues in *Frankenstein* is through choosing his sister as the recipient of his letters and thus making a woman the chief narratee of the novel: the first words of *Frankenstein* are, significantly, "To Mrs. Saville, England." Not only, then, is Walton an English writer, as was Shelley, but he is one who addresses a woman reader and evinces great concern about her: at the start of his first letter, he states, "I arrived here yesterday; and my first task is to assure my dear sister of my welfare" (p. 9).

Names consistently have symbolic significance in Shelley's novel, and both Walton and his sister's names are no exception. His name, with its connotation of "forest" (from the German *Wald*), suggests an unbroken tie with benevolent nature, the same tie that Frankenstein's kindly and enlightened professor Waldman retains. Her name connotes "city" (from the French *ville*), and perhaps more importantly, as Knoepflmacher observes, "civil," the British pronunciation of her name.[21] Also noteworthy is her first name, Margaret, which has the same earthy connotation of the French flower marguerite noted in the last chapter in connection with *Paul et Virginie.* She is a civilizing force but of an earthy and flowering kind; he is a man of the forest. Thus together brother and sister, in their close and crucial familial and narrative relationship, combine city and country, wild and civilized nature, man and woman; together they thus offer a positive solution to Frankenstein's conflictual world view.

Thus although a man, Walton, resolves the oppositions developed in *Frankenstein*, a woman plays a key role in enabling him to provide such a resolution. That woman is M. S.—the woman writer Mary Shelley and the woman narratee Margaret Saville. As Mary Poovey observes regarding the crucial importance of Mrs. Saville, "Walton's letters, as the dominant chain of all the narrations, preserve community despite Frankenstein's destructive self-devotion, for they link him and his correspondents (Mrs. Saville and the reader) into a relationship that Frankenstein can neither enter nor destroy."[22] It is only through writing, then—but through writing by and for women—that an escape can be discovered from the prototypically male, modern prison of Frankenstein's oppositional thought.

5

Politics and Landscape:

Les Chouans and Le Lys dans la Vallée

Monarchism and the Novel

When, in France, Balzac uses description of nature in the novel some thirty years after Chateaubriand, his landscapes take on a far more concrete, overtly political significance than those of his celebrated predecessor: this is not surprising since the thirty-year span from 1800 to 1830 encompasses the entire post-Revolutionary period with its sudden, disruptive shifts in government from Republican to oligarchical, imperial, and finally monarchical rule. By virtue of becoming more overtly political, however, landscape does not cease with Balzac to follow the conflictual path traced in the preceding chapters. On the contrary, Balzac's conception of both landscape and politics is fraught with conflict. It centers on Monarchism, a political system to which Balzac adhered (as did many other sincere, serious nineteenth-century thinkers) but to which he adhered in what was perhaps a uniquely ambivalent way. The ambivalence consists in Balzac's understanding, on the one hand, that the monarchy and its aristocratic adherents had withdrawn from the reality of the modern world and were ultimately doomed while, on the other, that monarchy constituted the sole political system capable of inspiring hope and dignity for the future.

Balzac's ambivalent view of Monarchism is manifest throughout *La Comédie humaine*, but nowhere perhaps more dramatically than in the novels that make an extensive and elaborate use of landscape, notably, *Les Chouans* (1829) and *Le Lys dans la vallée* (1835). Through novels such as these, Balzac develops a textual tradition in which narrative landscape centers on the thematic notions of support for or rebellion against authoritarian rule. Nature tinted with the colors of Monarchism becomes with Balzac another one of those grids imposed on landscape like Rousseau's oppositional grid and Chateaubriand's or Bernardin's exotic one.

A close look at Balzac's treatment of Monarchism in relation to landscape reveals that the narrative mechanisms at work in the Balzacian novel are subtle and frequently disguised. Monarchism is to the forefront; but how and for whom are questions that cannot immediately be answered. The chief reason is that the important role of narrators in the Balzacian novel often goes unnoticed, as does the degree to which Balzac's descriptions are related to characters and their points of view. Scenes that display a high degree of what has been defined earlier as "focalization"—that is, scenes that are marked by both the physical vision and the mental outlook or attitudes of characters—appear at first glance to derive from an omniscient narrator. The initial task is then to detail the hierarchical pattern of interrelated narrators and focalizers through which landscape is presented in *Les Chouans* and *Le Lys*, a pattern that a number of modern critics have identified and described.

Following the path traced by Gérard Genette, Mieke Bal and Susan Lanser stress the importance of, first, distinguishing between the two components of narrative voice and point of view—between Genette's *voix* and *mode*—and, second, perceiving the relations that unquestionably exist between these two components.[1] On the one hand, the two are not identical and should not be lumped together as critics have often tended to do; but on the other, they are not unrelated and should not be considered in isolation from each other.

According to Bal, a hierarchy exists that places the various narrative participants in a variety of dominant or subordinate positions. High in the hierarchy appear those narrators whom Genette calls "extradiegetic" and Lanser calls "public"—narrators who stand outside the fictional world of the novel and whose audience does not comprise other characters. Next appear those secondary or embedded narrators whom Genette calls "intradiegetic" and Lanser "private"—narrators who are part of the fictional world and who do address other fictional entities. Last appear those characters who do not actively speak as narrators but who assume the more passive, indirect roles of viewers or focalizers. These characters will frequently—and this point is of the utmost importance for Balzac—take over for the narrator, whether that narrator be of the public sort (as in *Les Chouans*) or the private sort (as in *Le Lys*). Bal notes in this respect that parallel roles devolve to the narrator and the focalizer; and Lanser stresses in the same vein the importance of the focalizer as an index of the fundamental values that the narrator plays the chief (but not sole) role in promoting: "the focalizing character also signals an affinity between that character and the narrative voice, and thus constitutes an important index of the narrator's psychological stance."[2]

It is in terms of such an interplay between narrator and focalizing character that the Monarchist grid appears in the Balzacian novel. Each is responsible for certain of the text's political implications. Yet meanwhile each manages to achieve relative invisibility and political neutrality. The invisibility and neutrality are not quite the same as the containment strategies discussed in chapter 3, in which an attempt is made to pass off as general, universal truth what is in fact a social and political content. Such content is without a doubt far more overt with Balzac than with Bernardin and Chateaubriand. Rather, invisibility and neutrality are new aesthetic standards for nineteenth-century novelists, attempts at eschewing didacticism and achieving "objectivity." What is denied is not the political nature of the literature per se but rather any evidence of political bias in that literature.

In *Les Chouans*, the narrative voice seems to be neutral and objective but in fact plays an important social and political role. It is especially relevant with respect to *Les Chouans* to note, following Fredric Jameson, the close community ties that Balzac's narrators have. Jameson shows that in his treatment of narrative voice, Balzac reestablishes ties with the ancient practice of storytelling and thus reinstitutes narration as an act of communication and community. In contrast to a writer like Flaubert, whose attempts to make the narrator silent and invisible reflect "the disappearance, under capitalism, of some socially sanctioned *institution* of storytelling in which the activities of both sender and receiver, narrator and public, correspond to roles recognized and codified within the social order itself," Balzac attempts "to revive an old pre-capitalist mode of storytelling, to combine elements of the old storyteller of inn or village with those, equally feudal, characteristics of the high-society wit and *raconteur*."[3]

The storyteller who serves as narrator in *Les Chouans* reveals himself and performs the social and political functions that devolve upon him chiefly at the beginning of the novel; later he is replaced by the novel's focalizers. Even at the beginning the narrator's appearance is infrequent, and many readers might well not notice him. He nonetheless succeeds in setting a tone whereby all the narrative participants—narrator, characters, and readers alike—are assumed to have common social and political concerns. The narrator differs from the other participants only to the extent that he is a somewhat older and wiser member of the community, as is evident in remarks such as the following: "It would have been easy for an observer aware of the internal discords then agitating France to pick out . . ." or "as those who were not involved in the drama of the Revolution may need to be told. . . ."[4]

The narrative voice in *Les Chouans* can thus be said to derive, however mutedly and indirectly, from a concerned, responsible political presence in the novel. His actual preferences and political stands are never directly apparent. He is capable of making relatively pointed remarks—for example, that Republican decrees are losing force and influence, because they "were no longer backed by grand idealistic conceptions, patriotism or the Terror, which formerly had made them effective" (p. 44). But even in such cases, the reader cannot actually decide whether the narrator is for or against a Republic versus a Monarchist form of government. This is not surprising in view of the conflictual nature of Balzac's political attitudes and his ambivalence toward Monarchism. The fact remains, however, that the narrator introduces a political presence and tone into the novel. The way is thus prepared for those characters whose political points of view will constitute the center of interest throughout the rest of the novel.

In *Le Lys*, a similarly significant political presence and tone are established, superficial differences notwithstanding. Thus although *Le Lys* has a private narrator who speaks in the first person while *Les Chouans* has a public narrator who never directly identifies himself as a speaking voice, the same indirect, only partially acknowledged preoccupation with Monarchism hovers over both texts. In *Le Lys*, this preoccupation reveals itself in the crucial role played by political events in a narration that on the surface is strictly personal. The novel begins with a letter in which the aristocratic narrator, Félix de Vandenesse, agrees to comply with the wishes of the narratee, his lover Natalie de Manerville, and recount his past life, thereby explaining the oddly distracted behavior he manifests in her presence. The reader assumes that the narration would then proceed along strictly personal and romantic lines. In point of fact, however, Félix immediately casts his life in a political light, and this in two different ways. The first way concerns the family. At the very moment in history that the drama of absolute, monarchical rule is being enacted in society at large, this same drama is being enacted within his own family. His mother is presented as a tyrant; his brother Charles is introduced as "my family's hope; consequently king of the household"; his aunt, the marquise de Listomère, as living "as if Louis XV had never died."[5] As for the narrator himself, the unwanted outcast in this aristocratic family, he is compared to Marat ("Marat was an angel beside me," p. 9). Indeed, virtually every aspect of the narrator's early life, as he presents it, concerns matters of justice, freedom, and social class—the very matters being decided in the political arena at the time.

Félix also introduces political preoccupations focused on Monarchism through his treatment of the parallel chronology of public and private events. Events in his own life are measured and punctuated by major political upheavals. Thus Napoleon's attempted return to power is the occasion of the narrator's abandoning his studies in Paris; and Louis XVIII's triumphal restoration of Bourbon rule, for his entering aristocratic society as the family's representative. More generally, his growth and development —from a sickly child to an insecure adolescent and finally to a strong and confident adult—mirrors that of the restored Monarchist regime. Moreover, in the presentation of his childhood, he often emerges as the same concerned, responsible political presence as the public narrator of *Les Chouans*. Consider for example his remarks about the yearnings for power and glory that the early days of the Restoration stirred in him and in others:

> Who has not envied that adulation, an awe-inspiring repetition of which was offered me some few months later when the whole of Paris rushed to meet the Emperor on his return from Elba? This sway exercised over the masses, whose lives and feelings flow into a single soul, pledged me, there and then, to glory, that priestess who slaughters the Frenchmen of to-day, as in bygone days the Druidess sacrificed the Gauls. (pp. 14–15)

If the first step in understanding how Balzac creates a Monarchist grid for viewing landscape in *Les Chouans* and *Le Lys* is to identify the narrative voice and the indirect political role that devolves upon that voice, the second step is to acknowledge that in the Balzacian novel narrative voice and focalization are two compatible and closely linked novelistic components. Focalization is not tantamount, pace Jameson, to silencing and depersonalizing the narrative voice. It does not necessarily produce, as he and other Marxists contend, an undue emphasis on individual psychology and subjectivity; nor is it always indicative of "the fragmentation of middle-class life towards the end of the nineteenth-century" or reflective of "a monadized society."[6] Rather, Balzac uses focalizers as a normal adjunct and extension of the narrative act, as indeed do all the writers in the literature of images. Jameson would have it that Balzac writes "something like a pre-individualistic narrative" in which "the concepts of identification and point of view *have not yet* become relevant." And as proof he adduces what he calls Balzac's indifference to the choice of focalizers: "no analysis of Balzac is satisfactory unless it comes to terms in one way or another with this profound *indifference* of Balzacian narrative with its 'bearers,' who are distanced or suppressed with an arbitrariness that is properly meaningless in terms of the ethical criteria of point of view theory."[7] Careful consideration of *Les Chouans* and *Le Lys* will reveal that, contrary to what Jameson contends, Balzac is anything but indifferent to the choice of focalizers. On the contrary, they are consistently chosen in relation to the larger political outlook that the novel as a whole acts to further and develop.

Balzac's use of focalizers in *Les Chouans* and *Le Lys* develops that indirect focus on Monarchism which the narrative voice introduces into the novel. In *Les Chouans*, the process will be seen to be relatively complex. Suffice it to say here that after the opening pages in which the public narrator's voice is often heard, a series of Republican focalizers take over. The most noteworthy among them is Hulot, the military leader sent to Brittany to suppress the Chouan uprising, and Marie, the young spy sent there to seduce and betray the Monarchist leader Montauran. To dismiss as insignificant the coherent Republican outlook of these and other focalizers in

Les Chouans is to fail to perceive many of this novel's crucial features. It is surely to fail to perceive the significance of its landscapes, as critics have tended for the most part to do.

There are undoubtedly a number of reasons for critics having over-looked or undervalued the role of focalizers in works such as *Les Chouans*. One is that their role is played in a largely unobtrusive, indirect way. An-other is that, as Jameson indicated, their role is not essentially psycho-logical in nature: since the point of view of a particular character is not al-ways interesting in terms of insights into his individual psychology, the reader is tempted to dismiss that point of view as being gratuitous or insignificant. Consider the opening lines of the first landscape presented in *Les Chouans*:

> From the top of the Pellerine the great valley of the Couesnon lies spread out to the traveller's view, with the town of Fougères rising as one of the most prominent focal points on the horizon. Its castle from its rocky height dominates three or four important roads, a po-sition which formerly made it one of the keys to Brittany. From their point of vantage the officers could see the whole expanse of this ex-tremely fertile valley with its notable variety of scenery. (p. 46)

Initially only the narrator's voice is heard. Then gradually a point of view emerges ("From their point of vantage the officers could see . . ."). Now, upon analysis of the intricate ties that link the Republican viewpoint of these officers with that of the novel's other focalizers, it appears that the lengthy landscape that follows these opening lines is everywhere marked by that viewpoint. The significance that thereby accrues to the landscape says little about the psychological importance of the officers in the novel; but it says much about their political importance as characters and about the political importance of landscape to the work as a whole.

The focalizers in *Le Lys* present different problems from those in *Les Chouans*. The chief problem in such a work is the confusion between two different though related narrative presences who happen to bear the same name: one, Félix as an adult, who acts as the narrator of events in his past; the other, Félix as a child and young man, who acts as a participant in those events at the time they occurred. It is in keeping with the strategy deployed in the novel generally that the difference between these two presences—and accordingly the difference between voice and vision—is consistently blurry and ambiguous. That strategy acts among other things to play one presence off against the other, thereby producing an effect of political neutrality and objectivity.

One typical move in the strategy is for Félix as youthful participant to protest his innocence and naïveté, while at the same time seeing both na-ture and politics with the wisdom or experience of his older, narrating counterpart. The very first landscape in the novel provides an example. Should the reader wonder how the eye of an adolescent who has lived a virtually sequestered life can be as perceptive as that of an experienced, widely traveled adult, the narrator notes, "Although completely new to the poetry of place, I was unconsciously demanding, just as those who, without any practical knowledge of an art, imagine, first and foremost, its ideal" (p. 18). In point of fact, however, the experienced eye in this landscape is an instance of a dual focalization in which the narrator's vision temporarily coincides with the participant's. Thus focalized scenes, which do derive from the participant's naïve vision, also take on a coloration that can be traced to the narrator's active participation in the political arena. Consider the following descriptive passage, in which an autumnal scene reflects Félix's sadness: "The fields were shorn now, the poplars were losing their leaves, and those that remained were the colour of rust; the vine shoots were burned, the tree tops wore the sombre hues of that tan colour which the kings of old used to adopt for their dress and which hid the purple of power beneath the brown of sorrows" (p. 112). Political concerns and attitudes here recall the older, disabused narrator; yet at the same time the younger, romantic focalizer's viewpoint is the center of interest.

It is important in conclusion to emphasize the crucial role that focalization plays in Balzac's use of landscape to reveal a political point of view. In *Le Lys*, all of the descriptions of nature derive from the point of view of Félix, who has a clear propensity for seeing what he wants to see in nature, for example: "Moved to my very soul, I went down into that basin, and soon saw a village which in my overflowing lyricism seemed to me quite matchless" (p. 19). A comment such as this reveals the unduly subjective, even solipsistic vision that characterizes Félix's deformed vision of nature, love, and politics. In *Les Chouans*, the deformation is more subtle and variously applied to different characters and points of view; but it is nonetheless a fundamental ingredient of landscape. In the landscape near the beginning, it affects the inexperienced Republican officers whose perceptions of nature evince their inability to comprehend the military significance of their surroundings. In other important landscapes, Marie de Verneuil is the center of interest: her blurred visual perception serves to reveal her only partial ability to understand the confusing contemporary conditions in which she lives.

In short, the vision that Balzac's characters, and by extension his readers, have of nature is emblematic of their vision of the problematic political reality of the times. And that vision perhaps best explains what Monarchism represents in the Balzacian novel: it is a critical stance, a way of exposing to view and enabling the reader to experience directly the problematic political responses to which contemporary events give rise. The events in question are Napoleon's coming to power in 1799, recounted in *Les Chouans*, and the Hundred Days and beginning of the Restoration some fifteen years later, recounted in *Le Lys*. In both novels, certain privileged characters can, in moments of lucidity, see these events as inaugurating the modern era and heralding the demise of all that was held in past centuries to be noble and worthwhile. It is within a global atmosphere of criticizing this modern era, notably its self-serving and materialistic form of individualism, that Balzac depicts the adherence to Monarchism and that he develops his ambiguous attitude to that adherence—at times viewing it as noble and admirable, at others dismissing it as futile and stemming from ignorance.

Ideology, Plot, and Landscape

Although Monarchism acts as a grid through which landscape is viewed in *Les Chouans*, it is not the political allegiance of the characters who view nature: on the contrary, they are the Republican characters who have been sent to Brittany to quell the Monarchist uprising that occurred there during the closing years of the eighteenth century. Nor is Monarchism either implicitly or explicitly endorsed: even in the revised versions of the novel that date from after Balzac's "conversion" to Monarchism in 1830, no such endorsement is to be found. Very simply, Balzac saw the Chouan revolt, as did many other royalist adherents and supporters, as an ill-conceived, futile attempt to restore legitimate rule carried out by persons who tended in the main to be ignorant, fanatical, or selfish. What is important in Balzac's novel is less an allegiance than the lived reality of Monarchism, notably, experiencing on the spot the indissoluble ties linking the Breton Monarchists to their land. In *Les Chouans*, Balzac chooses to convey this lived reality through the adoption of a Republican point of view; in *Le Lys*, he achieves the same goal by adopting a Monarchist point of view. The result in both cases is the same. Monarchism emerges in both novels not only as the chief subject but also as the chief locus of political ambivalence and conflict, which becomes an integral part of describing nature.

Before turning directly to the political significance of *Les Chouans*, however, a number of preliminary clarifications are in order, the first and perhaps most urgent of which is a brief plot summary. *Les Chouans* recounts an aborted attempt to restore legitimate monarchy in France by insurgents from the western departments. The events occur in and around Fougères in Brittany, the focal point of *chouannerie* or Breton rebellion, in the fall of 1799, the time of Napoleon's triumphant return from his Egyptian expedition against the English and the coup d'état that marked the beginning of his rule as First Consul. Chapter 1, "The Ambuscade," begins with a military confrontation between Republican troops and the Monarchist insurgents. The Republicans, led by Colonel Hulot and his seconds in command Merle and Gérard, are victorious, though their victory clearly cannot permanently stem the tide of rebellion. Chapter 2, "An Idea of Fouché's," is almost twice the length of the first. In this chapter it becomes apparent that attempts of a different sort have been made to end the Chouans' persistent guerrilla warfare: the powerful leader of the secret police, Fouché, has sent a spy, the beautiful Mlle. Marie de Verneuil, to seduce and betray the insurgents' young leader, the marquis de Montauran. Circumstances beyond her control have forced this young woman into the ignoble role of spy: the illegitimate offspring of a noble family, she became the innocent but maligned protégée of an older man, and was subse-ʃ̣_ ̣_ :y left alone, penniless, and unprotected. When she and Montauran meet, they fall in love; however, all sorts of misunderstandings and ambivalent feelings, political and personal, arise between them. Chapter 3, "A Day with No Morrow," is the longest and most complex of the novel's three chapters. A tangle of events occurs, all closely linked with the geographical setting of the Chouans' activities. Both political sides, Republican and Monarchist, now close in on the lovers who, unable to withstand these external pressures, are entrapped and die. A similarly tragic note is sounded on the political level. The Chouans' defeat follows close after Montauran's; and so too, ironically, does the Republicans': for without their knowing it, they were fighting in Brittany to defend pure, genuine Republican government at the very moment that Napoleon was acting to undermine and destroy it. In neither love nor war is there a "morrow" to the tragic events described in *Les Chouans*.

Other preliminary clarifications regard the problems that arise in reading landscape in *Les Chouans*. Balzac himself highlights one such problem, that of length, in the preface to one of his longest descriptions of nature: "As the concluding events of this story were affected by the terrain where they took place, in the town and its surroundings, a detailed description is indispensable at this point; otherwise the unwinding of the plot would be difficult to follow" (p. 229). And a "detailed description" is indeed what follows: a seven-page-long detailing of the city of Fougères (the arrangement within the city of fortifications, ramparts, walls, terraces, as well as the locations of surrounding mountains, valleys, gorges, rivers, winding country roads)—all of which would probably make more sense to city planners, geographers, or mapmakers than to the typical reader of novels. Yet the reader cannot merely dismiss this extremely detailed landscape, just as he cannot skip over the other geographical facts and lengthy descriptions in the novel. The reader who fails to form some mental picture of the setting finds that the events recounted and their larger significance indeed become, as Balzac warns, "difficult to follow." Exactly how are events related to landscape in *Les Chouans*, and to what end? I shall answer these questions by considering three distinct but closely interrelated topics: geography, military strategy, and visual perception.

Another problem that arises in connection with landscape in *Les Chouans* involves the accumulation of detail. To many critics, the extreme intricacy of *Les Chouans'* landscapes can be adduced as proof of either the accuracy or the clarity of the description, or both. The introduction to the Garnier edition, for example, provides a map of the "real places" described in the novel, with no mention whatsoever of the strictly extratextual nature of this information: the assumption presumably is that understanding the "real" geography of the place will clear up any confusion that arises from the literary presentation of that place. It is also assumed that the precision of Balzac's descriptions attests to their clarity. Closer to the truth regarding *Les Chouans* is the view that Leo Bersani has articulated about Balzac's descriptions in general: "Compared with the extraordinary distinctness and precision of descriptive language in Proust, Balzac's descriptions seem designed to substitute the dizzying effect of a scene for the visualization of that scene."[8] How and why this dizzying effect is produced in *Les Chouans* and what the readers' reactions are to the complexity and confusion that surround landscape in Balzac's work will be the concerns below.

It becomes apparent that the structural coherence of Balzac's *Les Chouans* depends on the existence of three geographical entities: first, a straight road between Brittany and Paris along which the main characters travel in the first two chapters; second, a large, vaguely defined international area in France and England that provides the larger political context of the novel; and third, a vertical axis formed by the mountains, terraces, and valleys in and around the city of Fougères, an axis along which the main characters ascend and descend in chapter 3. These entities are all presented in the novel as both crucial to an understanding of plot and yet paradoxically confusing at the same time.

The first geographical entity, the Brittany–Paris road, derives its importance from the fact that movement along it signifies movement either into or out of the region of Chouan dominance—a region that is presented in Balzac's novel as unfamiliar and often confusing to the characters and readers alike. Such a presentation can be understood as an attempt to cast the reader in the role of a non-Breton and strengthen his adherence to a Republican ideological outlook. At the beginning of the novel frequent reference is made to cities (Fougères, Mayenne, Alençon, Pontorson, Mortagne) as if all readers could immediately situate them on a map. In the very first paragraph of the novel the author is more quick to dispel the reader's confusion about the date than about the location of the story:

In the New Year of the year VIII, one day at the beginning of the month of Vendémiaire, or towards the end of September 1799 in the present calendar, a crowd of about a hundred peasants together with a large number of townsmen were climbing the Pellerine Mountain. They had left Fougères that morning to march to Mayenne; the Pellerine lies about half-way between Fougères and the little town of Ernée which is a usual halting-place for travellers. (p. 39)

Only gradually does the reader become familiar with the confusing geography of Brittany, just as he only gradually makes sense of the confusing facts of the plot. The reader at the start is thus like the Republicans who enter Brittany with the expectation of acquiring a greater understanding of an unfamiliar place. This expectation clearly is an ingredient in the reader's willingness to explore the intricate paths of the novel's lengthy, at times even labyrinthine landscapes.

The crucial relation to plot of the second geographical entity, the extended area of the Chouans' activities in France and England, derives from the fact that *chouannerie*, far from being autonomous, is inextricably linked with external forces. Achieving their political goal is contingent upon creating a unified and extensive Monarchist front, notably by joining forces with the insurgents to the southwest in Vendée; and achieving their military goal requires receiving support, men and arms, from England, which in turn requires having access to the northern coastal regions. But as with the geography of Brittany, so too with this larger geographical context, Balzac does more to create than to dispel the reader's confusion. Reference is made to a "vast and formidable plan of operations" of which the Chouans' activities are a part, and such northern regions as Normandy and Morbihan are said to be involved; but the exact perimeter of the area in which these operations are taking place remains vague. References are made to Paris, but the reader is in the same confused, disoriented position as the characters, vaguely sensing that major upheavals are occurring there (in fact the Directory is collapsing and Napoleon is coming to power), but never having a firm grasp on events outside the geographical reality beyond the confines of Brittany. With respect to England, the reader knows only that it is the distant, foreign place whence Montauran departed to enter France somewhere in Brittany or Normandy. Not only is England unfamiliar; it also is presented from a Republican viewpoint as guilty of intervening in French affairs. The text also makes repeated references to "our peasants," "our rough ancestors," and the like, which foster a sense of nationalistic, patriotic complicity between the narrator and the reader. By thus appealing to the reader's nationalistic sentiments, the novel also appeals indirectly to his putative interest and pride in the regional and geographical features of France which are dwelled on in landscape.

The importance to plot of the third geographical entity, the city of Fougères and its immediate surroundings, emerges in chapter 3, where the reader must be able to picture the relative location of the combatants in various military encounters. Sometimes it is a matter of figuring out which troops have captured the high places and are shooting down at the opposing side. Other times it is necessary to determine the direction of the line of fire in a battle by figuring out on what mountain or in what valley the soldiers are hiding. In one instance, the reader needs to know where the Promenade is located in relation to the Chouan hiding place, since the Promenade is both the spot where Marie's Chouan enemies shoot at and miss her and the point of departure for her subsequent nocturnal pursuit of them. But despite the importance of geographical considerations, their presentation by Balzac is of a decidedly confusing, even obfuscating sort. The presentation of Fougères indeed involves far more confusion than that of the road and western departments, owing to the intricate detail in which it is described—or, perhaps, overdescribed. An example of such overdescription is the following passage, one of several to present the geography of Fougères as an intricate series of descending planes:

> In front of this church, dedicated to Saint Leonard, there lies an irregular-shaped little *Place* terraced by a wall rising to form an ornamental parapet, and leading by a ramp to the Promenade.
>
> A few fathoms below the Place Saint-Leonard on a second rocky ledge the Promenade winds about the height, opening out into a wide expanse planted with trees, built at its lower end on the ramparts of the town.
>
> Then, some sixty feet below the walls and rock supporting this esplanade . . . there is a spiral way called the *Queen's Staircase* cut out of the rock, leading to a bridge built across the Nançon by Anne of Brittany.
>
> Finally, below this way which forms a third cliff balcony, gardens fall from terrace to terrace, in tiers filled with flowers, down to the river. (p. 230)

A description such as this is likely to interest and confuse the reader at the same time. On the one hand, he has been conditioned by metanarrative statements about the importance of descriptive detail to be eager to have an accurate description of the scenery. But on the other, he is likely to be disoriented by this and similar descriptive passages at the beginning of chapter 3 which make of Fougères's rocky, mountainous terrain a veritable labyrinth of winding paths and treacherous turns.

Why does Balzac seek thus to disorient the reader? It is to make him feel like an outsider, one who has a very imperfect, partial knowledge of the geography of Brittany. It should be noted, incidentally, that the text provides frequent explanatory notes concerning regional terms and objects, such as "A *piché* is a kind of brown earthenware jar found in a similar design in several parts of France, and a Parisian can picture it for himself if he imagines . . ." (p. 262); such a comment clearly assumes the reader to be unfamiliar with Brittany and its customs. As an outsider to the region, the reader is also an outsider to the Chouan cause; for the novel would have it that this cause cannot be understood without actual knowledge of and ties with the land: "Mademoiselle de Verneuil then began to understand the kind of war the Chouans were waging. Moving along these roads she could appreciate better the nature of the country which had appeared so entrancing to her viewed from above—only by walking through it was it possible to form a conception of its dangers and inescapable obstacles" (pp. 278–279). The reader may well, and probably does, come to have some sympathy for the Chouans; often the narrator actually encourages such sympathetic response. *Les Chouans* clearly does not present a black-and-white world in which the good guys oppose the bad. But the reader's sympathy for the Chouans is sporadic. What is constant is his being an outsider—like the Republican soldiers in never really understanding the Chouan viewpoint from within. The reader actually is "with" the Republican, not the Chouan, characters throughout most of the novel—and indeed in all the landscapes. Formally, then, the reader has no choice but to adopt the Republican viewpoint—to see Brittany as the soldiers sent there to squelch the rebellion see it; to discover, with them, the strategic dangers its labyrinthine lands present. There is a reason for Balzac's obfuscating, disorienting geographical descriptions: they help to cast the reader as a non-Breton and thus strengthen his adherence to the Republican ideological outlook.

In military strategy, landscape again bears a significant relation to plot. Balzac emphasizes the inherent military dangers that the Breton land presented as well as the tactical advantage that its inhabitants derived therefrom: Scott's treatment of Scotland and its intractable Highland inhabitants in *Waverley* is similar. A wide range of features assumes military importance. Not only is there the rocky, mountainous terrain of Fougères discussed above, but in presenting the surrounding countryside, Balzac makes much of the special way that fields are separated by hedgerows ("banks of earth, six feet high, triangular in section, from the ridge of which grow chestnuts, oaks or beech trees"), *échaliers* ("a tree-trunk or heavy branch one of whose ends has a hole bored through so that it fits on another piece of unshaped wood which serves as pivot"), and high brush ("giant furze, a shrub so well treated here that it rapidly attains a man's height"; pp. 239–240). Along with these, other obstacles in the Breton countryside are highlighted: the deep ditches that parallel the hedgerows, the slippery steps that scale them, the blocks of granite that stick up in the soil, the muddy paths that provide the sole access to the fields, and so on. An example of how these obstacles can affect plot is the key episode in which the Republicans chase Montauran but fail to capture him because of their unfamiliarity with the fields. Balzac makes much of the symbolic significance of each field being closed in on itself as is Brittany, geographically and politically, in relation to the rest of France. Speaking of the hedgerows and *échaliers*, he says that these objects "covering the land make it look like a vast chessboard, of which each square is a field completely isolated from the others, sealed off like a fortress with rampart-like defences" (p. 280). For Balzac, the Chouans ultimately were people who, from their remote province, "had never been able to appreciate the facts of Revolutionary events, and were bound to regard as reasonable assumptions what were really hopes founded on nothing" (p. 298). The hedgerows and *échaliers* are thus both symptom and symbol of Brittany's tragic geographical and political insularity.

Balzac also stresses the Chouans' ability to derive tactical advantage from the land they know so well, with the result that the reader's understanding of the military strategy is contingent upon an understanding of the landscape. Much is made in the novel of the Chouans' guerrilla warfare, their skill in finding hiding places underground, behind rocks and trees, in crevices and turns in the road: "The hedges of these lovely valleys with all their flowers were hiding invisible enemies. Each field was a stronghold and behind every tree lurked an ambush, and some murderous booby-trap was set in every hollow old willow stump" (p. 55). Indeed, the Chouans are presented as physically indistinguishable from the landscape in which they hide, their goatskin attire having the same rough, brownish texture and color as their mountains and fields: at one point, in a strikingly beautiful image, hundreds of them are seen clinging to and blending with the rocky surface leading up to the Promenade, "giving it the appearance of a thatched roof darkened by time" (p. 256). There also is the fact, as the narrator points out, that the Republicans can never really win a battle because, when victory is near, the Chouans disappear en masse into the surrounding brush, a military tactic known in the region as *s'égailler*. All in all, the Chouans seem to be everywhere, as if one truly could not take a step in the countryside or turn around for a moment without falling into a trap. Indeed, this is why Marie has been sent to deceive and betray Montauran: the "idea of Fouché's" is that the physical features of Brittany provide natural hiding places and advantages for the rebels, "making the country impregnable and military manoeuvre impossible" (p. 280); thus, only through espionage, not through direct combat, can the Chouans be defeated.

It has just been seen that there are indissoluble connections between landscape and the military situation in *Les Chouans*; but to understand fully the precise nature of these connections, it is also necessary to consider the novel's use of point of view. Nature becomes linked with military strategy because the two are linked in the minds of those characters through whose eyes the reader sees the landscape. Similarly in other Balzac novels—in Le Lys most noticeably—the peculiar perceptual or psychological conditions of the act of viewing colors, and at times even deforms, scenes in nature. In Les Chouans, it is significant to note the contrast that is established early in the novel between two related but opposing points of view. One is the vivid imagination of Hulot, wise veteran of innumerable battles fought in defense of his cherished Republic. It is he who suspects everything and is seen peering suspiciously into the vegetation along the side of the road, examining the sand, or listening in the sound of dry leaves for footsteps. Hulot's almost paranoid way of looking at landscape is not only the first major point of view to be utilized in the novel; it also turns out to be one with the most profound effect on the reader.

There is the similarly Republican but contrasting naïve point of view of Hulot's young seconds in command, Gérard and Merle. The following passage, part of the first major landscape in the novel, is typical of their way of looking at their surroundings:

> In the whole vast expanse of sky as the officers gazed to the far horizon there was not the smallest cloud to show by its silvery reflection that the immense blue vault was the firmament. It looked more like a silken canopy supported at varying heights by the mountain summits. . . . The officers gazed absorbed by . . . the warmly-coloured fields, in some of which sheaves of harvested buckwheat were stacked in conical piles like soldiers' guns at a bivouac. (pp. 46–47)

This passage is not without ironic qualities. These are educated young officers: "These were intelligent young men, torn like so many others from their studies to defend their country, and war had not yet blunted their aesthetic sensibility" (p. 45). The irony is that at the very moment that the two young men are suspended in a state of aesthetic rapture by the beauties of the countryside, the enemy is actively gathering around them and preparing to attack. Hulot, unlike them, is quick to envision this eventuality: "However, Hulot . . . was not the kind of soldier to let himself be captivated by the charms of a landscape, even an earthly paradise, in the face of impending danger" (p. 48). Balzac's use of symbolic touches emphasizes Gérard and Merle's inability to comprehend the military significance of their surroundings: they fail to see any clouds on the horizon or signs of the imminent battle and defeat; they fail to see the "silken canopy"—in French, the dais—as a symbol of the spread of

Monarchist sentiment covering the region they are entering or the sheaves of buckwheat as a warning of the arms soon to be pointed at them. Not surprisingly, the two officers later lose their lives, precisely because of their failure to learn to see the treacherous Chouan landscape through Hulot's eyes.

The fact of the reader's close association with Hulot's point of view early in the novel promotes a Republican bias in the reader's mind. By emphasizing the treacherous nature of the Breton landscape, he is in some sense validating the Republican military action, making it seem not only an appropriate response to the menace posed by the Chouans and their land but a necessary and even an heroic one. Ultimately it is Hulot, not Montauran, who is the hero of the battle fought in Brittany; Gérard and Merle, not the Chouans, who are its most tragic victims. The way the novel comes to an end is significant in this regard. First Montauran sends a message to his exiled brother to abandon the revolt and entrusts that message to Hulot, thereby tacitly expressing approbation of both Hulot's character and his commitment to the future instead of the past, the whole of France instead of just one of its parts. Next one of the most savage and bellicose of the Chouans, Marche-à-terre, is seen, weary and old, peaceably selling livestock at the market, "although he was the killer of more than one hundred persons" (p. 388). The fact that a passerby views him with sympathy ("There's a fine honest fellow!") strikes an ironic note, given the brutal acts he has committed in earlier times. But above all, whether the book's final image of the last Chouan evokes sympathy or blame, it serves as a poignant reminder of the defeat, the futility, and above all the irrevocable pastness of the Chouans' revolt.

To turn away from geographical and military matters and toward visual perception is to focus on the central character and heroine of *Les Chouans*, Marie de Verneuil. Her major role in the novel can be said to follow Hulot's: whereas the reader is with Hulot through most of chapter 1 and part of chapter 2, he only begins to be with Marie in chapter 2 and to identify fully with her point of view in chapter 3. Balzac's concern would appear to be first to establish firmly Hulot's straightforward Republican viewpoint before introducing Marie's politically more ambivalent, though ultimately also predominantly Republican, outlook. She then dominates the second half of the novel, with her unusual kind of visual perception of landscape assuming significance with respect to both plot and politics.

Along with the shift to Marie's point of view, a subtle but significant shift occurs in the role that the novel indirectly assigns to the reader. An appeal is made more frequently to the reader's taste for romantic effects than for accuracy of geographical detail. An appeal is also made to the reader's ability to see the symbolic significance of landscape more clearly than can Marie, the chief participant in the drama.

There are two main series of events in chapter 3, both of which depend directly on Marie's visual perception. The first involves her pursuit of Montauran, beginning with the shooting episode on the Promenade and ending with their reconciliation at Saint-James. The second involves their plans for marriage and escape, beginning with his early morning signal that he will be arriving that night and ending with their deaths the following morning. In both series of events, Marie's life literally depends on her ability to see. In the first, she is making her way over the hills and through the fields to a countryside in which hidden Chouans are omnipresent and nature seems to conspire with the enemy to obscure her vision of the way. At first it is nighttime, and accordingly everything seems especially dark and treacherous. Like Hulot in the first chapter, Marie must be acutely aware and suspicious of every shadowy form or crackling leaf. The way things in nature look under these conditions is not only eerie but at times even hallucinatory and grotesque. It is in this part of the novel that Balzac most visibly appeals to the contemporary taste for the Gothic, Romantic effects in nature made popular by Ann Radcliffe and her followers. The reader's expectation that such effects will occur in a novel like *Les Chouans* derives from the literary status of description at the time.

Marie's pursuit of Montauran continues in the early morning hours, but even sunrise does not dispel the obscurity and danger that surround her in nature. At night, darkness had fallen "like a black curtain." In the morning, fog similarly interposes a perceptual screen that blocks her vision: "swirls of vapour spread into sheets, filled the valleys and rose to the highest hills, shrouding the rich basin in a snowy mantle" (p. 255). That Marie is literally on a battlefield at this point in the text, where seeing clearly and escaping from the enemy are one and the same, is brought out symbolically in this passage through the image of violently agitated waves of fog: "Then this cloudy air heaved up waves like the ocean, raised opaque billows which softly swayed, eddied, violently swirled, took on tints of bright pink in the sun's rays, with transparent openings here and there apparently revealing a fluid silver lake." The agitation is especially pronounced in the French text where the misty atmosphere "souleva des lames impénétrables qui se balancèrent avec mollesse, ondoyèrent, tourbillonnèrent violemment, contractèrent aux rayons du soleil des teintes d'un rose vif." Agitation is suggested here in the polysemous use of the word *lames* as well as in the rhythm of the sentence due to the repeated use of long, third-person forms of the *passé simple* such as *tourbillonèrent* and *contractèrent.* Balzac is at his most poetic in a passage such as this one: indeed, he reveals here a distinctly modern side of his use of narrative description, very much at odds with the stereotypical notion of this use as strictly referential or "realistic." He also reveals his poetic side as a describer. A basic affinity exists in this regard between Balzac and such other novelists of the nineteenth century as Gautier and Flaubert.

The role of perceptual screens such as darkness and fog is even more salient in the second major series of events in chapter 3 than in the first. To begin with, perception plays a peculiar role with respect to the signal that has been agreed upon between the lovers as the sign that Montauran will come to marry and leave with Marie: that signal is the smoke from a fire which the wife of the Chouan traitor Galope-Chopine has been instructed to set to some branches on the rocks of the Saint-Sulpice mountain. Now, the very fact of the signal's consisting of smoke bespeaks the importance of perception: smoke is less distinctly visible under certain conditions of lighting or direction than solid substances. And there are other factors that increase the importance of perception, notably fog and dim light. With respect to both, I might add, echoes of Scott can be discerned: in *Waverley*, changing atmospheric and perceptual conditions also emerge on several occasions as integral components of a dramatic presentation of battle scenes.

Fog sets in, as in the first series of events, but this time so heavily that, as one character observers, "One can't see anything six paces away" (pp. 364). Thus when Marie scrutinizes the distant landscape to perceive the smoke signal, her vision is obstructed:

> The fog had gradually thickened, and enshrouded the whole district in a grey veil that obliterated the landscape masses even near the town. She looked with a tender anxiety in turn towards the cliffs, the Castle and the buildings that loomed through the fog like darker patches of fog. Near her window some trees were dimly visible against the bluish background like branching coral apprehended in the depths of a calm sea. The sun lent the sky the dull tones of tarnished silver, and the almost bare branches of the trees where a few last leaves still hung were touched with vague reddish colour by its gleams. (p. 353)

The reader plays an especially active role at this point in the novel, for it is the reader who perceives here the symbolic significance of landscape, which Marie is unable to see. The reader will note that even the sunlight acts oxymoronically to obscure rather than illuminate this scene, giving it "the dull tones of tarnished silver"; later when moonlight replaces the sun's dark rays, it similarly seems to make vision less rather than more clear ("The moon shone out, making the fog look like white smoke," p.

373). The reader will also note the "vague reddish colour" in this landscape—a symbolic touch that evokes both the blood that has just been
shed, the Chouans having brutally beheaded the traitor Galope-Chopine,
and that of the two ill-starred lovers, which will be shed within the day.

Not only are plot and perception of nature inextricably linked near the
end of the novel, but both are connected in close and important ways with
politics. For what is emphasized and dramatized by Marie's inability to
perceive such features of the landscape as the path to Saint-James or the
smoke signal is her concomitant inability to perceive clearly such issues as
which side, Republican or Monarchist, is the more just and sincere and
how the interests of the country as a whole can best be assured—hence the
odd, risky romantic involvement in which she and Montauran become
embroiled. According to Reinhard Kuhn this involvement reflects in both
cases an equivocal view of history, a desire to evade confusing, problematic political realities:

> Her Republic is on the point of disintegration, and his royalty in ex-
> ile is equally threatened by the conflicts of shabby self-interests.
> They are both engaged in losing causes, and their only hope for indi-
> vidual salvation lies in the determination that they cannot muster to
> disentangle themselves from a complex web of intrigues. Their pas-
> sion for each other provokes an impotent nostalgia, a terrible desire
> to escape from what Eliade has described as the "terror of history."[9]

Marie thus plays a very different role in *Les Chouans* from Hulot's. Upon
him devolves the role of introducing a straightforward version of the novel's ideology; upon her, that of presenting its problematic, nuanced side.
And indeed, Balzacian scholars like Pierre Barbéris warn against simplis-
tically viewing *Les Chouans* as "a left-wing novel," a blanket endorsement
of the liberal bourgeois ideology.[10] Marie is truly a figure whose vision is
obscured: by her being in love, by her having an equivocal past life, and
probably (in Balzac's view) by her being a woman. But more important
than her passion, reputation, or gender are her times. A generation
younger than Hulot, she comes to Republicanism during the problematic
post-Revolutionary period when little more than expediency and self-
interest motivated most adherents to political parties, Republican and
Monarchist alike. As Barbéris says, "The primordial novelistic material of
Le Dernier Chouan is a certain historical decay."[11] Landscape was not the
only, but one of the important means Balzac had at his disposal for evok-
ing the obscure and impure nature of the historical period he chose to
treat. Notably it was one that had the merit of enabling the reader to join
actively and directly with the characters to "see"—or rather to fail to
see—the meanings of past events and distant places.

Monarchism thus functions as the locus of conflict in Balzac's novel, as a way of enabling the reader to experience the confusing, conflict-ridden political responses of both the Chouans and their Republican opponents. It also functions as a critical stance, as a way of enabling the reader to pass judgment on both the blind and backward provincial aristocracy that adhered to Monarchism in the nineteenth century and the modern, degraded political figures in whose ignoble hands the future lay. It plays a similar role elsewhere in Balzac's works. *Le Lys dans la vallée* provides a representative example of the curious double-edged sword that Balzac yields. There too Monarchism is shown to be an unviable solution adopted by aristocrats who are remote from the reality of the contemporary world; yet at the same time it emerges as a better solution in many ways than its modern, unprincipled counterparts.

The Ambiguous Lily Motif

The strategy Balzac deploys in *Les Chouans* of adopting a Republican point of view riddled with confusion and conflict results in the distinctive Monarchistic stamp of that novel's landscapes. A different strategy found in *Le Lys* consists of adopting a Monarchistic point of view that is systematically presented in the novel in terms of ambiguity. There is ambiguity in *Le Lys* and its landscapes insofar as phenomena consistently emerge as having two levels of meaning, a duality that can be traced directly to the novel's main character and his confrontation with the social and political conflicts of his times. What is at issue is not merely symbolism—a multiplicity of connotative meanings that the reader and character may or may not perceive in nature. Rather, *Le Lys* displays a process whereby nature is willfully given two meanings, misread, and its true meaning rendered obscure.

The narrative source of the ambiguity is the first-person narrator and describer of nature in the novel, Félix de Vandenesse. In the opening pages of the novel Félix depicts his unfortunate childhood and the overly studious, sheltered, penurious existence his unfeeling parents forced him to lead. Everything changes, however, when he leaves home to pay an extended visit to some family friends, the Chessel family, who live in the country and when he meets their neighbors, the Mortsaufs—representatives of the old aristocracy now seeking refuge in the backwaters of the provinces from the changing conditions of modern life. The novel traces the ecstatic joys Félix experiences on having formed an intense, obsessive passion for the extremely pious Mme. de Mortsauf—Henriette to him. It also traces the torments, of which there are two main sources: first that, for a variety of reasons, their mutual love remains platonic; and that he must watch his adored Henriette suffer at the hands of her tyrannical, maniacal husband. Near the end of the novel, Félix must leave for Paris, where new interests, political and romantic, attract his attention and cause him to neglect his distant "lily of the valley." This neglect contributes to her growing despondency, perhaps even to her untimely death, and on his part to the constant feelings of guilt and nostalgia for the past that his lover Natalie complained about at the outset. As the novel comes to a close, Natalie chooses, having heard his story and recognized how unfit he is for any romantic involvement whatsoever, to break with him, leaving the reader in doubt as to the course of his future life.

This, then, is the character who describes nature in the novel and who endows it with a peculiar coloration, even deformation. The fact of Félix's being the source of the ambiguity is not tantamount, I hasten to add, to his fully comprehending it. Indeed, dramatic irony is very much a feature of the novel: the reader, seeing Félix see nature, comprehends certain facets of the visual act to which the character remains blind. The process is not unlike the ironic one utilized by Constant in *Adolphe* or by Gide in his *récits*. The first-person narrator looks back and seeks to understand or excuse a presumably reprehensible past conduct. But the retrospective vision, like the past conduct—and indeed the very act of narration itself—ultimately founders on the shoals of profound, irreconcilable conflicts. To say that the narrator fails to understand the past or resolve the conflicts it poses is of course not totally to dismiss or denigrate his attempt. It simply recognizes that this attempt is complex and problematic—as indeed were the conflictual contemporary conditions that produced it.

There is one especially important nature description in *Le Lys*, which illustrates the way in which the expression of political conflict occurs in landscape: it occurs near the beginning of the novel, where it serves almost singlehandedly to establish the overall descriptive tone and thematics of the novel. That description's chief interest lies in its ambiguous presentation of natural phenomena like the eponymous "lily." On the surface, the meaning of the lily image is unequivocal: at numerous places in the text it is treated as a symbol of purity and equated with the novel's pristine, virtuous heroine, Mme. de Mortsauf. On a deeper level, however, another meaning can be discerned, although it is never openly proclaimed in the text and Balzac may well not have consciously "intended" it as a symbol. That second meaning is that of the fleur-de-lis, symbol of monarchy. The fact that Mme. de Mortsauf serves throughout the novel as both the metaphorical link with the lily as purity and the novel's chief spokesman and emblem for Monarchism in itself constitutes prima facie evidence of the ambiguity. But there is other evidence to be found as well, as an analysis of the lengthy opening description of nature in *Le Lys* will reveal.

Highlighting the importance of plant images, the description immediately stresses that it is as a distant "white dot" surrounded by the green valley and the green plants in her garden that Henriette first appears to Félix and assumes in his eyes the resemblance to a lily of the valley: "Her muslim dress produced the white dot which I noticed under a peach tree, among her vines. She was, as you already know, though you know nothing yet, the lily of this valley, where she grew for Heaven, filling it with the perfume of her virtues" (p. 18). Also emphasized are the spiritual, transcendent qualities that simultaneously make the lily a symbol of Henriette's purity and virtue. Elsewhere in the novel she is constantly compared to stars, sun, and other celestial bodies; and in the opening description, her capacity to capture and reflect light is repeatedly stressed: at one point the text states that "the midday sun was sparkling on the tiles of her roof and the panes of her windows" (p. 18); later in the passage she is referred to as "the woman who shone in this vast garden just as, in the midst of green hedgerows, the white bell of the convolvulus, withering at a touch, might strike the eye" (p. 19).

The reader might be tempted to go no further and accept the lily-of-the-valley symbol at face value, were there not odd indications in the text that another level of meaning is at issue. One such indication is found in the comparison of Henriette to the "bell of a convolvulus," "withering to a touch" (in French, "flétrie si l'on y touche"). This phrase evokes not only her own vulnerability and fragility but that of the declining, slowly degenerating aristocracy in general and of a certain blind, backward-thinking provincial aristocracy in particular. This aristocracy is depicted in the novel as clinging desperately to the outdated Monarchist cause. Another indication that a second level of meaning is at issue occurs in the following very curious instance of flower imagery: "Amaryllis, reeds, yellow pond lilies and phlox adorn the banks with their tapestried magnificence. A rickety bridge, composed of rotten beams; its piles covered with flowers; its handrails, encrusted with hardy weeds and velvety mosses, leaning outwards over the river" (p. 19). An emphasis once again is placed on the lily, the *lys* of the title. This emphasis is especially salient in the French text where the reference to the related species of the water lilies entails mentioning both the *lys d'eau* and its synonym *le nénuphar* and where there is a homophonic effect in the naming of the *amaryllis*. What is most striking here, however, is not just the recurrence and modulation of the lily motif but its peculiar function, that of acting together with the other flowers to cover up the "rickety bridge, composed of rotten beams"—in French, "Un pont tremblant composé de poutrelles pourries, dont les piles sont couvertes de fleurs, dont les garde-fous plantés d'herbes vivaces et de mousses veloutées se penchent sur la rivière et ne tombent point." Once again, vulnerability, fragility, even degeneracy and ultimate destruction are the key notions that nature imagery serves here to evoke.

M. de Mortsauf, a character whom Balzac designated in a letter to Mme. Hanska as "the statue of Emigration,"[12] plays a special role in this regard in the novel. The text portrays him as having all the physical, mental, moral, and intellectual infirmities of an old, genuine aristocracy that has suffered through the deprivation of exile and is tragically lacking in the regenerative powers necessary for a true Restoration to occur. Not surprisingly then, in the opening description, the notions of vulnerability, fragility, and degeneracy of the aristocracy seem to focus on M. de Mortsauf. It is he whose seemingly inevitable destruction has for whatever reason still not come to pass at the end of the novel, whose debilitated physical and mental structures "se penchent sur la rivière et ne tombent point." It is he whose decadent, even demented state is covered from public view by his wife: "its piles covered with flowers, its handrails [in French, the *garde-fous*] encrusted with hardy weeds and velvety mosses." Later in the novel, significantly, the same image of flowers masking a crumbling wooden object—in this case, a door—reappears. In both cases, the connection with M. de Mortsauf is made explicit. Referring to Henriette, Félix says, "No one, moreover, had any inkling of Monsieur de Mortsauf's real inadequacy, for she draped his ruins with a heavy cloak of ivy" (p. 32). Elsewhere he recalls, "We were within sight of a wooden gate leading into the grounds of Frapesle, the two derelict posts of which, overgrown with moss and creepers, briars and weeds, I still see in my mind's eye. Suddenly a thought flashed like a dart across my brain, the thought of the Count's death" (p. 72).

It is interesting to note regarding plant imagery that aristocratic overtones appear in the text in connection with trees; for these overtones extend beyond the trees and affect the reader's interpretation of other botanical phenomena, the lily not least among them. What is at issue is the personification of the trees, as if they were the elegant inhabitants and supporters of Monarchism in the world of nobility Félix is entering, along with the metaphorical designation of the trees as crowns, tapestries, laces, and other typical accoutrements of the aristocratic or regal appearance. Early in the description, Félix notices the rows of poplars that decorate the valley "with their quivering lace" (Garnier, p. 29; my translation). Later he notes in a similar vein the islands "crowned with a few clumps of trees" and the trees and flowers that "adorn the banks with their tapestried magnificence" (Garnier, pp. 30, 31). Aristocratic overtones are also produced through the emphasis placed on the age of the trees—the "ancient walnut trees" and the "century-old trees" (Garnier, p. 31)—as if they were as old and dignified as the aristocratic families Félix will soon meet, or as the chateau that is one of the first objects he perceives in the valley. It is not surprising that later in the novel, when Henriette argues the case for Monarchism with Félix, she has recourse to a symbolism of trees and plants. The principle upon which

Monarchism is based, she says, "is a sort of sap which must spread along the tiniest capillaries in order to give life to the tree, help it keep its foliage, develop its blossom and improve its fruit so magnificently that it excites general admiration" (p. 114).

Aside from the botanical images, there are two separable but related images of the river and the road displayed in the opening description. Both of these images are traditionally taken as analogues for progressive historical time. With regard to both the flow of the river and Felix's movements on the road that runs alongside it, it is interesting that throughout the description Félix describes nature and himself through a strange, even paradoxical combination of movement and stasis, as if wanting at the same time to affirm and to deny temporal movement and change. At the beginning, all movement seems arrested: Félix presents himself seated under his walnut tree; the noonday sun seems to be immobilized, as does the river, "streaming in the sunlight between two green banks" (pp. 18–19). Yet at the same time, he seems to attribute to nature a will, if not a compulsion, to interrupt the descriptive stasis that he himself has imposed. The trees are active in decorating the valley, the woods move forward to the river, the river establishes the contours of the hills: "Boundless love . . . of which my soul was full, found expression . . . in those rows of poplars adorning with their quivering lace this vale of love; in the oak woods thrusting between the vineyards upon slopes which the river rounds in every varying curve" (pp. 18–19). Through Félix's use of active verbs and personified natural objects, movement seems to inhere not only in the river itself but in all of the natural phenomena that surround it.

Later in the description, there is a repetition of this pattern. Félix's movements in this case are limited to his entry into the valley and the perceptual activities he performs ("I saw," "my eyes kept on turning to") or invites the reader to perform ("Imagine"). With nature generally and the river especially, however, there is no such diminution of movement. Especially important in this regard is the emphasis placed in the following passage on the tumultuous flow of the river and the trees growing on its islets and banks:

> Imagine three watermills, set among gracefully chiselled islets crowned with a few clumps of trees, amid a water-meadow—what other name can one give to that aquatic vegetation, so hardy and so bright, which carpets the river, undulates with it, yields to its whims and bends to the storm waves lashed by the millwheels? Here and there mounds of gravel rise, on which the water breaks, forming fringes which glisten in the sun. (p. 19)

Now, if we take the trees as symbols of the aristocracy—as the text invites doing, as does the example of other descriptive novelists, Chateaubriand for instance—then it is significant to note the way the trees passively submit to the river's flow: the vegetation "carpets the river, undulates with it, yields to its whims and bends to the storm waves lashed by the millwheels." The trees submit to the tempestuous flow of the river as the aristocracy was forced to do to the tumultuous process of historical change.

Immobility and movement are also contrasted on another occasion in the opening description, although in this case they are not attributed to nature but to Félix alone:

> Frame the whole with ancient walnut trees and young poplars with pale golden leaves; set graceful workshops in the midst of the long meadows where the eye loses itself beneath a warm and hazy sky, and you will have an idea of one of the thousand viewpoints of this lovely place.
>
> I followed the Saché road along the left side of the river, looking at the contours of the hills which crown the opposite bank. Then, at last, I reached an estate, adorned with century-old trees, which told me I was at the castle of Frapesle. I arrived just as the bell was ringing for luncheon. (p. 20)

At the beginning of this passage, movement seems to be arrested. Directly addressing the reader, Félix proposes framing the scene, thereby fixing it outside progressive historical time like an aristocratic family portrait hung on the wall of a chateau. Also noteworthy with regard to the cessation of movement is the fact that between noon evoked earlier and lunchtime here, time has barely seemed to progress. Near the end of this passage, however, movement seems to be emphasized. Félix now actually progresses along the road leading to the chateau. Moreover, his movements occur on the left side of the river inhabited by the Chessel family, representative of the new, changing bourgeois way of life as opposed to the old, unchanging, aristocratic way of the Mortsauf family on the right side. (The similar opposition in Proust's novel between "Swann's Way" and the "Guermantes's Way" comes to mind.) Félix's movements here on the left side of the river prefigure the denouement of the novel. Eventually he will join the changing modern world and will leave behind the world of the Mortsauf family where "the eye loses itself under the warm misty sky," that is, in a world of irrevocable, unchanging pastness.

What conclusions can be drawn from the existence of the ambiguous nature imagery in *Le Lys*? The first and most obvious one is that Félix, the viewer and describer of nature in this novel, evinces a peculiar, persistent urge to impose his subjective vision on nature. The existence of this urge is even emphasized within the description itself. At one point Félix says that he took the river to be a symbol of boundless love "without other nourishment than an object, scarcely perceived, of which my soul was full" (p. 18). Later he states that he viewed the village as special and unique because of his "overflowing lyricism" (p. 19). Such an emphasis on the subjective quality of landscape alerts the reader to the possibility of an ironic interpretation of Félix's vision of nature in particular and of himself as a character in general. If Félix's visual perceptions are not accurate and objective, then his account of his actions, motives, feelings, and the like—indeed all of the explanations he gives to Natalie during the course of the narration—are perhaps not accurate or objective either. Later in the novel the subjective quality of nature images becomes increasingly manifest. One especially striking example is the lengthy description of the bouquets Félix gives to Henriette, which serve as a disguised expression of his passionate sentiments: here, Félix's personal drives and desires almost totally determine the "meaning" of natural phenomena.

Other conclusions about the ambiguity of nature in Le Lys follow from the first, which concerns Félix's subjective vision. One of these conclusions is that Félix's perception of nature mirrors and explains his perception, or rather misperception, of Henriette herself. It is not only as a lily of the valley but also as a fleur-de-lis that he sees both her and nature, that is, as epiphenomena of the nobility: the aesthetic accoutrements and values of aristocracy are the grid for filtering nature and Henriette into his and the reader's consciousness from the first page of his narrative to the last. In addition to Félix's claiming to see as a lily of the valley what he often sees as a fleur-de-lis, there is of course the further misperception of his seeing Henriette as a lily of the valley in the first place: her deathbed letter reveals that she was tormented by sensual desires and was not the embodiment of virtue he had conjured up in his imagination. There is a fundamental sense then in which Félix never succeeded at all in seeing her as a person in her own right, beyond her social class, just as by blithely recounting to Natalie his enduring love for Henriette he reveals that he has never succeeded in seeing her as a person, or in being aware of her needs or desires.

Félix seeks not only love but also success and political stature, although to the end he remains blind to his own materialistic motives—which in the final analysis are perfectly concordant with those of the Restoration as it is depicted in the novel. Significantly, the first real event in the novel, after the exposition of Félix's unhappy childhood, is the ball given by the duc d'Angoulême to celebrate the Bourbon Restoration, where Félix first meets Henriette. He subsequently recounts that meeting as follows: "Then, all of a sudden, I met the woman who was to be a constant spur to my ambitions and who was to crown them by throwing me into the very heart of royalty" (p. 15). The failure at issue in the novel is perhaps less

Henriette's in satisfying Félix's desires than his own in knowing what those desires really were, and acknowledging that they were perhaps more social and political than personal and romantic. There plainly is an ironic ring to Félix's frequent protestations that he had absolutely no interest in politics: "I had no idea what the Privy Council was; I knew nothing of politics nor worldly matters. I had no other ambition than to love Henriette" (p. 75). In fact it is Henriette, as Natalie points out at the end, "who raised you to the peerage" (p. 254), just as it is the Monarchist cause to which he is so totally devoted—"he saw that I was devoted to the Bourbons, head, heart and limb" (p. 127)—that enables him to achieve the lofty political position to which he aspires. There is also an ironic ring to Félix's name, Vandenesse, an anagram of his family motto— "ne se vend pas"—as well as of the Vendée, the reactionary rebellion in which Félix plays a role. He is a reactionary in the opportunistic, vaguely unprincipled sense that characterized the period of the Restoration for Balzac, a period in which selling oneself and success were largely synonymous.

Félix's misperception of time, like his misperceptions of Henriette and Natalie, is also deducible from his ambiguous perception of nature. With respect specifically to the lily motif, O. N. Heathcote notes that there is a dislocation of the sense of time in Félix's very invention of the lily of the valley metaphor.[13] It is worth remembering the enigmatic, even incoherent phrase quoted earlier—"She was, as you already know, though you know nothing yet, the lily of this valley"—in which Félix presumes that the reader of his account knows what he is saying before he says it. Heathcote concludes from a phrase such as this that "the novel takes place in a kind of eternal present" and that Félix's misperception of time is such as "to destroy any sense of past which may otherwise be created"; he further concludes that "Natalie's reply shows the reader that Félix does indeed . . . remain for ever trapped in his own a-temporal, verbal creation."[14] Again there is a connection between Félix's way of seeing the world and his aristocratic outlook, that connection being an unconscious need to deny time and change. Such a denial enables the aristocrat to believe that there exist eternal, God-given structures of monarchy and social class and that these structures are the ballast on which he can build edifices of the future. Such a denial similarly enables Félix, as describer of nature, to believe that landscape exists as some static aesthetic phenomenon in the eternal present of his own subjective vision. Only reluctantly, it would seem, does he resume his normal movements on the left, progressive side of the river as the description comes to a close. His heart, his mind, his eye remain riveted to the other side—the unchanging, eternal, atemporal world of "Mortsauf's Way."

Another conclusion that can be drawn from the ambiguous treatment of nature in *Le Lys* concerns the aristocracy itself. It is important to remember that a symbolic reference is made to Henriette in the flower "withering to a touch" and to her husband in the "rickety bridge composed of rotten beams," and moreover that both of these references suggest the vulnerability, fragility, even degeneracy of the aristocracy. The novel's presentation of the members of the Mortsauf family (other than Henriette, who paradoxically is the one who dies) as debilitated, feeble, and sickly supports such an interpretation. Nor is the presentation of other representatives of the nobility more positive. Both Félix's and Henriette's aristocratic mothers are, like M. de Mortsauf, tyrants; the king and members of his court emerge as essentially weak and indifferent to any serious human problems and values. Externally and aesthetically the aristocratic way of life may be pleasing and may seem to be an appealing model for the future. But plainly it lacks the substance to sustain serious Monarchistic convictions. What then does Félix's adherence represent, both for him personally and for the reader?

It is perhaps best to answer this question in terms of the ambiguity discovered and discussed above. Félix's ambiguous perception of nature perhaps derives from another, more profound ambiguity implicit in the novel regarding the aristocracy in general. It involves a nostalgic, aesthetic attraction on the one hand and a lucid, critical rejection on the other. In this vein, Bersani observes that "*Le Lys dans la vallée* is an extraordinarily pessimistic critique of Balzac's conservative principles; it dramatizes both the need for those principles and the bankruptcy of the institutions which embody them."[15] The nostalgic, aesthetic attraction to Monarchism is apparent in Félix's dwelling on images of flowers, trees, chateaux, and the like in the landscape examined here. It is also apparent more generally in the novel's poignant portrayal of the Mortsauf family, even the demented count. Enfeebled, remote from contemporary reality, and doomed to extinction, this family nonetheless embodies a genuine, ancient aristocracy, which contrasts sharply with the degraded, materialistic counterpart that arose and prospered during the Restoration. It is that genuine aristocracy which is symbolized by the lily and which inspires Félix's respect and allegiance.

However profound Félix's attraction to the Monarchist cause may be, the rejection of that cause to which the novel ultimately gives rise is no less profound. Here, the reader plays an active role, that of seeing issues more clearly and critically than the novel's protagonist and narrator. Félix—like the others of his time who rallied to the Monarchist cause, who echoed the then-popular phrase "Where the fleurs-de-lis lie, There the nation lies"[16]—does not distinguish clearly between politics and love, between nostalgia for the aristocratic way of life and Monarchism as a viable political alternative. Félix's lack of lucidity in this regard does not escape the reader: indeed it is perhaps the true subject and focus in the novel. To promote this focus, Balzac uses ambiguity to dramatize this character's misperception of his own feelings and those of the "lily of the valley" he claimed to love. By surrounding the central metaphor of the novel, the lily, with obscurity, Balzac brings into the penetrating light of novelistic inquiry that similar obscurity which for Félix and others of his time seemed to enshroud a rapidly changing, profoundly problematic society.

The perspective established above makes it possible to summarize some of the salient differences and similarities in Balzac's treatments of landscape in *Les Chouans* and *Le Lys*. The differences are pervasive: the two novels display dissimilar settings, historical events, political points of view, even narrative techniques for landscape. The setting of one novel is the rugged terrain of Brittany; that of the other, the lush valley of the Loire. One recounts the Eighteenth Brumaire, whereas the other focuses on the Hundred Days. One exhibits a Republican outlook and the other an ardent Royalism. One contains a technique that dwells on various characters' geographical, military, and perceptual confusions; the other, a technique that dwells on a single character's willful, ambiguous misreading of nature. Pervasive as the differences between the two novels' landscapes may be, however, the affinity of basic conception is no less pervasive. To an equal extent, but in different ways, landscape in *Les Chouans* and in *Le Lys*—as in Balzac's novels generally—is indissolubly linked to the cause of Monarchism. Monarchism is the grid for viewing landscape and the locus of conflict in these works.

A further affinity of basic conception between *Les Chouans* and *Le Lys* can also be noted, concerning the distance established between the reader and the landscape. No longer, as with Rousseau, Bernardin, and Chateaubriand, does the reader accept landscape at face value for the positive attributes it displays: with Balzac the reader has entered, to borrow Nathalie Sarraute's famous phrase, the age of suspicion. For the viewer of nature to be confused, guilty of deception, or simply not in total possession of the descriptive act has now become a crucial strategy in the description of nature.

6

Transcending History:

Salammbô and L'Education sentimentale

The Transcendent Point of View

The indissoluble ties that Flaubert's landscapes have with history and the social and political conflicts of his times have for several reasons not been sufficiently observed. One is the failure to recognize that the formation of such ties constitutes an integral part of the intertextual history of narrative landscape. Just as the landscapes of Chateaubriand, Balzac, and others have far more than a merely decorative, digressive role to play, so too have those of Flaubert, a writer whose affinities with his predecessors in the literature of images cannot be overemphasized. Another reason is that at first glance, nature description in novels like *Salammbô* and *L'Education sentimentale* seems to be a locus for an escape from history rather than for a preoccupation with it: indeed, not only with landscape specifically but with the novel generally, charges of escapism and indifference to genuine social concerns have repeatedly been leveled at Flaubert.[1] I shall argue that Flaubert's descriptions of nature consistently proceed from an urge to transcend rather than to turn away from historical, social concerns. By "transcend," I mean for Flaubert not the action of passing over the existential domain to reach some spiritual, immaterial realm. Rather, I refer to a tendency to push experience of the external world to some outer limit of plenitude and perfection, to go beyond that experience in the sense of exceeding its disillusioning limits. Flaubert's urge to transcend is thus two-sided and indicative of conflict. On the one hand, it is an implicit acknowledgment of the existence of limitations and of the solidity and stability, if not inescapability, of what is. On the other hand, however, it reveals the existence of aspirations and a belief in the possibility of change for the future; it bespeaks a vision of, if not perhaps a true commitment to, what might be.

If we return now to questions posed in earlier chapters—Who views or describes landscape, and to what end?—three approaches to matters of narrative voice and vision can be adopted. All are directly relevant to the topic of transcendence: for to speak of transcendence is tantamount to singling out some consciousness—some describer or viewer—whose presence in the text, apparent or implied, is the locus for that transcendence. The first approach, largely psychological in nature, focuses on the protagonist and takes his point of view as providing unity and coherence. With this approach, the transcendent urge would be that of the individual. The second approach is essentially textual or poetic; it eschews unity and coherence and focuses instead on such features as the irony, indeterminacy, or effect of distancing displayed by the Flaubertian text. This approach focuses not on the characters in the novel but rather on the author and reader and the transcendence they derive from the textual features of writing itself. The third approach is political; it focuses on some social group, which the protagonist embodies and which serves to provide unity and coherence. Here, the transcendent urge would be that of a collective, social entity. Since all three approaches have some validity, a synthesis that acknowledges the varying degrees of applicability of the three will best account for the far-reaching significance of Flaubert's landscapes.

To focus first on the individual as the locus of transcendence, we discover three individuals whose aspirations are recorded in *Salammbô*: first and most frequently the barbarian chief Mâtho; next, in one central chapter of the novel, the leader of the Carthaginian army, Hamilcar; last, and in only a few short passages, the Carthaginian princess, Salammbô. Common to these characters is their superiority over their debased compatriots and political fellow travelers; indeed they form a transcendent triad, which contrasts sharply with that formed by the three other important characters in the novel: Salammbô's fiancé, the Numidian leader Narr'-Havas; Mâtho's right-hand man, the former Greek slave Spendius; and finally Hamilcar's chief political rival, the Carthaginian leader Hannon. The sole motivations of this debased triad are material wealth and personal power; the motivation of the transcendent triad is, in contrast, a sincere but primitive will to understand the mysteries of society and the cosmos. In terms of the religious symbolism of the novel, this is tantamount to saying that they believe in the *zaïmph*. The *zaïmph* is the veil belonging to the Carthaginian moon goddess Tanit; it plays a central role in the plot when Mâtho steals it and then when Salammbô eventually retrieves it by delivering herself into Mâtho's hands. The fact that the search for transcendence evinced by these three characters centers on religious symbols such as the veil is of the utmost importance for an understanding of their peculiar way of viewing landscape. As R. J. Sherrington observes, theirs is a world view that constantly centers on the symbolic significance of the external world.[2] Not surprisingly, then, their vision of landscape is heavily tinted with the colors of symbolism, as it is with the colors of Flaubert's odd blend of eroticism and religion. This is especially true of Mâtho, who discovers in Salammbô's natural surroundings, as in her physical presence, the realization of his curiously combined sexual, social, and metaphysical aspirations.

With *L'Education sentimentale*, it is the character of Frédéric Moreau who embodies individual transcendence in the novel. The transcendence in his case, as in that of such other Flaubertian characters as Saint Antoine, is largely pantheistic in nature: Frédéric evinces a marked proclivity to fuse and be one with the external world, in all of its diversity, profuseness, and plenitude. Jean Levaillant spells out the nature of such transcendence thus:

> The original need to be united with God—but it no longer is God —can only be accomplished through multiplicity: one must identify with everything, communicate with everything, to attain the happiness of fundamental union. . . . With totality and continuity thus obtained, happiness consists in a union with living matter, in an absorption in which existence finds its meaning and transcends pure knowledge.[3]

Georges Poulet emphasizes in this regard that, unlike the Romantics, Flaubert depicts a transcendence essentially centrifugal in nature. Frédéric and other Flaubertian characters move toward the outside world, not toward their own inner being, in their drive to achieve the metaphysical fullness of meaning and being that they crave.[4] Not surprisingly, nature looms as a privileged locus for such transcendence. Indeed, the only moments in which Frédéric comes close to realizing his transcendent desires will be seen to be during three outdoor scenes—first with Louise at Nogent, next with Mme. Arnoux at Auteuil, and most importantly with Rosanette at Fontainebleau. In all three scenes, it is less the presence of the woman than that of her setting in nature that leads to Frédéric's experience of an epiphany.

Other critics, who adopt the textual approach referred to earlier, denounce the unitary, unified transcendent point of view that the first critical approach discovers in Flaubert's novels, and especially in *L'Education sentimentale*. They maintain that it is wrong to conceive of narration as one psychological monolith, that such a conception leaves to one side those features of the text that create a distance between the reader and the text and prevent the reader from ever being entirely "with" the principal viewer of a scene. This approach emphasizes the fact that the Flaubertian text routinely draws back from the viewer to suggest the presence of some unidentified and ultimately unidentifiable narrative source—a presence felt in such diverse and heterogeneous textual phenomena as contrived effects of style, ironic contrasts, clichéd echoes of social discourse, and even subtle authorial intrusions. All of these textual phenomena are interpreted as functioning to undermine the notion of a unified psychological point of view. An articulate spokesman of this approach is Jonathan Culler. He contends that there is an insidious danger in point-of-view criticism insofar as it produces what he calls a process of "recuperation," which "suggests that the details of every description are justified and given a function by virtue of the fact that someone noticed them. It denatures strangeness by personalizing it, making it a function of a particular optic."[5]

According to the textual approach, the indeterminacy in Flaubert's novels makes it both possible and impossible to identify the text with the viewpoint of individual characters or of the author. As Culler observes,

> we can never be sure when the author is responsible for his language, when he may be citing sources which we happen not to identify but which represent a limited position like any other, and consequently the general sense of potential irony, a sense of the possibility of distancing ourselves from any of the sentences which the text sets before us, comes to hover over the book as a whole.[6]

Other critics agree. With respect specifically to *Salammbô*, Veronica Forrest-Thomson observes that there is no unifying basis for understanding the text, not even irony; for "there is no consistent factual element against which the characters' fictions may be exposed as illusory."[7] According to Forrest-Thomson, description enacts the process whereby readers, like the characters, seek and ultimately fail to achieve understanding. And speaking of *L'Education sentimentale*, Levaillant observes that description routinely records more than what an individual viewer would see: "An analytic, separating consciousness—that of the author—is substituted for the living and global consciousness of the perceiving subject." He goes on to note that description acts to produce its own narrative code—"a sort of collective consciousness, within things themselves."[8] It is clear, in short, that the accent must be placed on the author, the reader, or the text itself—but not on the characters—as the privileged loci of transcendence for Flaubert.

Now, it may be true, as the textual approach would have it, that attempts to identify the point of view in Flaubert's descriptions presuppose more order and coherence than the text ultimately displays. But it is also true that to make no such identification is to fail to account for the inescapable fact of description's crucial relation to character development. Noteworthy in this regard is the often-quoted remark Flaubert made about *Salammbô*, which also applies to his other works: "there are no isolated, gratuitous descriptions in my book; all of them *serve a purpose* in relation to my characters and have a distant or immediate influence on the action."[9] To navigate between the often-competing demands of accounting for the patterns whereby landscape connects itself to character and avoiding an undue emphasis on individual psychology requires some nimble footwork, but this is what must be done. Rather than totally reject either the psychological or the textual approach, we must achieve some synthesis in which the two are equal partners. It is no longer enough to cast Flaubert in the exclusive mold of precursor to a New-Novel aesthetics of fragmentation and discontinuity, as it was popular to do in the late 1960s and early 1970s, when the textual approach became popular. It is time now to acknowledge the literary contexts and conventions in which he wrote, one of the foremost of which plainly is the symbolic use of description in relation to character and social themes.

The third approach to point of view and transcendence in Flaubert's novels, the collective and historical approach, entails broadening the notion of point of view to encompass the social or political group to which the individual viewer belongs. According to this approach, the eye of Mâtho or Frédéric scrutinizing a nature scene is not only that of an isolated psychological entity but also that of a larger collective force of which he serves as the reflector or representative. Such a critical perspective is clearly warranted for *Salammbô*, a novel that regularly adopts the viewpoint of both the Carthaginians and the mercenaries. As Jean Rousset notes,

> Insofar as the three individual heros are treated as representatives of their communities, one can with a few rare exceptions subordinate their narrative role to the general system of oppositions underlying the whole story—Carthaginians against barbarians—and relate all key positions in space to those of antagonists in war who are incessantly spying on, pursuing, or besieging one another.[10]

And other critics agree that by thus identifying the point of view in *Salammbô* as that of a social or political group, it becomes possible to discern important motives for description. Sherrington notes that the attentiveness to detail in many long descriptive passages can be explained by the status of Mâtho and the mercenaries as foreigners, struck by the strangeness and most of all by the excessive wealth of Carthage, of which the countryside is to them an extension and reflection (pp. 157–158). And Victor Brombert notes that the transcendent will which the descriptive act evinces in *Salammbô* has privileged links with the peculiar psychology of the mercenaries: "the Mercenaries' impulse to 'devour with their glances' what they cannot seize and possess corresponds to the Flaubertian nostalgia for the unattainable."[11]

It should also be noted that although the points of view of Mâtho and the mercenaries are not the exclusive perspectives of nature adopted in the novel, they are the predominant ones. A majority of the extended nature descriptions in *Salammbô* have Mâtho and his followers as the viewers. The mercenary point of view is also a privileged one. One reason is that the revolutionary uprising, and concomitantly the aspirations and transcendent urges evinced by the revolutionary masses, are central to the novel's plot and fundamental thematic content. What Mâtho and his fellow soldiers experience in nature is the very essence of their being, to wit, absence, desire, the urge to achieve fullness of being and meaning. Another reason for the privileged status of the mercenary point of view is its historical nature. Victims of a host of political and economic ills—poverty, oppression, injustice, alienation—the mercenaries emerge in the novel as the chief actors in the saga of social change. In contrast to Salammbô, who remains fixed in a contemplative state of mysticism and religious fanaticism, and Hamilcar, who fails to transcend a conservative adherence to the status quo, the mercenaries consistently evince the will to go beyond the historical limitations of their times.

Focusing on the centrality of the revolutionary aspirations in *Salammbô* sheds light on the point of view and transcendent themes displayed by *L'Education sentimentale*. To be sure, the later work does not present nature or the world of the novel through the eyes of the working class—the seething masses of oppressed, rebellious people who would be the French counterpart of the mercenaries in *Salammbô*. Rather, the point of view in *L'Education sentimentale* is that of a character who occupies a border position between the impoverished provincial aristocracy and the bourgeois idle class. Yet however profound the class difference between Frédéric and the mercenaries may be, revolutionary aspirations and historical transcendence emerge in *L'Education sentimentale* as no less central to the plot and basic themes than in *Salammbô*. The process simply is less direct, the tone less positive and straightforward: *L'Education sentimentale* might be called an ironic version of *Salammbô*. The ironic way of enacting the historical aspirations of the revolutionary masses in 1848 is through Frédéric's ahistorical ones; the people's dreams and illusions are doubled, and in the process ultimately destroyed and denigrated, in his corresponding ones. As Brombert quite rightly notes, the inescapable parallelism in *L'Education sentimentale* between the personal and collective domains— between Frédéric's longings and those of society at large—produces an oddly ambiguous, negative relation between the two domains: "For paradoxically, the parallel thematics that are permanently maintained among different levels (the individual, the group, History) constitute a partition between the private and collective realms. Articulation here does not produce meaning; redundancy contributes to negativism."[12]

To focus on the centrality of revolutionary aspirations and historical transcendence—and to acknowledge, accordingly, the importance to a consideration of the Flaubertian landscape of this approach to point of view—is to discover that a common bias in favor of the revolutionary masses, however attenuated and ill-defined, hovers over both *Salammbô* and *L'Education sentimentale*. To be sure, the bias is at best only relative in nature. The mercenaries are more loyal and courageous, less cruel and corrupt than the Carthaginians. Similarly in *L'Education sentimentale*, the revolutionary forces are more capable of heroism, less selfish and blind than the reactionaries. Flaubert said to George Sand that in this novel, "the reactionaries . . . will be treated less kindly than the others, for they seem to me to be more criminal."[13] Flaubert's novels clearly do not display a love for the people; they clearly are not the products of a writer who shares the illusions of those who took up arms, in Carthage or Paris, in the common man's behalf. The fact remains, however, that those illusions are the fulcrum of Flaubert's two novels and the key features of the landscapes they contain, the author's political cynicism notwithstanding. To illustrate exactly how those illusions find expression in nature description and how they relate to the individual, textual, and collective points of view discussed above, it will be useful to consider a short proleptic passage from *L'Education sentimentale*.

This is the first time the novel presents more than a fleeting, one-line glimpse of nature. Placed in the second chapter, it presents Frédéric and his boyhood friend Deslauriers pacing back and forth between the two ends of a bridge:

> On the side toward Nogent they had immediately in front of them a block of houses which projected a little. At the right was the church, behind the mills, whose sluices had been closed up; and, on the left, were the hedges, covered with shrubs, skirting the wood, and forming a boundary for the gardens, which could scarcely be distinguished. On the side toward Paris the high road formed a sheer descending line, and the meadows lost themselves in the distance amid the vapours of the night. Silence reigned along this road, whose white track gleamed through the surrounding gloom. Odours of damp leaves ascended toward them. The waterfall, where the stream had been diverted from its course a hundred paces farther away, rumbled with that deep harmonious sound which waves make in the night time.[14]

In an important though not exclusive way, this passage focuses on Frédéric—on his point of view and his personal aspirations. The nature of these aspirations is highlighted by his pacing back and forth between the two ends of the bridge and by the contrasting value systems represented by the two ends: in the novel Frédéric will have to choose between the value system associated with his home town of Nogent, to which one end leads, and the opposing value system associated with Paris, to which the other end leads. The one associated with Nogent involves here such characteristic features as home, garden, church, and industry; that of Paris, opposing features such as open space, distance, mystery, and an invitation to glamor. Nogent thus emerges as the antitranscendent alternative—a place for familial continuity, economic stability, and bourgeois respectability, but not for dreams and desires. Paris in contrast emerges as a privileged locus for Frédéric's transcendent goals. This is not to say of course that he actually perceives or understands such features of the scene as the symbolic significance of the two ends of the bridge. But these features are nonetheless focused on him and his point of view; they emerge as important because of the importance accorded in the text to his vision of his surroundings.

Shifting now from the psychological to the textual, it is possible to observe that this passage succeeds in bringing about, under the aegis of Frédéric's vision, a number of striking poetic effects. Not only is Frédéric unaware of these effects, they also do not really focus on or concern him at all. An example is provided in the French text by the striking alliteration of the sounds / d /, / p /, and / r / to produce a soft, lilting movement:

> Mais, du côté de Paris, la grande route descendait en ligne droite, et des prairies se perdaient au loin, dans les vapeurs de la nuit. Elle était silencieuse et d'une clarté blanchâtre. Des odeurs de feuillage humide montaient jusqu'à eux; la chute de la prise d'eau, cent pas plus loin, murmurait, avec ce gros bruit doux que font les ondes dans les ténèbres. [15]

Flaubert also elaborates a highly artistic, impressionistic scene in this description of the road leading to Paris. The contours of the meadows dissolve into the night air; the road is a splotch of white light; the surrounding vegetation and water are reduced to fleeting olfactory and auditory impressions. With effects of this sort—a true hallmark of Flaubert's prose—a special kind of transcendence, the artistic kind of which Flaubert speaks so frequently in his correspondence, is achieved: not through the psychology of the characters but through the artistic sensibilities of the author and certain of his more perceptive, lettered readers.

Finally the possibility exists of reading this passage in terms of a collective transcendence, one that Frédéric's whole social group seeks to achieve. The presence of Deslauriers along with Frédéric, and consequently the use of the pronoun "they" throughout the passage, especially invites a transindividual reading. The transcendence occurs not only for one isolated individual but for others like him as well, his whole generation, for example. The collective transcendence, like the personal sort, is centered in Paris; but upon a social, historical reading, Paris is not only the locus of mystery and glamor. Nearer the mark is Paris's identity as a place in which change is possible: in which there is movement, loss, danger, but also the promise for a better future ("this road, whose white track gleamed through the surrounding gloom"). Read thus as a proleptic version of the significance that the events soon to occur in Paris assume for Frédéric's generation, the rumbling, harmonious sounds of the waterfall in this passage are significant. They evoke the revolution itself and the oddly ambivalent way it is presented in the novel: on the one hand as a moment of meaningless violence, on the other as a fleeting realization and fulfillment of revolutionary aspirations.

It is thus never possible to account for Flaubert's landscapes in terms exclusively of either a psychological, a poetic, or a political transcendence; all three are always present, together, in nature description. The interaction of the three kinds of transcendence provides an intricate nexus of personal, artistic, and collective motives, a complex context within which individual and group seek to go beyond the narrow confines of their historical conditions. And if ultimately defeat occurs on the immediate personal and political levels, the artistic transcendence achieved by the very act of recording the failed historical transcendence in some measure compensates for or neutralizes this defeat.

The Revolutionary Dream

Having uncovered the multifaceted character transcendence assumes in Flaubert's novels makes it possible now to focus on the ambivalent expression of that transcendence in *Salammbô*. The ambivalence assumes especial importance with regard to the novel's central theme of social change, notably of the violent, disruptive form, revolution. Flaubert views such change, as Anne Green argues persuasively, in both positive and negative terms: positive insofar as it shakes a complacent society out of its lethargy, negative in that it ultimately accomplishes nothing, the new regime more than likely being no better than the old one, and the human weaknesses that marred the established society inevitably resurfacing in its revolutionary successor.[16] Green also makes a convincing case for taking the Revolution of 1848 as the model for Flaubert's two-sided conception of revolution. Viewed from such a perspective, Flaubert's preoccupation with the events of 1848—and his conflictual interpretation of those events as dream and as disillusion—provides the common denominator and true thematic core of his writing throughout the period of the 1860s, as much in *Salammbô* in 1862 as, more directly, in *L'Education sentimentale* in 1869.

In a striking number of the novel's some fifteen nature descriptions, the predominant psychological presence is that of Mâtho, both as an individual and as a representative of his social group. Landscape serves thus to enact and dramatize the mercenaries' point of view and transcendent desires, notably during the more successful of the two phases in their drive for political dominance; it acts there to express the positive features and realization of the mercenaries' goals. But the realization is never complete, not even during this early successful phase. From the very start intimations arise of the negative features that will undermine and ultimately destroy altogether the revolutionary dream.

An appropriate starting point is the first of several striking nature descriptions in the first chapter of *Salammbô*. At the beginning of the novel the mercenary soldiers, substantially responsible for the Carthaginian victory against Rome, have been treated to a lavish feast at the home of the absent Carthaginian general, Hamilcar. As the reader will learn shortly, Hamilcar has left the country because of his obdurate compatriots' unwillingness to make peace with the mercenary masses and pay them the wages to which they are entitled. By having the feast there, Hamilcar's rivals hope to placate the rebellious soldiers and at the same time wreak havoc with his cherished home and worldly possessions. It is in the context of this feast at Hamilcar's palace that the following passage needs to be read:

> Fig-trees surrounded the kitchens; a wood of sycamores stretched away to meet masses of verdure, where the pomegranate shone amid the white tufts of the cotton-plant; vines, grape-laden, grew up into the branches of the pines; a field of roses bloomed beneath the plane-trees; here and there lilies rocked upon the turf; the paths were strewn with black sand mingled with powdered coral, and in the centre the avenue of cypress formed, as it were, a double colonnade of green obelisks from one extremity to the other. [17]

This passage is the first of several that symbolically enact the transcendent desires of the mercenaries. Especially noteworthy here is the thematic importance of the notion of plenitude—the sense of the richness and fullness of being. Objects in nature make their appearance not as isolated, individual entities, separated from one another by open space, but rather in profuse, all-encompassing groups: a wood of sycamores, masses of verdure, grape-laden vines, a field of roses, an avenue of cypress. The plenitude of nature here evokes the metaphysical character of the mercenaries' transcendent urges. What they seek is not only to possess the Carthaginian plenitude that their longing eyes devour but, as it were, to be themselves that plenitude. Brombert makes an apt observation in this regard when he notes that, "what really counts in *Salammbô*—as in most other works of Flaubert—is the drama of an impossible desire. This quest for the unattainable, this boundless appetite for that which can never be seized, and much less appropriated, is without a doubt the main tragic theme of the novel." [18]

This passage also attributes vitality to the masses of objects in nature —the same quality that the novel highlights in its treatment of the masses of people who are pictured in nature. Throughout the passage,

Flaubert uses active verbs that seem to endow the vegetation with the attributes of movement and will. Near the end, these attributes seem proleptically to assume military significance—to suggest the mercenaries' dream of triumph over Carthage—in the paradelike formation of the "double colonnade of green obelisks from one extremity to the other." Vitality is also suggested in the sharply contrasting colors, which introduce into an otherwise calm and idyllic nature scene a note of dynamic discordance: specifically, the brilliant red of the pomegranate, which "shone amid the white tufts of the cotton-plant," and the paths "strewn with black sand mingled with powdered coral." Later in the novel, reddish colors such as these—in contrast notably with the colors white or black —assume a privileged thematic significance. They are part of a network of mythical and symbolic meanings related to the active and destructive masculine principle embodied in the sun, the sun god Moloch, and his earthly counterpart Mâtho.

Further evidence of the relation between nature description and the mercenaries' transcendent urges appears in another key descriptive passage, near the end of the first chapter. By now, the reader has become familiar with the internecine struggles in Carthaginian politics and with the nature of the conflict between Carthage and the mercenaries. The major characters have also emerged. The mercenaries have freed the Greek slave Spendius, and he has manifested his devotion to Mâtho and their common cause. Salammbô has made an appearance and has aroused in Mâtho a profound and all-consuming passion. The following passage needs to be read in terms of all of the above factors—political conflict, the common mercenary cause, Mâtho's intense passion. In this passage, Mâtho, accompanied by Spendius, perceives the sun rising over Carthage:

> They were on the terrace. A huge mass of shadow stretched before them, looking as though it contained vague accumulations, like the gigantic billows of a black and petrified ocean.
>
> But a luminous bar rose towards the East; far below, on the left, the canals of Megara were beginning to stripe the verdure of the gardens with their windings of white. The conical roofs of the heptagonal temples, the staircases, terraces, and ramparts were being carved by degrees upon the paleness of the dawn; and a girdle of white foam rocked around the Carthaginian peninsula, while the emerald sea looked as though it were curdled in the freshness of the morning. (p. 14)

Transcendence is expressed in this passage chiefly through light imagery, the light of the rising sun heralding both a different, brighter vision of the future and a clearer, more meaningful awareness of the present. The transcendence is announced in the striking light image that begins the second paragraph: "a luminous bar rose towards the East." It then continues in the related image of the water glimmering in the sun, standing out against the green vegetation to produce the effect of "windings of white." With both images, nature assumes the same dynamic, vital character attributed to the mercenaries. The gradual rising of the sun in this passage sounds a striking diachronic note. The mercenaries and the threat to the status quo of bourgeois Carthaginian society posed by their rising political and military power sounds a similar note in the novel generally. (That threat is suggested symbolically in this passage in the "huge mass of shadow" and the "gigantic billows of a black and petrified ocean".) Another facet of the mercenaries' vigor and vitality becomes apparent later in the passage when, as is often the case in Flaubert's novels, metaphysical or social transcendence merges with sexual desire. In this case, the light image is that of the "girdle of white foam rocked around the Carthaginian peninsula." Numerous similar associations between sexuality and landscape are established later in the novel, for example in chapter 2: "The mountains at their summits were crescent-shaped; others were like women's bosoms presenting their swelling breasts, and the Barbarians felt a heaviness that was full of delight weighing down their fatigue" (p. 24).

Other important facets of the mercenaries' revolutionary transcendence become apparent in this passage in connection with the workings of point of view. There are two viewers of the scene, Spendius and Mâtho. This dual point of view provides an immediate justification for the use of the third-person plural—which helps to shift the meaning of the passage at least in part beyond the purely personal level and onto a collective, social plane. Moreover, Mâtho and Spendius occupy an elevated position in space—that view from on high which Jean Rousset calls the *vue plongeante* and identifies as a key theme and technique for Flaubert. Through the use of the *vue plongeante*, Flaubert equates the mercenaries' psychological and visual dominance in description of nature with the political dominance, even the metaphysical transcendence, that is the goal of their revolutionary uprising. In his illuminating analysis of *Salammbô*, Rousset shows the vital extent to which the structural and thematic unity of that novel relies on the contrast between, on one hand, Mâtho's position on high and thus his spatial dominance over Carthage at the beginning of the novel and, on the other, his relinquishing of that position and thus his spatial inferiority at the end.

If the two passages examined above reveal certain positive features —plenitude, vitality, power—they also have a distinctly negative side. Conflict thus arises in the Flaubertian landscape, and the revolutionary transcendence assumes the ambivalent colors of the author's two-sided conception of revolution. What is negative in both passages is chiefly the people's inability to produce a truly meaningful transcendence of their own—their inability to do more than mimic or be unwitting tools in an enactment of those very bourgeois values which it is presumably their mission to oppose. In both passages, for example, the mercenaries covet the material and political dominance of the Carthaginians: in this regard Sherrington notes that one of the chief functions of description in *Salammbô* is to reflect the voracity of the mercenaries as they cast their longing eyes on the external manifestations of the vast Carthaginian wealth.[19] Similarly, in the first passage the trees serve as symbols of the dominance and oppression that the mercenaries both oppose and yet unwittingly repeat and perpetuate within their own transcendence; and in the second passage the fixed geometrical shapes and especially the "fixed and petrified ocean" evoke an espousal of the Carthaginian unwillingness to change and commitment to the status quo. Thus the mercenaries, like the French masses of Flaubert's time, come to exemplify a promise for change in the future while at the same time exemplifying their own inability to effectuate or even truly envision that change.

The issue of the mercenaries' inability to produce a meaningful transcendence of their own also arises in relation to the subject of point of view. It is manifest to the reader of both passages that the perceptions recorded are too subtle, their arrangement far too artistically contrived, to originate in the minds and eyes of the two barbarian soldiers. As with material and political drives, so too with aesthetic perceptions, the mercenary transcendence is thus a borrowed one, in this case borrowed from the highly civilized, educated mind of the bourgeois writer of the novel. Especially striking among the numerous examples of the subtle aesthetic properties of these texts are the pictorial and poetic features of the second passage. Pictorially, the scene is static and carefully circumscribed: the waves seem to be petrified; the pale sky forms a background against which such geometrical shapes as the temple roofs stand out; the white of the canals and the ocean foam creates a sharp contrast with the green of the gardens and the emerald sea. Poetically, it displays features such as the metaphoric evocation of the early morning sea air as a frothy sash. But perhaps its most distinctive poetic effects are to be found in its effects of sound and rhythm. Consider for example the poetic beginning of the second paragraph in the French text: "A gauche tout en bas / les canaux de Mégara." Megara—distinctive because exotic and remote from any identifiable referent—stands out, creating echoes throughout the passage with the numerous variations on the sounds / é /, / a /, and / r /. At the end of the passage "couleur d'émeraude" seems particularly reminiscent of the earlier "canaux de Mégara." Needless to say, such intricate poetic effects leave Mâtho and Spendius far behind. They are present here, but only as participants in an aesthetic drama which, like the political one, they can neither control nor even understand.

Subsequently, the negative features within the revolutionary trans-cendence assume larger and more thematically significant proportions. Among these features are weakness and apathy, an inability or unwilling-ness to maintain the visual control over landscape, which comes in the novel to symbolize political and military control. Significantly, a reversal of the implicit power structure of the two opposing forces, the mercenar-ies and the Carthaginians, occurs at the midpoint of the novel in chapter 7. Hamilcar returns from abroad and sets the Carthaginians on the road to their eventual victory over the mercenaries. Not surprisingly, his return —and the menace to the mercenary control it signifies—is marked among other things by a landscape in which his transcendent desires rather than theirs are inscribed in nature. "The town sank downwards in a long hollow curve with its cupolas, its temples, its golden roofs, its houses, its clusters of palm trees here and there, and its glass balls with streaming rays, while the ramparts formed as it were the gigantic border of this horn of plenty which poured itself out before him" (p. 94). Else-where in chapter 7 there occur long descriptive passages—undoubtedly the longest and most detailed of the entire novel—in which Hamilcar surveys his riches. Jacques Neefs notes that in these passages, as in the landscape cited above, description becomes a novelistic equivalent of power and control: "The attention to minute detail brought to description . . . is also the affirmation of a political will to make power and the social order coincide, be it through destroying or radically transforming the ba-sis of their original division."[20]

The negative features and loss of control within the mercenaries' rev-olutionary transcendence are further highlighted in chapter 8 by a system of images that emphasizes formlessness—the lack of precise visual limits or shapes—in the natural phenomena they observe. Consider for ex-ample the following passage, where they view the approaching Carthagin-ian army:

> something of enormous size continued to advance. Little vapours, as subtle as the breath, ran across the surface of the desert; the sun, which was higher now, shone more strongly: a harsh light, which seemed to vibrate, threw back the depths of the sky, and, permeat-ing objects, rendered distance incalculable. The immense plain ex-panded in every direction beyond the limits of vision; and the almost insensible undulations of the soil extended to the extreme horizon, which was closed by a great blue line which they knew to be the sea. (p. 132)

A passage such as this forms a striking contrast to the highly geometrical, structured view of Carthage by Mâtho and Spendius in the first chapter. There, as the enemy sleeps, passive and defenseless, the city assumes ever greater clarity in the light of the dawning sun. Here, as the enemy approaches, active and menacing, the plain looms as limitless and invincible as Carthage itself.

Another way in which the negative features and loss of control within the mercenary transcendence emerge in chapter 8 is through the curious technique of presenting landscapes that patently have no identifiable viewer. The use of this technique suggests the diminution and even destruction of individual control over events that undermines the mercenaries' rebellion in its later stages:

> Night fell. Carthaginians and Barbarians had disappeared. The elephants which had taken to flight roamed in the horizon with their fired towers. These burned here and there in the darkness like beacons half lost in the mist; and no movement could be discerned in the plain save the undulation of the river, which was heaped with corpses, and was drifting them away to the sea.
>
> Two hours afterwards Mâtho arrived. He caught sight in the starlight of long, uneven heaps lying upon the ground (p. 138).

Now, clearly, it is not Mâtho who is the viewer here; he only arrives on the scene some two hours after it occurs. There is a distinct absence here of an individual point of view such as Mâtho's; and this absence is itself pregnant with meaning. Through it is suggested the void within the revolutionary dream and the reasons for its ultimate failure. What emerges in this text by Flaubert is, again, a characteristically two-sided conception of the mercenaries' cause, one that records the persistence of Mâtho's transcendent desires at the end of the passage while earlier recording that character's inability to realize those desires.

The use of landscape in *Salammbô* subsequent to chapters 7 and 8 can be summed up in terms of the same loss of individual control over historical events. On several occasions, the same technique recurs whereby the landscape viewer's identity is rendered vague and problematic. But for the most part, landscape simply disappears gradually from the novel, the only exceptions being a couple of instances in which perceptions of a static, silent outside world are filtered through the vague, mystical consciousness of Salammbô. Consider, for example, the moment that she approaches Mâtho's tent to regain possession of the *zaïmph*:

> No one was to be seen around Carthage, whether on the sea or in the country. The slate-coloured waves chopped softly, and the light wind blowing their foam hither and thither spotted them with white rents. In spite of all her veils, Salammbô shivered in the freshness of the morning; the motion and the open air dazed her. Then the sun

rose; it preyed on the back of her head, and she involuntarily dozed a little. (p. 168)

A similarly silent, static, even somnolent state is recorded when her engagement to Narr'Havas is made official: "Domestic animals, grown wild again, fled at the slightest noise. Sometimes a gazelle might be seen trailing scattered peacocks' feathers after its little black hoofs. The clamours of the distant town were lost in the murmuring of the waves. The sky was quite blue, and not a sail was visible on the sea" (pp. 254–255).

Landscape thus supports plot in suggesting as *Salammbô* draws to an end that the status quo has been restored and that the static, complacent bourgeois society embodied by Salammbô herself has successfully vanquished the forces of change and revolt that Mâtho and the mercenaries have served to represent. All that is left of the revolutionary dream at the close of the novel is the overwhelming frustration and futility felt by the dying mercenaries as they cast their eyes one last time on Carthage at the end of the novel: "they felt, in a confused way, that they were the ministers of a god diffused in the hearts of the oppressed, and were the pontiffs, so to speak, of universal vengeance! Then they were enraged with grief at what was extravagant injustice, and above all by the sight of Carthage on the horizon" (p. 263). For the oppressors—the Carthaginians and the French bourgeoisie they represent—Flaubert clearly reserves no sympathy; whatever sympathy his novel displays is reserved for the oppressed. It is worthwhile to draw attention in this context to what Green takes to be the guiding principle of Flaubert's political philosophy: "His political views are based on his hatred of any form of constriction, any political dogma which attempts to force society into its mould. Even more, he fears the stultifying effects of a régime which seeks to level society by crushing individualism and minority groups, and which he believes can lead only to utilitarianism and mediocrity."[21] But at the same time, the forces of individualism —minority groups or the people—are subjected to a treatment that is at the least ambivalent and at the worst filled with disillusion and even disgust.

The People as Transcendence

A prime illustration of the importance of reading narrative landscape in relation to the novel's other landscapes as well as to its other narrative and socio-political elements is provided in Flaubert's *L'Education sentimentale*. Although it contains one of the lengthiest and most celebrated landscapes in the literature of images—the description of the forest of Fontainebleau —which numerous critics have subjected to minute, detailed scrutiny, it has not been sufficiently observed that this description constitutes the true culmination of the series of personal and political crises enacted by the novel. Flaubert's presention of the scene in the Fontainebleau forest as simultaneous with the February Revolution of 1848 is a salient example of the profound and pervasive conjunction of politics and landscape that marks the presentation of nature scenes throughout *L'Education sentimentale.*

A brief summary will help to situate landscape and explain its significance in *L'Education sentimentale.* The novel comprises three parts, the first of which situates an impoverished young aristocrat from the provinces, Frédéric Moreau, on a boat returning to his home town of Nogent. The time is September of 1840. On the boat he meets Mme. Arnoux, the wife of an enterprising, vulgar merchant; she will throughout the novel constitute a romantic ideal for Frédéric. The remainder of the first part, covering a period of roughly five years, introduces most of the issues that will subsequently assume importance in Frédéric's life. Among them, two stand out. The first is his odd passivity, his unwillingness or inability to value and participate in anything other than his idealized, unrealizable passion for Mme. Arnoux. Nature is first presented in *L'Education sentimentale* in terms of this passivity—fleeting perceptions of the river banks or of Nogent suggestive of Frédéric's propensity for retreating from the present reality into some dreamlike state. It is also in terms of this passivity that Frédéric later seeks transcendence in nature. The second issue introduced in the first part is the political malaise that is making itself felt in French society, notably in Paris, where uprisings by the needy, angry masses are already occurring.

The second part of the novel, covering the period from December 1845 to February 1848, records an increased complexity in both the personal and the political domains. Frédéric's romantic life now involves three women: the elegant and unattainable Mme. Arnoux; the simple and rustic Louise, his neighbor from the provinces; and the sensual and sophisticated Rosanette, M. Arnoux's mistress and soon Frédéric's as well. Until the end of this part, Frédéric's transcendent yearnings are directed at the first two of these women, and in an outdoor setting in both cases. First with Louise at Nogent, and then with Mme. Arnoux at Auteuil, he achieves a true but transitory sense of union with others and with the external world. Politically, there is increased unrest, culminating at the end of this part in the outbreak of revolution in February 1848. At the very moment that the fighting begins, Mme. Arnoux fails, because of her child's illness, to arrive at a clandestine meeting with Frédéric. He then, in a mood of despair and frustration, begins his affair with Rosanette.

Part 3, covering the years from 1848 to 1867, begins with Rosanette and Frédéric fleeing the political violence in Paris and seeking fulfillment in love and nature at Fontainebleau. From this point on, the novel records the progressive decline of Frédéric's life and of society at large. His romantic relationships disintegrate, not only with the three women mentioned above but also with a fourth: Mme. Dambreuse, wife of a wealthy industrialist and member of the conservative Parisian high society, whose return to power is ushered in with the Second Empire. Rosanette's child by Frédéric dies; Mme. Arnoux's beauty, and concomitantly his passion for her, fade with time. When the novel comes to a close, both the revolution of 1848 and his illusions and transcendent desires are things of the past. Little has changed, and nothing has improved.

Seen thus in the context of the work as a whole, landscape in *L'Education sentimentale* displays a number of striking features. The most striking perhaps is its extensive, almost exclusive occurrence in one particular segment of the narrative syntagma. That segment spans roughly the last third of part 2 and the first third of part 3. By its placement there —in a part of the novel that records a growing political tension, culminating in a collective will to change through violent, revolutionary means —it not only expresses conflict but actually echoes the movements and rhythms of revolution. Already in *Salammbô*, there was a close correspondence between the pattern of revolution and that of landscape's presentation in the novel: the incidence of landscape in that novel corresponded to an initial rise of power for the mercenaries. In *L'Education sentimentale*, there is a similar correspondence between revolution and landscape, but one that is more striking because more suggestive of a true dramatic high point both in the novel and in history.

Another striking feature of landscape in *L'Education sentimentale* concerns its association with character and social class. As already noted, each of the objects of Frédéric's love or romantic attentions—most notably Louise, Mme. Arnoux, and Rosanette—is presented in connection with an important outdoor scene. Each of the women involved also originates from and indeed personifies a distinct social class or sociological group. Thus Louise is associated in the novel with provincial society generally, and the lower middle classes in particular. Her distinguishing features apply to those classes as well: ignorance, illegitimacy, vulgarity, sentimentality, earthiness, newly acquired money. Mme. Arnoux is clearly associated with the bourgeoisie: as with that class generally, her concerns are domestic and financial; her values confined to marriage, children, and virtue. The appropriate association for Rosanette—and this association is crucial for the argument I shall be developing—is with the Parisian proletariat. Like that class, she is raised in poverty and need. Like Mâtho, Rosanette displays an odd blend of positive and negative characteristics. On the one hand she exhibits an intense vigor, sensuality, and capacity to love that may be the most genuine human qualities displayed in the novel. On the other hand her character is marred by gross shallowness, ignorance, and materialism. Finally there is Mme. Dambreuse, a character who can be considered representative of the moneyed elite of the upper middle classes and new aristocracy. With those classes she has in common a certain coldness, cruelty, and emptiness which make her the most negative of the four women depicted in the novel. It is not totally surprising to discover then that with her, Frédéric experiences virtually no transcendence whatsoever and that with her, there is no major landscape scene.

In the series of nature scenes in which Frédéric seeks to satisfy his transcendent desires with women, nature images suggest that the obstacles to the transcendence are not unrelated to the woman's social class. The first example is the scene in Nogent, where Frédéric experiences a brief moment of happiness and fulfillment with Louise. Initially, the accent is on the same kind of transcendent motifs—for example, water, whiteness, distance—detected earlier in the scene in which he paces back and forth between the two ends of the bridge at Nogent. But as was true in connection with the end of the bridge representing the homey values of Nogent, the transcendence is soon blocked; for example, "the horizon in front was bounded by a curve of the river. It was flat, like a mirror" (p. 328). So too is Louise's life, and that of her entire sociological group, both bounded and flat. But there is more, as is evident in the following passage:

> This piece of land had been under the Directory what is called "a folly." The trees had, since then, grown enormously. Clematis obstructed the hornbeams, the walks were covered with moss, brambles abounded on every side. Fragments of plaster statues crumbled in the grass. The feet of anyone walking through the place got tangled in iron-wire work. (p. 329)

What is evoked is thus not only obstruction and limitation but also the decaying political and material structures of the past. What once may have seemed to hold a promise for the future—the countryside, a society based on cultivating the land—is now as devoid of aesthetic as of political value. Frédéric will almost immediately come to see the product of that countryside and that society, Louise, in a similar light.

Shortly after the scene at Nogent, Frédéric replays his transcendent search with Mme. Arnoux at Auteuil. The transcendence is in this case more lofty and intense, as the images of height and heaven in the following quotation suggest: "They often stood at the top of the stairs exposed to the free air of heaven. The tops of trees yellowed by the autumn raised their crests in front of them at unequal heights up to the edge of the pale sky" (p. 360). But many of the same qualities can be discerned. Consider for example the epiphany Frédéric experiences in the presence of Mme. Arnoux:

Sometimes the rays of the sun, passing through the Venetian blind, extended from the ceiling down to the flagstones like the strings of a lyre. Particles of dust whirled amid these luminous bars. She amused herself by dividing them with her hand. Frederick gently caught hold of it; and he gazed on the twinings of her veins, the grain of her skin, and the form of her fingers. (p. 360)

In the earlier scene with Louise, "as the light fell through the irregular gaps on the green herbage, Frederick, turning his head to speak to Louise, noticed the shadow of the leaves on her face" (p. 329). With Louise as with Mme. Arnoux—and later with Rosanette too—effects of light produce an intensifying of an aesthetic, almost religious present moment, an arresting of real, historical time. The epiphany in question here is not only or even primarily psychological in nature. As indicated earlier, description with Flaubert enacts a transcendence that extends to the individual's social group as well as to the reader and author of the novel.

The scene with Mme. Arnoux also intensifies and dramatizes the sense of material and historical decay associated earlier with Louise and provincial or peasant society. Thus with her the reader learns that "she had reached the autumnal period of womanhood" (p. 360) and that in the summer house where she and Frédéric meet, "black specks stained the glass; the walls exhaled a mouldy smell" (p. 361). With Mme. Arnoux, even more than with Louise, there is no future; indeed, other than the few fleeting moments of epiphany, there is not even any present. For her, as for the bourgeoisie which saw its heyday during the July Monarchy, there is only decay and decline. If there is movement over time, it only brings this class ever closer to the kind of violence and destruction that will erupt in February of 1848. It is interesting in this regard to note the political significance implicit in the following description of Frédéric's and Mme. Arnoux's mounting sexual desires: "They experienced a sensation of delight at the odour of moist leaves; they could not endure the east wind; they got irritated without apparent cause, and had melancholy forebodings. . . . They felt as if they were being pushed toward the edge of a chasm. They were surrounded by a tempestuous atmosphere" (p. 362). Since this scene occurs on the very eve of the Revolution, it seems plausible to associate the rising tension occurring thus in the realm of nature and love with that occurring in the social and political arena.

Considering Mme. Arnoux as emblematic of the bourgeoisie—as Salammbô, that other romantic ideal, was in Flaubert's earlier novel[22]—can illuminate the nature of the obstacles that prevent Frédéric from realizing his transcendent desires with her. Like Salammbô, she is an exterior shell, emptied from within: in the passage quoted earlier, she is associated, significantly, with particles of dust suspended in the sunlight.

With her there is desire without the realization of that desire, form but not substance, the old cut off from the new. Viewed thus, she assumes an even more striking contrast than is commonly acknowledged with her rival and lower-class counterpart, Rosanette.

With Rosanette at Fontainebleau, Frédéric comes closer than at any other moment in the novel to realizing his search for transcendence. With her, the moments of epiphany are similar to but far more intense and protracted than those observed elsewhere. The following passage, notably, presents in its most developed form the highly sensitive perception of light and its effect on natural phenomena noted earlier in connection with both Louise and Mme. Arnoux. Frédéric and Rosanette, reclining in a carriage, are in this case driving through the forest at the very moment that the Revolution has broken out in Paris:

> The midday sun, falling directly on wide tracts of greenery, made splashes of light over them, hung gleaming drops of silver from the ends of the branches, streaked the grass with long lines of emeralds, and flung golden spots on the beds of dead leaves. Looking upward, they could distinguish the sky through the tops of the trees. Some of them, which were enormously high, looked like patriarchs or emperors, or, touching one another at their extremities formed with their long shafts, as it were, triumphal arches; others springing forth obliquely from below, seemed like falling columns. This heap of big vertical lines gaped open. Then, enormous green billows unrolled themselves in unequal embossments as far as the surface of the valleys, toward which advanced the brows of other hills looking down on white plains, which finally lost themselves in an undefined pale tinge. (pp. 438–439)

The epiphany in this case assumes strong monarchical connotations. Earlier in the description of Fontainebleau, Frédéric and Rosanette were presented admiring the regal splendors inside the château; now it is as if aristocratic riches—silver, emeralds, gold—were similarly displayed in nature. And just as the château's interior bespeaks its former noble inhabitants, so too its exterior seems peopled by patriarchs and emperors. That the trees are the vehicles here for monarchical or aristocratic meaning is not surprising in view of the decisive intertextual example set by novels such as *Atala* and *Le Lys dans la vallée*. (A marginal note in one version of the manuscript, which reads "Watch out for *Le Lys dans la vallée*,"[23] can be adduced as proof that Flaubert was himself aware of the intertextual tradition.) Later in the Fontainebleau episode, the text states that the trees "twisted their tops together" (in French, "entremêlaient leurs couronnes"), that they were like bronze, that they were "bent into elegiac attitudes"; all of these details evoke their noble and regal nature.

The symbolism of the trees in Flaubert's Fontainebleau landscape does not bespeak the political viability of the monarchical system they evoke. A number of critics have indeed noted the incoherent presentation of that system within a single sentence in terms of both "triumphal arches" and "falling columns."[24] Rather, the trees assume importance here as participants in a vast, intensely vigorous collective movement that affects all of nature, including the lovers. In the passage quoted above, it is the movement whereby "enormous green billows unrolled themselves in unequal embossments as far as the surface of the valleys." And later in the description, there is an even more forceful expression of the trees' movements: "There were gigantic oaks with knotted forms, which had been violently shaken, stretched out from the soil and pressed close against each other, and with firm trunks resembling torsos, launched forth to heaven despairing appeals with their bare arms and furious threats, like a group of Titans struck rigid in the midst of their rage" (p. 439).

The movement evoked in descriptive passages such as these bears a distinct relation to the similar movement which, as the reader knows, is occurring simultaneously in the streets of Paris. Speaking about Flaubert's descriptive technique generally, Michael Danahy observes that "many descriptive sequences are written about a set of objects while something else is also accomplished without being directly narrated. At the end of the description, the reader realizes that this other action has actually occurred at the same time as the description, in other words, in the meantime"; and speaking about the Fontainebleau description specifically, Brombert notes that "the forest becomes ironically and in what one might call a mythical way the mirror and echo of the upheaval in Paris."[25]

Now, by contrasting the dynamic, energetic movement of both nature and Revolution with the passive, static quality of Frédéric's own life, it is possible to grasp why the scene in the forest constitutes a moment of true transcendence for him. Something finally seems to be happening; action and life seem at last to be possible. He is not seeking to escape from history here: on the contrary, he has for perhaps the only time in the novel the illusion of being intensely involved in history. Not surprisingly, he will run off shortly to rejoin his friends and seek an active role in the Revolution itself. The moment evoked in the forest is the moment of his transcendent dream, as it is similarly the moment of the people's dream. As noted earlier, the fact that his dream proves to be so ephemeral can be seen as calling into question and even providing a negative, ironic statement about theirs.

Rosanette plays an important role in the Fontainebleau scene. One of the main functions of her presence there is to introduce the typical Flaubertian blend of erotic and metaphysical desire. For Frédéric, as for Mâtho, sexual desire provoked by a woman is inscribed in nature; landscape then becomes a concrete, immediate object of a desire that is of a far more vast but vague and abstract kind. Flaubert's characters ultimately have no true or abiding interest in either landscape or romance. Nature for them is the locus of transcendence; woman is the pretext.

There is, however, a notable difference between Salammbô, the pretext for Mâtho's sexual and metaphysical desires, and Rosanette, the pretext for Frédéric's; and it is a difference that closely concerns the social classes of the women involved. Salammbô, like Mme. Arnoux and the bourgeoisie generally for Flaubert, exhibits an external beauty and mystery along with an internal emptiness and absence. These women are personifications of perfect form, of the ideal, even perhaps of Art. The presentation of Rosanette, in contrast, is everywhere marked by the same sense of fullness, presence, and substance that Flaubert attributes to the proletariat. Jean-Pierre Richard aptly characterizes Rosanette when he observes, "To her Flaubert assigns the role of incarnating, as opposed to Mme. Arnoux's modesty, the immodest plenitude of nature and the flesh. Everything around her becomes thicker, more dense, including the landscapes themselves. When she walks with Frédéric in the Fontainebleau forest, the trees swell in a powerful movement of luxuriance."[26] A similar plenitude is characteristic of Zola's treatment of the forest in La Faute de l'abbé Mouret, a novel that unquestionably resonates with intertextual echoes of Flaubert's Fontainebleau landscape.

Frédéric rejects the transcendence exemplified by Rosanette, the luxuriant forest, and the people because it is blocked, as it was with Louise. As the lovers move farther and farther into the depths of the forest during the Fontainebleau episode, they have an increased sense of silence, of immobility, of time standing still. Frédéric thus finds himself trapped in a full but homogeneous present moment with Rosanette, one that allows for no movement beyond, no vague or idealized future time. The same is true of the people and the Revolution. Like Rosanette, both of these social phenomena are ultimately inadequate to meet Frédéric's transcendent desires. They possess the same vigor and vitality as the mercenaries in Salammbô but also the same inability to realize or sustain an ideal. A dramatic high point is reached, but it is almost immediately subjected to the forces of degeneration and decline.

As an epilogue to Frédéric's failed search for transcendence through nature in L'Education sentimentale, it is worth considering the children associated in the novel with Mme. Arnoux, Rosanette, and Mme. Dambreuse. The fate of these children summarizes and symbolizes the fate of the union of woman, nature, and the external world that Frédéric dreamed of achieving. The first of these women has been identified as exemplifying the bourgeoisie, notably that in power during the July Monarchy. During the course of the novel, her child suffers the same life-threatening ordeal as does Frédéric's search for transcendence in nature with a woman who personifies the bourgeoisie. And as with his search, so too with the child, there is little hope for the future at the end of the novel. The child endures, but in a less-than-robust condition. Similarly, the bourgeoisie lives on, but without any hope for fulfillment through nature or love. No more encouraging is the fate of Rosanette's child as an embodiment of the people. Like Frédéric's failed transcendence with Rosanette at Fontainebleau, and like the people's revolt, the child dies. Frédéric's illusions and the hopes fostered for a time by the people and their uprising in 1848 were as transitory as the fleeting perceptions of nature that he and Rosanette shared in the forest. Both the child and the perceptions were doomed, as was the Revolution. Finally there is Mme. Dambreuse, who exemplifies another, different bourgeoisie, the moneyed elite of the Second Empire. As noted earlier, no transcendence is possible with her; nor is she associated, significantly, with any substantial scene in nature. And not surprisingly, the child to whom she serves as substitute mother is not only her husband's illegitimate offspring but also, as it turns out, a greedy and ungracious child. To this child and the class she personifies Flaubert leaves the final, pessimistic word in the novel. As for Frédéric's transcendent desires, they are merely a memory at the end, as are nature and Revolution.

7

The Woman's Eye and Voice:

Jane Eyre

Female Narrators and Narratees

The female protagonist of Charlotte Brontë's celebrated *Jane Eyre* has a special relationship with landscape that derives from her special attitude to women and work. She articulates that attitude at one point in the following terms:

> women feel just as men feel; they need exercise for their faculties, and a field for their efforts as much as their brothers do . . . and it is narrow-minded in their more privileged fellow-creatures to say that they ought to confine themselves to making puddings and knitting stockings, to playing the piano and embroidering bags.[1]

Just such an "exercise for their faculties" is provided by the activities of narration and landscape description, a type of "work" that women perform repeatedly over the pages of *Jane Eyre* and which that novel presents as exemplary from both an intellectual and an economic point of view. If women follow Jane's example in practicing these activities, the novel suggests, a middle ground can be discovered that reconciles the opposing poles of revolt and subservience.

Before examining the narrative and descriptive activities proposed in *Jane Eyre*, we must distinguish three distinct but closely interrelated narrative voices in the novel: indeed they are so closely interrelated as to seem at times identical. First there is the character Jane Eyre, who occupies center stage, who is quoted in reported dialogue, and who often seems to be speaking, in the voice of the character as she was between the approximate ages of ten and twenty. Next there is Jane Rochester, narrating some ten years after the facts recounted in the novel, whose "I" and whose superior knowledge and maturity in relation to the character Jane Eyre make themselves heard sporadically throughout the novel. And finally, there is the implicit presence of an invisible, unidentifiable authorial figure who stands behind and ever so slightly apart from Jane Rochester, the narrator. This figure, whom I shall call the "fictional author" (although others might equate her with the "real" author Charlotte Brontë), makes her presence known through certain signs—addresses to the reader are one example—or such authorial activities as irony or contrived effects of style that call attention to the act of writing itself. And indeed, a number of modern Brontë critics agree that there is evidence of a literary self-consciousness in *Jane Eyre* that had formerly gone unnoticed.[2] If it is more appropriate to speak of a "fictional author" than a "public narrator," as with other novels in the literature of images, it is because there are actual or implicit references to writing in *Jane Eyre*. And indeed, the first edition did present an editor, Currer Bell, as one of the narrative participants, thereby acknowledging the role of an authorial figure in relation to the novel.

Addressing an audience in which women readers clearly form a major segment, the fictional author of *Jane Eyre* dwells on the important ties that narrating and describing nature have with the related activities of reading, teaching and writing. She proposes these activities as providing ways of valorizing the woman's "voice" and thus enabling women to discover viable models for life and work. She also proposes them as providing ways of valorizing woman's solidarity with other women and thus enabling her to discover viable relationships with other women in society. The woman reader would then gain a significant measure of independence from those "masters" whose close relationship with narration and landscape in *Jane Eyre* will be examined later.

That for women, the activities of narration, nature description, and reading are closely connected is a point made by the narrator and fictional author at the very start through the presentation first of the ten-year-old Jane and then of the servant Bessie. Both female characters are readers— Jane reads Bewick's *History of British Birds* and Bessie reads *Pamela* aloud to Jane—but they are readers of a special, feminist kind that recurs throughout Charlotte Brontë's writings. These female readers read women's books—books by, to, for, or about women—in order to derive strength themselves or to pass strength on to other women. They do not read passively, as recipients of messages sent out by predominantly male authors. Instead, they actively discover meaning relevant to women, which furnishes models for living and for work. Theirs is truly a "poetics" of reading, with that term being taken here, as in Aristotle's *Poetics*, as a manual for how to do something or make an artistic object, such as a nature description. Proposing the adoption of such a poetics is the fictional author's purpose.

It is not surprising then that the first part of *Jane Eyre* where the reader is offered an example of how the female protagonist learns to "read" and describe nature, takes place at the homonymic home of Mrs. "Reed" and that the first paragraphs of the novel highlight the importance of "leaves." From the second sentence ("We had been wandering, indeed, in the leafless shrubbery an hour in the morning"), where leaves are absent out-of-doors, the novel immediately shifts to their presence inside the house in the form of the leaves of a book ("At intervals, while turning over the leaves of my book, I studied the aspect of that winter afternoon," p. 2). Incapable of discovering beauties in her cold, barren surroundings, Jane turns to Bewick's *History of British Birds*, which acomplishes the study of winter nature that she is vainly attempting to achieve by looking out the window.

If becoming a reader helps women to become narrators or describers themselves by presenting models of writing, it also helps them by presenting models of women writers and characters. As feminist critics Gilbert and Gubar explain, a woman who engages in literary activities must "redefine the terms of her socialization" and, to do so, she must actively seek "a *female* precursor who, far from representing a threatening force to be denied or killed, proves by example that a revolt against patriarchal literary authority is possible."[3] There is a subtle indication in *Jane Eyre* that suggests that the fictional author agrees and is seeking to propose models of female writers to the reader. I refer to the presentation near the end of *Jane Eyre* in which Jane, alone and starving, arrives at the Rivers's cottage and sees a happy, congenial threesome through the window. That presentation is strikingly reminiscent of the similar scene in which the monster looks into the DeLacey cottage in Mary Shelley's *Frankenstein*. Although admittedly only a detail, such an instance of intertextuality is significant because it enables the fictional author to acknowledge the strength she derived from her female precursors in the literature of images and to propose them as examples.

Another female reader, whose importance to Jane cannot be overemphasized, is Bessie. Bessie is Jane's first friend and mentor, the person who helps her to understand the necessity of speaking up to assert herself and thus of acquiring a voice ("you're such a queer, frightened, shy, little thing. You should be bolder," p. 36), both to survive and to earn her living. It is Bessie, in explaining what school will be like, who first tells her about landscape: "She boasted of the beautiful paintings of landscapes and flowers by them executed" (p. 20). Landscape painting will subsequently be an important accomplishment, enabling Jane to acquire employment as a governess and teacher. Though only a servant, Bessie thus assumes the role that so many other women fill in Charlotte Brontë's works of reading and passing books on to other women. These women thus duplicate the fictional author's own efforts in showing women the way to gain strength through language and work.

Bessie's choice of *Pamela* is also important because it furnishes the fictional author with another instance of intertextuality. In this case, the intertextuality is ironic, that is, it emphasizes the important differences between two different kinds of texts; in conscious protest against works like *Pamela*, *Jane Eyre* alludes to it and signals it as a target. Goran Hermeran refers to such allusions and signals as "antithetical similarities" and observes that "there are similarities between the two authors—they deal with the same topic, they discuss it from the same aspects, they can be compared to each other on a number of specific points"; yet at the same time, "what one author says on these points is the antithesis of what the other says."[4] In a book like *Jane Eyre*, which dwells on female freedom and independence, it seems far more likely that Pamela would emerge as an object of irony than as a serious model of female conduct.

There are important feminist implications to *Jane Eyre*'s adoption of an ironic attitude to *Pamela*. As Gilbert and Gubar state, "women writers in England and America, throughout the nineteenth century and on into the twentieth, have been especially concerned with assaulting and revising, deconstructing and reconstructing those images of women inherited from male literature"; they also note that Pamela would be an especially important image to deconstruct, stressing as it does to "female readers that they can hope to rise only through male intervention."[5] I might add parenthetically that it is the very garden scene analyzed in chapter 1, in which Mr. B declares his love to Pamela, that the fictional author singles out and deconstructs when Rochester proposes marriage to Jane. Whereas Brontë's female predecessors in the literature of images are alluded to indirectly and seriously, her male predecessors are referred to directly and ironically. Such references implicitly encourage women to reject models proposed by male writers and adopt those proposed by their female counterparts.

It is also worth noting that a degree of narrative distance is maintained in *Jane Eyre* regarding narrative models generally. This distance fosters literary self-consciousness and encourages women to examine carefully the literary examples they choose to follow. Rosemarie Bodenheimer states in this regard that "Brontë continually asks us to think about typical plots in order to disengage them from her own"; and she concludes that "at every turn the novel is conscious of its status among fictions."[6] The adoption of a prototypically female generic model in the middle of *Jane Eyre*, to wit, the Gothic novel, can best be understood then as a self-conscious move whereby a woman writer writing largely for women chooses a woman's genre, but in full awareness of the strengths and weaknesses of that genre and of popular woman's literature in general.

Closely related to the significance attributed to women as readers in *Jane Eyre* is their significance as teachers. Indeed, that significance perhaps emerges more strongly in this work than in other novels by Brontë that depict women teachers because here, with the possible exception of St. John Rivers, no competing male "master" exists, such as Paul Emmanuel in *Villette*. The world of education in *Jane Eyre* is indeed the veritable *gynécée* that radical French feminists consider the only solution for modern women. And although the fictional author of *Jane Eyre* does not propose a separatist society for women, nonetheless she tells a story in which women alone are responsible for the intellectual training of other women. Her own training will indeed come only from women, with the minor exception of the instruction that St. John Rivers imposes on her. After Bessie, Jane will receive that training from her fellow student Helen Burns, from the various teachers at Lowood School, and from that school's directress Maria Temple; later in the novel Diana and Mary Rivers will teach her German and share the world of books with her, when they are not themselves employed as governesses. Jane, in her turn, will become a teacher at Lowood School, then Adèle's governess, and then again a teacher of working-class children at Morton School.

For women in Brontë's novel, teaching provides an "exercise for their faculties"—speaking, reading to girls, telling them stories, describing or painting nature scenes—along with a way of earning a living and thus of obtaining their independence. Indeed, it is the only viable solution proposed in the novel short of receiving an inheritance, as Jane happily does at the end of the novel. Teaching and the activities with which it is closely related need not, of course, be confined to the classroom. Thus when Miss Temple leaves for "a distant country" with her clergyman husband there is no reason to believe that she will cease to be a teacher but may simply direct her attention now to underprivileged children in that distant land or even to her own husband or children. Similarly for Jane and for her cousins Mary and Diana Rivers, marriage is presented as merely a different kind of "work," but one in which the woman's narrative, descriptive, and pedagogical talents can still be employed to obtain satisfaction and independence.

From teaching, it is easy to move now to the related activities of *speaking* and, indirectly, of *writing*. For it is only indirectly, as a disguised form of speaking, that women's writing is presented in *Jane Eyre*. Other than the indirect intertextual allusions to women writers noted earlier, writing seems, in the public domain at least, to be the unique purview of men. It is interesting that Jane comments at one point that she learned of the fleeting character of love "in books written by men," as if those were the only kind of books there are in her eyes. And it is also interesting in a similar vein that Rochester appears in a key scene, recounted once by the narrator and again quoted later in his direct discourse, as being the person who performs the activity of writing: "I sat down to rest me on a stile; and there I took out a little book and a pencil, and began to write about a misfortune that befell me long ago, and a wish I had for happy days to come" (p. 285).

With Jane as a character, in contrast, there is no comparable reference to her finding consolation in writing or even, for that matter, in her engaging in writing at all. Nor, at the end of the novel, when she acknowledges herself as the narrator, is Jane depicted as putting her story down on paper. Almost the only times that Jane writes anything at all are associated with economic independence: on one occasion she writes an advertisement to obtain employment as a governess and on another she writes to her uncle John Eyre to obtain an inheritance that will assure her financial freedom from Rochester's control.

If the female narrator of *Jane Eyre* is not presented as an actual writer, she nonetheless performs the same activities that writers do, such as telling stories and describing nature; and thus the perceptive reader senses the presence of the fictional author, who refuses to acknowledge her presence, behind the narrator who says "I" and agrees to acknowledge openly her existence in the text. At times, the narrator even comes close to revealing her identity as a writer, for example in the following comments at the beginning of chapter 10: "Hitherto I have recorded in detail the events of my insignificant existence: to the first ten years of my life, I have given almost as many chapters. But this is not to be a regular autobiography" (p. 83). What is at issue, clearly, is the narrator's hesitation to acknowledge herself as a female writer and thus to valorize fully the profession of writing as a viable option for women. As Gilbert and Gubar observe, nineteenth-century women writers frequently resorted to "evasion and concealment" in their writing; and they note that "Brontë's women artists withdraw behind their art even while they assert themselves through it."[7] The hesitation that nineteenth-century women writers felt about the activity of writing translates itself in *Jane Eyre* as an unwillingness to acknowledge narration or description of nature as "writing" and a desire to pass them off instead as "speaking" or even such a presumably natural and acceptable female activity as landscape painting. Thus the issue of male authorship and the exclusive male right to exercise the profession of writer are simply not addressed. An acceptable middle ground of oral or pictorial landscape is proposed whereby women need neither rebel against social conventions nor subserviently accept them.

Such an attitude to the activity of writing helps us to understand the novel's numerous references and addresses to the "reader." That these references and addresses bear the name "reader" rather than "listener" is surprising since their tone, and indeed the tone in the novel generally, is a distinctly oral one, as if Jane were telling her story rather than writing it. Speaking of Helen Burns, for example, the novel first poses a rhetorical question ("And where, meantime, was Helen Burns?" p. 78) and then develops the matter as if the reader were participating in a conversation on the subject with the narrator ("True, reader; and I knew and felt this"). But in light of the female narrator's hesitation to acknowledge her activity as a writer, such addresses are understandable. By naming the reader while at the same time adopting an oral tone, the narrator can appear to be speaking while actually writing.

The same evasion and hesitation that surround the narrator as a writer in *Jane Eyre* surround the implied reader to whom the novel is addressed and notably the matter of that reader's gender. Sylvère Monod reaches the provocative but to my mind largely unsupported conclusion, frequently mentioned, that it is a male reader whom *Jane Eyre* addresses, a "contemptible being, conventional, silly, cowardly, ignorant, and vain" who "coincides at every point with the image which the Brontë girls pictured to themselves of the average male"; he goes on to say, "the tone which Charlotte uses to address the reader . . . is what she fancies to be the tone of a conversation between men."[8] Not only is there little evidence in the text for what Monod interprets as a condescending and hostile attitude to the reader or of a "conversation between men"; I would argue that on the contrary many of *Jane Eyre*'s salient narrative features lead to the conclusion that the narratee is a woman to whom the narrator and fictional author seek to impart insights about life and work. One of those features, as seen above, is the relationship between female teacher and female student in which women speak to women, care for them, and train them to be better and more useful members of society. Relevant in this regard is the slightly didactic tone the fictional author at times assumes, as if her audience were a group of girls, as it indeed was at the Lowood and Morton schools: for example, "Good fortune opens the hand as well as the heart wonderfully; and to give somewhat when we have largely received, is but to afford a vent to the unusual ebullition of the sensations" (p. 416). It is also worth mentioning such addresses to the unidentified reader as the following, which seem clearly directed at women: "oh, romantic reader, forgive me for telling the plain truth!" and "Gentle reader, may you never feel what I then felt!" And as Jerome Beaty explains, it is a fact, though an admittedly external one, that similar addresses were commonplaces in such female genres of the nineteenth century as the "governess novel."[9]

Another important narrative feature that supports the identification of a female narratee are the repeated defenses of women's actions in *Jane Eyre*. These defenses seem to be intended by the fictional author to further a sense of solidarity among the women to whom she is speaking or writing. In the first section of the book, for example, the narrator insists repeatedly on defending Mrs. Reed. And elsewhere, the narrator comes to the defense of other female characters for whom she might be expected to have mixed or even negative feelings, such as Rochester's first wife Bertha, Blanche Ingram, his former mistresses, Adèle, and even the women who refuse her food when she is starving in Morton. Additionally, Gail B. Griffin notes that Bertha, with all her madness and rage, never harms either Jane or her female keeper Grace Poole, whereas she mercilessly attacks her husband and her brother. In fact, states Griffin, "she issues to Jane a significant gesture of help and sisterhood in the torn veil, a warning from one Mrs. Rochester to another."[10] It is the same sisterhood that Bessie feels for Jane and Jane for Mrs. Reed, a compassion for women that the narrator clearly seeks to foster among her readers.

It is worth noting that foreign women are less favorably treated in *Jane Eyre* than the English women to whom the novel is in large part addressed. The complicity based on a common nationality between the narrator and the narratee also fosters sisterhood and solidarity among women. Although, as noted above, Jane defends foreign women like Rochester's first wife or his former mistresses, she is still concerned at the end of the novel, for example, that Adèle receive "a sound English education" that will correct "her French defects" (p. 483).

All critics would not agree that there is sisterhood and solidarity in *Jane Eyre*'s attitude to English women. At least one argues that the attitude is a politically conservative one and thus calls into question Brontë's achievement as a feminist writer:

> *Jane Eyre* constructs a new female stereotype: the highly principled, unattractive woman, the anti-woman to the French coquette. Her role is to protect the English male from falling into "French" ways, and thus, indirectly, she becomes the pillar of the nation. Jane, from being governess to a child becomes governess to a man and governess to the nation. This type of female perfectly suited the imperialistic, militaristic temper of the period. . . . Charlotte Bronte . . . set out to liberate woman from the representations in which Victorian ideology held her. She also set out to vindicate the socially underprivileged woman. Yet *Jane Eyre* comes to celebrate the very *ethos* upon which bourgeois capitalism and its patriarchal ideology rest.[11]

Such a critical position overlooks the myriad specifics in the text that actively promote the goals of liberating and vindicating women. Admittedly, conservative elements do appear in *Jane Eyre*: distancing revolutionary politics as typically French is indeed an intertextual marker in the literature of images that was amply recorded in chapter 4 with respect to the writings of Radcliffe and Shelley. But those elements are outweighed by many others, which challenge a "patriarchal ideology" rather than promote or support it.

In short, *Jane Eyre* speaks clearly to its predominantly female, English audience; and it does so in a voice that valorizes women's activities—their asserting sisterhood, their writing, their teaching, their narrating and describing. Through these activities, the fictional author proposes the ways of dealing with male authority that will be examined in the analyses to follow of two very different kinds of "masters": the repressive one, represented by Jane's cousins John Reed and St. John Rivers at the beginning and end of *Jane Eyre*, and the benevolent one, represented by Edward Fairfax Rochester in the novel's lengthy middle section.

Landscape as Revolt

In the opening and closing sections of *Jane Eyre*, male cousins of the female protagonist attempt to exercise the total dominance over her existence to which a master is presumably entitled. It is as a form of revolt against the common, though admittedly very different, dominance exercised by these two characters—one bad and one good—that landscape can best be understood in those sections of the novel. Describing nature is one of a cluster of activities that the fictional author proposes for women, activities that enable them to acquire a voice and to assert their independent economic identity.

Before we examine the specific activity of landscape in detail, it would perhaps be well to elaborate upon the important narrative parallels established by the novel between Jane's two male cousins. As a needy, homeless orphan, Jane is taken into the homes of two families of cousins, each comprising two girls and a boy named John who is the sole, living male member of the household and thus an apt symbol of male authority. John Reed, at the beginning, insists significantly that Jane call him "Master" (p. 4); and in the novel's last paragraph, St. John Rivers writes to Jane, "My Master has forewarned me," thereby reminding her, as was his wont, that in his eyes she is subservient to God and indirectly to St. John's own saintly person.

The differences between the two masters only sharpens and emphasizes the commonality of their treatment of their female cousin. It is true that John Reed has dark skin and big lips (pp. 10, 92) whereas St. John Rivers is fair, blond, and endowed with a "Greek face, very pure in outline" (p. 368), and that the former is a model of moral baseness while the latter is a model of spiritual elevation. But by emphasizing the similarities between the two cousins, the narrator makes the point that what counts for her story is that their male dominance has equally nefarious effects on Jane. And indeed, both cousins make Jane profoundly uneasy and unhappy. The bad cousin throws a book at her and the good cousin pressures her to learn Hindustani: the one almost kills her with hatred and the other with love. Most importantly, both cousins singlehandedly create an atmosphere that imprisons her and against which she must revolt and even flee to survive.

Landscape's role in the first section of the novel needs to be understood in response to the kind of dominance exercised by John Reed. That section is aptly presented as taking place first at the Reed home and then at

Lowood School, for it is as a frail reed that Jane begins the novel and as a silent piece of wood that she lives for many years. What transpires in the first section of the novel is that a poor, scared, tyrannized girl learns that by acquiring a voice to answer her masters and by performing meaningful, respected activities, she can assure her survival and even some limited degree of independence.

To acquire a voice, Jane turns to the closely interrelated activities of nature description and reading. But it is only at the very end of the Reed-house segment of *Jane Eyre* that a sustained, developed landscape occurs. Its placement there is significant. As Cynthia A. Linder observes, "Jane has grown older, and has now developed some talents of her own . . . which will enable her to express her thoughts and feelings more immediately than if she were to point to someone else's picture and say 'this is how I feel'"; and although Linder is wrong in saying that "this is the last reference to books in the novel," since numerous references to books in the St. John section parallel those found in the John Reed section, she is right in emphasizing the fact that the landscape at the end of the Reed segment "marks the beginning of passages of description of nature" in *Jane Eyre* and in interpreting that fact as a major step in Jane's development.[12] The passage begins with Jane picking up a volume of Arabian tales, which she soon puts aside as her attention and movements turn toward the out-of-doors:

> I found no pleasure in the silent trees, the falling fir cones, the congealed relics of autumn, russet leaves, swept by past winds in heaps, and now stiffened together. I leaned against a gate, and looked into an empty field where no sheep were feeding, where the short grass was nipped and blanched. It was a very grey day; a most opaque sky, "onding on snaw," canopied all; thence flakes fell at intervals, which settled on the hard path and on the hoary lea without melting.
> (p. 35)

If this landscape marks a new stage in Jane's development, it clearly marks a stage in which she views her surroundings with a lucid and even rebellious eye. For this description emphasizes above all the funereal, barren, lifeless setting of the Reed's existence, an existence in which neither Jane nor plants nor animals could find the barest minimum of warmth or sustenance. It is no wonder that in the short segment later in the novel, when Jane returns to visit her dying aunt Reed, landscape is completely absent. What is most significant about the single landscape Jane does produce in connection with the Reeds is not the fact that everything in it, as in the Reeds' life, is inimical to living nature, but the audacity and rebelliousness attributed to Jane in proclaiming that fact. This landscape can

indeed be read as a proclamation of Jane's newfound strength and independence, which make it possible for her to free herself from John Reed's
repressive rule.

At Lowood School, Jane is again dominated by a heartless and unthink-
ing male master—in this case the school's manager and final authority,
Mr. Brocklehurst—who, as John Reed's surrogate away from home, subjects her to the same humiliation, ostracism, and physical debilitation.
Her very existence at the school is a direct result of John Reed's unreason-
able treatment of her, since she would otherwise have been content to remain at the Reed house. At the same time, her female teachers enable her
to gain an ever greater strength and independence of which the ability to
produce landscape is emblematic. Thus the narrator observes, "in less than
two months I was allowed to commence French and drawing. I learned the
first two tenses of the verb Etre, and sketched my first cottage" (p. 74).
What Jane is acquiring at this stage is nothing less than her own identity—hence the French verb for "to be" and the French pronoun for "I"
which Mark M. Hennelly, Jr. perceptively observes in Jane's encoded ini-
tials "J. E."[13] Not surprisingly, in view of the crucial role of landscape in
the novel, her acquisition of an identity is intimately and profoundly tied
up with sketching her first cottage. That cottage indeed serves, as will
other landscapes later in the novel, as an identity symbol and thus allows
Jane to envision and ultimately possess a true home.

Only in the light of Jane's increased strength, which enables her to
fight back against an oppressor like Mr. Brocklehurst, can a curious, almost "engaged" landscape such as the following, occasioned by an outbreak of typhus at Lowood School, be understood:

> While disease had thus become an inhabitant of Lowood and death
> its frequent visitor; while there was gloom and fear within its walls;
> while its rooms and passages steamed with hospital smells, the drug
> and the pastille striving vainly to overcome the effluvia of mortality,
> that bright May shone unclouded over the bold hills and beautiful
> woodland out of doors. Its garden, too, glowed with flowers: holly-
> hocks had sprung up tall as trees, lilies had opened, tulips and roses
> were in bloom; the borders of the little beds were gay with pink
> thrift and crimson double-daisies; the sweet-briars gave out, morn-
> ing and evening, their scent of spice and apples; and these fragrant
> treasures were all useless for most of the inmates of Lowood, except
> to furnish now and then a handful of herbs and blossoms to put in a
> coffin (p. 77).

If it is remembered that Brocklehurst is held directly responsible for the
epidemic, because of the inadequate health and nutritional conditions of
the school, there is reason to conclude that the mordant ironic juxtaposi-

tion between malodorous death and sweet-smelling life established in this landscape is directed in some way at him and perhaps, beyond him, at his surrogate, that other mean-spirited and cruel male master early in Jane's life, John Reed. Whether the fictional author's goal here is to underscore Brocklehurst's evil ways or simply to allow the narrator to relive an especially dramatic and life-threatening episode in the past, a rebellious, almost incendiary tone and purpose seems to emerge. Bad masters, this passage suggests, should not be tolerated; and their victims should protest with whatever means they possess, be it nothing more than the simple ability to describe flowers in May.

Two social factors assume distinct importance in the presentation of Jane's second male cousin, a character who is presented as being far more positive than John Reed, though equally repressive with respect to Jane. One important factor is the elevated social class that the Rivers name connotes: Jane learns that "it was a very old name in that neighbourhood; that the ancestors of the house were wealthy; that all Morton had once belonged to them" (p. 395). No such aristocratic associations were established regarding the Reed family. Another important factor is Rivers's patrilineal connection with Jane (St. John's mother was the sister of Jane's father) as opposed to the Reed's matrilineal link with her (John Reed's father was the brother of Jane's mother). For according to the traditional conservative world view to which *Jane Eyre* seems here to conform, land is legitimately connected with the father. Not surprisingly, then, when Jane, true to her name, becomes an "heir," the money comes from her paternal uncle "Eyre."

An illustrative landscape from the St. John Rivers section of the novel can serve now to illuminate the reasons for Jane's rebellious response to her aristocratic male cousin, a response that is unquestionably milder and less virulent but no less significant than that provoked by John Reed.

> They loved their sequestered home. I, too, in the grey, small, antique structure, with its low roof, its latticed casements, its mouldering walls, its avenues of aged firs—all grown aslant under the stress of mountain winds; its garden, dark with yew and holly— and where no flowers but of the hardiest species would bloom— found a charm both potent and permanent. They clung to the purple moors behind and around their dwelling—to the hollow vale into which the pebbly bridle-path leading from their gate descended. (pp. 373–374)

If the similarly secluded cottage where the exiled French aristocratic DeLacey family lives in *Frankenstein* comes to mind in reading this passage, it is not only because of the common themes of loneliness, exile, and humble surroundings. There is further the fact of this passage's aristocratic connotations: in the mention, for example, of the "antique" structure, the "avenue of aged firs," the regal color purple, and the "charm both potent and permanent" of the entire scene. That charm strongly affects Jane who, like her female cousins referred to in the first sentence, deeply loves this "sequestered home." And indeed had St. John shared his sisters' and Jane's love of home and land, there is little doubt that Jane would have married him. Instead, he rejects those legitimate ties with nature that are manifest in his name "Rivers" and his aristocratic background.

Along with its aristocratic connotations, the passage quoted above also displays features expressive of the repressive atmosphere in which Jane will be enveloped by her cousin St. John. Like the trees, "all grown aslant under the stress of mountain winds," Jane's spirit will become withered and deformed under the iron rule of her cousin's lofty, ascetic mind. Passing through the strait gate of religion, she will indeed descend into a "hollow vale" in which all human love and warmth are absent. In St. John's religious world, if not in any religious world according to the fictional author, "no flowers but of the hardiest species could bloom." Along with St. John Rivers, the novel presents Eliza Reed and Mr. Brocklehurst as similarly cold, unfeeling, deprived individuals, who care more about their own spiritual well-being than about the real lives of other people. St. John, indifferent even to his own life, indeed invites death in almost as willing a fashion, as a missionary in India, as does John Reed by committing suicide.

This landscape occurs at the beginning of the St. John Rivers segment, when Jane is still free to enjoy and express herself through description of nature. The only other landscape in that section occurs at the end, when Jane forms her decision to flee her cousin's control. That landscape at the end is prefaced, significantly, by a statement about revolt:

> I know no medium: I never in my life have known any medium in
> my dealings with positive, hard characters, antagonistic to my own,
> between absolute submission and determined revolt. I have always
> faithfully observed the one, up to the very moment of bursting,
> sometimes with volcanic vehemence, into the other; and as neither
> present circumstances warranted, nor my present mood inclined me
> to mutiny, I observed careful obedience to St. John's direction; and
> in ten minutes I was treading the wild track of the glen, side by side
> with him. (p. 429)

The lengthy description that follows is a renewed commitment on Jane's part to assert her own identity through nature description, an indirect and perhaps even unconscious means to revolt against her cousin's efforts to squelch that identity. Also important are the powerful movements of living forces in nature: "the stream descending the ravine, swelled with past spring rains, poured along plentiful and clear," "the beck rushed down a waterfall," "the mountain shook off turf and flower." Although, as the narrator stated in her prefatory comments, no "present circumstances warranted" the moment of revolt Jane experiences here in nature, that moment is a profound and necessary response to her cousin's repressive rule which she has endured. Describing nature here, as at the end of the Reed-house section, is a proclamation of independence and strength.

The last segment of the St. John Rivers section involves a change of location, as was the case with the John Reed section. There, the change was to Lowood School and Brocklehurst as master; here, it is to Ferndean Manor and Rochester, whose special role as master will be examined next. Ferndean will, however, involve none of the alienation from nature that Jane experienced at the home of St. John Rivers. On the contrary, as the following passage reveals, to return to Rochester at Ferndean, "deep buried in a wood" (p. 461), is for Jane to return to the ferny Eden of her own profound and inextricable ties with nature:

> Even when within a very short distance of the manor-house, you could see nothing of it; so thick and dark grew the timber of the gloomy wood about it. Iron gates between granite pillars showed me where to enter, and passing through them, I found myself at once in the twilight of close-ranked trees. There was a grass-grown track descending the forest aisle, between hoar and knotty shafts and under branched arches. . . . The darkness of natural as well as sylvan dusk gathered over me. I looked round in search of another road. There was none: all was interwoven stem, columnar trunk, dense, summer foliage—no opening anywhere. (pp. 461–462)

What might seem dark, dank, and depressing to others will be Jane's freely chosen home. As she says here, she looked for another road but "there was none"; she contemplated a departure from nature's grip, and there was "no opening anywhere." But it is acceptance based on protection rather than oppression, not revolt, that is suggested in this description, in which Jane is protected and enclosed by such beneficent natural phenomena as "close-ranked trees," "branched arches," "natural as well as sylvan dusk," and "dense, summer foliage." In her final, freely chosen home, she will not only be far from the false values and demands of society. Above all, she will be free from repressive masters like her two paternalistic male cousins. Instead, she discovers at Ferndean, as at an earlier moment in the novel, that with nature she can replace masters with a beneficent, comforting mother: "Nature seemed to me benign and good; I thought she loved me, outcast as I was; and I, who from man could anticipate only mistrust, rejection, insult, clung to her with filial fondness. To-night, at least, I would be her guest—as I was her child: my mother would lodge me without money and without price" (pp. 345–346).

Landscape as Freedom

In the lengthy middle section of *Jane Eyre* located at Rochester's ancestral home of Thornfield, the narrator tells what is without a doubt a great and moving love story. Nor is there any doubt that one of the principle functions of landscape in the Thornfield section is to heighten the dramatic interest of that love story, to which most of that section's numerous nature scenes bear a highly conspicuous relation. That relation is indeed so conspicuous—and the landscapes themselves so studied and self-conscious—that it is difficult to imagine the fictional author formulating these landscapes merely as fond recollections of past places and happy moments. Instead, I shall argue that they are part of a threefold strategy whereby woman's work is upheld, romance is held at a distance, and freedom is created.

Since Jane's work is closely connected with landscape throughout the novel, it is not surprising that she is careful to maintain the connection at all times in her relationship with Rochester. After all, she is his employee, as she constantly stresses by addressing him as Mr. and Sir and referring to him as "my master." Only in the novel's last chapter and epilogue, after their marriage changes her legal status and her inheritance assures her financial independence, are the deferential terms Sir and Master replaced by the personal terms "my husband" and "my Edward." Until that time, Jane's chief concerns seem to be earning her wages and repaying through small services and attentions such as landscape description whatever kindnesses and favors she has received. Already at Lowood School, she had established her characteristic use of landscape. When Bessie asks whether she has learned to draw while at school, she replies: "That is one of my paintings over the chimney-piece." The narrator adds, "It was a landscape in water colours, of which I had made a present to the superintendent, in acknowledgment of her obliging mediation with the committee on my behalf" (p. 93).

It is in such a spirit that the initial landscapes in the Thornfield section can best be read. Literary sketches of the house and its surroundings, they are like eighteenth-century "prospects" in gardens, paintings, or poems, which celebrate the beauties of a rich landowner's property. Since Jane will later thank Rochester for his kindness to her on several occasions, offering these prospect landscapes to him would be for Jane an appropriate and characteristic form of repayment.

In the most striking of these prospect landscapes Jane, having climbed up to the attic and then to the roof, is presented looking down at Ro-

chester's property from on high, a characteristic perspective for a prospect
and a panoramic survey of the land:

> I surveyed the grounds laid out like a map: the bright and velvet
> lawn closely girding the grey base of the mansion; the field, wide as a
> park, dotted with its ancient timber; the wood, dun and sere, di-
> vided by a path visibly overgrown, greener with moss than the trees
> were with foliage; the church at the gates, the road, the tranquil
> hills, all reposing in the autumn day's sun; the horizon bounded by a
> propitious sky, azure, marbled with pearly white. No feature in the
> scene was extraordinary, but all was pleasing. (pp. 109–110)

As may be expected in a prospect, this landscape stresses the property's
artistic design, its rich if somewhat neglected plantings, its spaciousness
and ancient look, its integration into the surrounding community, which
it both crowns and complements. In this landscape, everything about the
property bespeaks order, tranquillity, and prosperity. Celebrating thus
the aesthetic and social virtues of Thornfield would of course have an
added value since, at the close of the novel, Thornfield exists no more,
having been burned to the ground by Rochester's mad wife: all the more
reason that a remembrance of it by someone who had observed it closely
and lovingly in the past would be of value to its former owner.

It is not surprising that later in the novel, Jane will articulate the feminist sentiments about women's right to meaningul work quoted before
from the same rooftop vantage point. For "work" is precisely what she is
doing when sketching Thornfield for its master. More generally speaking,
work is what Jane learns she and other women must do regardless of their
other choices and options. To be sure, at the beginning of her stay at
Thornfield, she goes up to the roof of the great mansion and dreams of distant places and transcendent goals in life. But increasingly, she comes to
understand that there is a place where she belongs—first Thornfield, later
Ferndean—and that working on, for, or about that place is the only transcendence that is necessary or even possible for women. It is through work
that women acquire freedom.

Jane's attitude to work and home sheds light on the ending of the
novel, notably her marriage to Rochester. It would be wrong, I believe, to
view that marriage as a cessation of work and an abdication of the feminist
values developed elsewhere in the novel. Landscape depiction, after all, is
an exemplary form of work for women; and it is precisely this work that
occupies Jane's time and efforts for the first two years of her marriage because of Rochester's b'indness:

> Literally, I was (what he often called me) the apple of his eye. He saw
> nature—he saw books through me; and never did I weary of gazing

for his behalf, and of putting into words the effect of field, tree, town, river, cloud, sunbeam—of the landscape before us; of the weather around us—and impressing by sound on his ear what light could no longer stamp on his eye. (p. 484)

According to Jane's work ethic and feminist convictions, describing landscape thus constitutes a significant exercise of her faculties and is therefore not without worth. Indeed, it is in many ways the perfect exercise, according to the values promoted in the novel. There is a relationship of near equality and meaningful solidarity between the narrator Jane Rochester and the narratee, her husband, as in the novel there is between the female narrator and the fictional author on the one hand and the female narratee and implied reader on the other. With Jane and her husband, the descriptive activity has a significant social function for both narrative participants: it enables him to endure his misfortunes and her to assert her independence through work. And finally, that activity suits Jane's profoundly social personality especially well. For as Rochester observes when, disguised as a gypsy, he analyzes Jane's mouth: "it was never intended to be compressed in the eternal silence of solitude: it is a mouth which should speak much and smile often, and have human affection for its interlocutor" (p. 212).

In view of these possibilities for personal and social fulfillment in Jane's activities at the end of the novel, I would disagree with Politi's comment that, "Once married, Jane Eyre can step into a light blue dress and spend her entire day talking idly with her husband . . . while income from investment and rents pours in."[14] Jane happens to be wearing her "light blue dress" at the moment that Rochester recovers his sight. Until that time, however, she has not been "talking idly" but talking with a distinct purpose, that of alleviating suffering in another person through the use of her special talents for narrating and describing nature. And after Rochester regains his sight, Jane becomes a mother and works at rearing a child; once that work presumably becomes less demanding, she turns to the further work of writing her autobiography.

A second function of landscape in the Thornfield section is to enable the narrator to propose a model for holding romance at bay, in much the same way that Jane as a character proposed a model of conduct when she kept Rochester's amorous advances in check during the weeks immediately following his first proposal of marriage to her. What is at issue is neither a shallow conformity to social standards of respectability nor a personal denial of normal sexuality. Instead, she recognizes that the myth of romantic love is a trap that induces women to abandon their will, judgment, and independence. Landscape provides an excellent alternative, for through it,

Jane can indulge in emotional feelings while maintaining some psychic and aesthetic distance. The following description of the moon, occasioned by Jane's first meeting with Rochester, provides an apt illustration:

> both my eyes and spirit seemed drawn from the gloomy house . . . to that sky expanded before me, a blue sea absolved from taint of cloud; the moon ascending it in solemn march; her orb seeming to look up as she left the hill tops, from behind which she had come, far and farther below her, and aspired to the zenith, midnight-dark in its fathomless depth and measureless distance: and for those trembling stars that followed her course; they made my heart tremble, my veins glow when I viewed them. (p. 120–121)

Significantly, this highly lyrical and romantic scene is abruptly cut off by the comment: "Little things recall us to earth: the clock struck in the hall; that sufficed; I turned from moon and stars, opened a side-door, and went in." Jane's strength lies precisely in her willingness and even dogged determination to experience love while at the same time controlling its effects on her life; as Rochester also said, when disguised as a gypsy, her mouth "is disposed to impart all that the brain conceives; though . . . it would be silent on much the heart experiences." She will speak of love, but only indirectly, as through landscape. Thus she acknowledges that the stars make her "heart tremble" and "veins glow," but not that the man she has just met has a dramatic effect on her feelings. It is the sky, not her own heart, that expands. The moon moves upward and outward, reaching some ultimate sense of "fathomless depth and measureless distance," not Jane herself seeking to satisfy her transcendent desires through love.

Another romantic episode provides an even sharper sense of Jane's strategy with respect to landscape and love: the summertime scene in which Rochester proposes marriage to her. Wandering alone in the orchard, Jane becomes aware of the characteristic odor of her master's cigar. She attempts first to flee and then to hide:

> Sweet briar and southernwood, jasmine, pink, and rose, have long been yielding their evening sacrifice of incense: this new scent is neither of shrub nor flower; it is—I know it well—it is Mr. Rochester's cigar. I look around and I listen. I see trees laden with ripening fruit. I hear a nightingale warbling in a wood half a mile off . . . that perfume increases: I must flee . . . I see Mr. Rochester entering . . . if I sit still he will never see me.
>
> But no—eventide is as pleasant to him as to me, and this antique garden as attractive; and he strolls on, now lifting the gooseberry-tree branches to look at the fruit, large as plums, with which they are

laden; now taking a ripe cherry from the wall; now stooping towards
a knot of flowers, either to inhale their fragrance or to admire the
dew-beads on their petals. (p.264)

What is most striking here is the half-playful, half-ironic transposition
into nature imagery of the lovers' romantic, even erotic feelings: images of
ripe and luscious fruit, of strong and alluring odors, of enticing light and
contented sounds. To combine the poetic smell of jasmine with the pro-
saic smell of a cigar creates a smiling, not a serious tone. So too does the
implicit reference to *Pamela* noted earlier. The movements of the actors
also have a gently comic effect, with Jane seeming to feign flight more
than actually to attempt it and with Rochester acting out provocative ges-
tures with fruits and flowers, not doubting for a moment that these ges-
tures receive Jane's full attention and understanding. In short, this is a
scene of play romance, which Jane in retrospect, as much as Rochester at
the time, can manipulate and enjoy at will.

A third function of landscape, finally, is to furnish an artistic image of
woman's freedom, a task that is accomplished through the novel's insis-
tent and unifying use of the imagery of birds. (A rough count reveals the
actual naming of some seventeen different species of birds during the
course of the novel.) In view of the thematic centrality of that imagery,
the initial description based on Bewick's *History of British Birds* mentioned
earlier is not out of place. On the contrary, it announces from the start one
of the narrator's chief goals in telling her story, inspiring others to soar as
high and as freely as she did, regardless of the social and material obstacles
they face. And therein lies what Igor Webb aptly terms the "radical
thrust" of *Jane Eyre*. In contrast with *Shirley*, in which Brontë "dramatizes
the split between freedom for one class and repression for another," Webb
finds that *Jane Eyre* "takes the dangerous position of celebrating individual
freedom from the point of view of the working class."[15]

The initial description based on Bewick's *History of British Birds* also
highlights the close connection that bird imagery has with the relationship between Jane and her "master" Rochester. A bird appears in that description which is indeed reminiscent of the main character, the lonely
seafowl. In the same set of pictures is found a "black, horned thing seated
aloof on a rock" (p. 3). What is most like Rochester, here, is less the bird
than the rock itself, a strong and striking feature of the dramatic, mountainous, arctic landscape. The stressing of the rock motif in this description ("solitary rocks and promontories," "the rock standing up alone in a
sea of billow and spray," pp. 2, 3), emphasizes the "rocklike" nature of
*Roche*ster, as in the French word *roche*. It is not surprising that the sublime
figure of Rochester is associated thus with rocks and mountains, if we re-

call the similar association made with such of his predecessors in the literature of images as Montoni and Frankenstein.

The bird imagery in *Jane Eyre* receives its most concentrated and consistent development in the Thornfield section of the novel. Indeed, birds are an integral part of the manor house itself. In Jane's first view of that house, she observes that "its grey front stood out well from the background of a rookery, whose cawing tenants were now on the wing: they flew over the lawn and grounds to alight in a great meadow" (p. 101). Birds also form an integral part of Rochester's conception of Jane. Thus he states on one occasion, "I see at intervals the glance of a curious sort of bird through the close-set bars of a cage: a vivid, restless, resolute captive is there; were it but free, it would soar cloud-high" (p. 145); and later, "Jane, be still; don't struggle so, like a wild, frantic bird that is rending its own plumage in its desperation," to which Jane replies "I am no bird; and no net ensnares me; I am a free human being with an independent will" (p. 270).

For if talk of birds may begin with Rochester, it certainly does not end with him. True, his influence is felt in the story's initial choice of the bird motif. As Jane Millgate observes, "Rochester continues to play with images drawn from Arabian Nights tales, fairy stories and ballads and with references to Jane as some kind of small bird, and no matter how much Jane may overtly resist this indulgence in fantasy, her Gateshead vignettes reveal how completely her imagination has been ensnared."[16] What is important, however, is the fact that as a narrator Jane consciously controls the implications of Rochester's images rather than being controlled by them. Not only is she free as a bird, she is free to conceive of the symbolic values of objects in nature such as birds as she chooses, regardless of whether they have been used and interpreted by others before her in different ways. As a narrator, Jane actually calls attention to the fact that she is thus reusing images taken from books or from the discourses of other narrators, as indeed Rochester took them from Arabian tales and elsewhere. To the attentive reader—or perhaps "rereader" would be more appropriate—it is interesting that the narrator writes at the very beginning of Jane looking at herself in the mirror and seeing a "half fairy, half imp . . . coming out of lone, ferny dells in moors" (p. 9) since the closing sections of the novel take place at *Fern*dean and *Moor* House. What she seems to be saying to the rereader is that she is not afraid to show that her nature images come from Rochester or from books; by using them anew in her story she exercises her freedom and literary control.

There is one further topic connected with bird imagery in *Jane Eyre* and its use to create an image of woman's freedom: the choice of Jane's last name, Eyre, with its studied plurality of associations. Considering this topic requires that we move beyond Jane as either a character or a narrator to that implied fictional author whose close connection to Charlotte Brontë herself was underlined earlier. All of those associations bear a relation to the novel's central theme of freedom developed through bird imagery. Jane gains her economic freedom at the end as an "heir" to an independent fortune, just as she gained her personal freedom as a child by learning to express her "ire" toward unjust masters and by learning to accept her fate in society of being "eerie," a word that appears on a number of occasions in the novel. But there also exists a triad of further associations—with "air," the French pronunciations of "air" and "*r*," and "eyrie" —which, to my mind, shed further light on the feminist treatment of women and landscape in Brontë's novel.

The most obvious association in this triad is that with "air," an association established in a way that is both conspicuous and critically self-conscious. Thus when Rochester calls Jane's beauty "delicate and aerial" she responds, "Puny and insignificant, you mean" (p. 276). When he tells Adèle that Jane is a fairy to be whisked off to the moon, Adèle speaks for her critical teacher in saying, "there is no road to the moon: it is all air; and neither you nor she can fly" (p. 284). When Rochester asks if it is truly Jane, in the flesh, who has come back to him, she responds: "You touch me, sir—you hold me, and fast enough: I am not like a corpse, nor vacant like air, am I?" (p. 465). As with the comparison to a bird, so too with Rochester's false designation of the air as her natural environment, it is Jane, not Rochester, who must give meaning to words and nature imagery.

As obvious as "air" is among the symbolic associations that readers are likely to make with Jane's family name, the second association—with the French pronunciations of "air" and "*r*"—is so obscure as to escape most readers. And yet the novel does call attention to it on one occasion. When Adèle first hears the name, her response is "Aire? Bah! I cannot say it" (p. 104). The perceptive reader will recognize the inaccuracy of this comment, since the French pronunciations for "air" and the letter "*r*" are both identical to "Eyre"; that name would thus be easy for a French speaker to pronounce. Should the inaccuracy then prompt the curious reader to wonder what is special about the French sound "*r*" in the novel, he might discover that all of Jane's masters—Reed, Rochester, and Rivers—have names beginning with a letter that has the same sound as her own name. At a playful, linguistic level, the fictional author is thereby perhaps making a statement that Jane is their equal; that servant and master, poor and rich, are all alike in the airy world of literature.

Still another, similarly obscure association can be discovered in the novel's single reference to an "eyrie," the home of a large bird such as an eagle atop a cliff or mountain. (The French translation of "eyrie" is, incidentally, "aire," the exact spelling of Adèle's version of Jane's name.) This association is especially apt in connection with the association mentioned earlier with "rock" in Rochester's name and the existence of the rookery as a distinguishing part of Thornfield. The reference occurs when Rochester's mad wife Bertha attacks her brother Richard Mason, tearing his flesh with her teeth. His piercing cry on that occasion is described as follows: "whatever being uttered that fearful shriek could not soon repeat it: not the widest-winged condor on the Andes could, twice in succession, send out such a yell from the cloud shrouding his eyrie. The thing delivering such utterance must rest ere it could repeat the effort" (p. 217). Rochester makes "such utterance" when, standing atop Thornfield in flames, he yells "Bertha" to his mad, dying wife, the cloud who has shrouded his "eyrie" for so long and kept him from his desired Jane Eyre. A wide-winged condor in the Andes furnishes an especially apt metaphor for the broad, powerful, rocklike master of Thornfield.

On another and more significant level, however, the description of the condor can be identified with Jane herself, as the conspicuous "ere" that immediately follows "eyrie" perhaps suggests doing. Admittedly both Jane's physical being and her "utterance" may initially seem less dramatic or powerful than Rochester's. The myth of the sublime male hero lingers on in reader's minds as it does in nineteenth-century literature. But Jane challenges the dominance of the male hero, just as she challenges the control over her life by a master: the good master Rochester as much as the less-good master Rivers or the bad master Reed. What she demands is nothing less than the highest of places in the manor house, nothing less than the "eyrie" itself, where the large and powerful birds live. More important than being a bird or flying through the air, then, is having a home, an important bird's home, which she is free to leave but where she chooses to remain. That home is the ultimate realization and embodiment of her very identity.

A logical outgrowth of the above remarks is to address the political implications of the feminist views that are fostered and developed by Jane Eyre the character, the narrator, and the implied fictional author of Brontë's novel. According to a number of critics, most notably Terry Eagleton, the freedom embodied in Jane Eyre is of a decidedly two-sided sort, as is perhaps reflected in the two-faced mythological figure Janus whose name resembles hers. Relevant to that two-sided freedom are the conflictual class values and allegiances that Eagleton discerns in Brontë's novels:

> We find embedded in Charlotte's work, for example, a constant
> struggle between two ambiguous, internally divided sets of values.
> On the one hand are ranged the values of rationality, coolness,

shrewd self-seeking, energetic individualism, radical protest and rebellion; on the other hand lie the habits of piety, submission, culture, tradition, conservatism . . . it is possible to decipher in the
conflicts and compromises between them a fictionally transformed
version of the tensions and alliances between the two social classes
which dominated the Brontës' world: the industrial bourgeoisie, and
the landed gentry or aristocracy.[17]

Jane's notion of freedom, according to Eagleton, must then be viewed
as a conservative compromise. He states, "Independence, then, is an inter-
mediate position between complete equality and excessive docility: it allows you freedom, but freedom within a proper deference."[18] And Jina
Politi goes even farther, to conclude that Jane's retaining the term "Master" in addressing Rochester is symptomatic of a submissive sexist and
even imperialist world view: "The political ideology behind the transfor-
mations of this term will be that people, i.e., races, nations, classes and
women are happy in inequality and have no reason to revolt against the
domination/subordination structure of their social existence so long as
they are free to *choose* their masters and so long as this freedom of choice
hides its exploitative purposes behind the humanitarian guise."[19]

Both Eagleton and Politi underestimate, to my mind, what Webb was
quoted earlier as calling the special "radical thrust" of *Jane Eyre*. Although
it may be true that Brontë held politically ambivalent views which found
expression in her other novels, the ambivalence is far from evident in the
telling of Jane's story. It is not certain, notably, that the term "master" is
treated respectfully and submissively in that story, as Politi suggests, or
that Jane can only conceive of "freedom within a proper deference," as
Eagleton states. Masters come in all sorts in *Jane Eyre* and are treated in all
sorts of ways, from outright rebellion to the establishment of a viable bal-
ance of power, as Jane does with Rochester. But nowhere does Jane become an apologist for the values of the upper classes or a compromiser
with respect to freedom. Jane may love her master at the end of the novel,
but to the extent that she is dependent on him neither for financial support, meaningful activity, nor self worth—to the extent that she has her
own "eyrie" for a home and her own story to tell—she can rightfully say,
"no net ensnares me; I am a free human being with an independent will."

8

Conclusion

When interviewed about how he created a nineteenth-century style in his recent novel, the popular contemporary novelist John Irving is quoted as saying that he "sets atmosphere, and creates a landscape."[1] His remark reflects what no careful reader of nineteenth-century narrative literature would seriously doubt and what I have attempted to indicate in this book: that during the historical period of the novel's full flowering, one of the hallmarks of that genre was the lengthy, highly detailed and symbolic description of nature, the narrative landscape.

Narrative landscape is, however, far more semiotically complex and elicits a far more complex process of reading than is commonly assumed by general readers or even by many literary critics. A concluding discussion of this complex semiotic process itself will make it possible to argue for the desirability of the relational reading of landscape that has been applied throughout this book—to argue not only that readers can read narrative landscape in the relational ways used here but that they thereby obtain a more complete and enriched literary reading of the novel than by other critical approaches.

A specific example of the limitations of one of those other critical approaches can serve to illustrate the need for the complete reading of narrative landscape supplied by the relational reading. In George Lukács's essay "Narrate or Describe," it is assumed that characters act as viewers or spokesmen *for* the author, in other words, that a direct equation can be made between landscape's significance for characters and for the behind-the-scenes entity whose moral and philosophical attitude is what most interests the reader and best assures a novel's coherence. For Lukács, unquestionably, it is the author who provides narrative coherence in description. Thus he states, "the author in his omniscience knows the special significance of each petty detail for the final solution and for the final revelation of character since he introduces only details that contribute to his goals. The reader takes confidence from the author's omniscience and feels at home in the fictional world"; and elsewhere he states in the same vein, "Compositional principles of a poetic work are a manifestation of an author's view of life."[2]

What is most striking, and nefarious for a complete understanding of landscape, is that, in Lukács's view, such "compositional principles" as

the various narrative mechanisms of voice and vision operative in landscape have no textual or intertextual life of their own. Thus they receive
short shrift, and an incomplete reading results: for as the analyses offered
in this book have shown, those mechanisms are highly complex and, when
carefully scrutinized, illuminate landscapes and entire novels. Lukács's
reading is literarily impoverished because, if taken to be strictly subordinate to the author's world view, neither landscapes nor novels themselves
ultimately receive much attention. Worse yet, should narrative mechanisms intrude or make their presence felt—in other words, should the
voice or vision of a narrative participant assume manifest significance
—such a narrative rather than authorial expression of attitude is either
downgraded or denied altogether. Lukács's reaction, for example, to the
phenomenon of a character's state of mind dictating a description is that,
"One state of mind at any moment and of itself without relation to men's
activity is as important or as irrelevant as another."[3] He refuses to see any
connection between the expression of a character's attitude in one descriptive passage and the text as a whole. Thus he condemns the genre in toto,
claiming that in description, "any artistic relationship to the composition
as a whole is lost."[4]

It is in the context of such a critical position, which promotes the author's expression of attitude and downgrades the characters', that Lukács's
diatribe against the technique of point of view can best be understood.
With that technique, he argues,

> Not only is a consequent representation of reality impossible . . .
> but, in addition, there is no possibility of artistic composition. The
> author's point of view jumps from here to there, and the novel reels
> from one perspective to another. The author . . . sinks consciously to
> the level of his characters and sometimes knows only as much about
> situations as they do. The false contemporaneity of description trans-
> forms the novel into a kaleidoscopic chaos.[5]

Mistakenly viewing the technique of point of view as a strictly modern
and modernist aberration, Lukács refuses to look beyond the limiting
confines of an authorial expression of attitude. His refusal thus to valorize
narrative subtlety and complexity—his assumption that the novel is a
simple and direct expression of the author's views—results in a less-than-
adequate reading because it takes the reader outside and away not only
from the landscape but from the novel itself, instead of into its richness
and complexity of meaning.

The special nature and significance of the relational reading adopted in
this book stands out most clearly in the light of Lukács's limited approach
to narrative description. Unlike Lukács's method, which leads *away from*
the text toward the author, the relational way of interpreting landscape is

"formal" and leads *into* the text. By formal, I first of all mean textual, that is, a reading that not only insists upon a consistent context for its relations of significance but requires that the context derive from some major discernible narrative property of the text. And it should be clear that the relational readings used throughout this book provide just such textual connections. Moreover, by formal I also mean linguistic, that is, a reading that is based on fundamental properties of language. Thus in the relational reading, landscape's connection to point of view stems from landscape's role in the enunciatory act; its relation to other descriptive passages stems from its association with narrative syntax; and its relation to socio-economic meaning stems from its link to narrative semantics. The significance of the relational reading is thus apparent. It is a reading that draws upon those elements which, as in language, are always present, together, in all speech acts. And it is on the basis of their common, fundamental status within language that the three relations find their interrelation. They are interrelated in the narrative text as they are within language.

It would perhaps be helpful to spell out in greater detail how the three relations are based on the fundamental properties of language. Concerning the first relation, to narrative point of view, it must be emphasized that formally speaking, what is at issue is not just one single narrative technique. As defined in the first chapter and used subsequently within these pages, "point of view" has been taken here in the broad sense of physical vision, narrative voice, and mental outlook and thus as involving any of a number of different narrative techniques. Only at times has the concern been centered narrowly on the technique of focalization. At other times, the concern has been instead with a first-person narrative voice or with an embedded narrative structure. What is important, then, is not a particular narrative technique but the larger acknowledgment that an eye that sees and a voice that speaks are fundamental properties of landscape description.

With respect to the second relation, to other descriptive passages, it is similarly the case that formally speaking, a number of different narrative techniques are involved. The broad, formal issue is narrative syntax and how landscape fits into and affects the larger significance of the narrative syntagma in which it is placed. Such a syntagma is made up of descriptive passages but also, naturally, of such more standard narrative elements as the unfolding of plot and the development of character. All of these together are inextricably connected, as can be seen most saliently in the foregoing analysis of plot, character, and landscape in Balzac's *Les Chouans*.

As for the third relation, to socio-political meaning, it can best be understood in formal terms as a semantic process. Its importance lies primarily in the way of discovering significance it provides, and only secondarily in the specific meaning or content that is thereby discovered. The process involves uncovering a system of oppositions in a text through which a largely unconscious search for resolutions to conflicts occurs. Objects in nature—trees, mountains, plains, riverbanks, flowers, the sun and moon—occupy crucial places in that oppositional system. And it is through those objects that conflicts frequently find indirect symbolic solutions—solutions that cannot be discovered on the more direct planes of plot resolution or explicit philosophical statement.

In the final analysis, the relational reading resembles other critical approaches to narrative description—be they referential, biographical, psychological, historical, or textual in nature—in one important respect. For like those other approaches, it inevitably involves establishing relations between descriptive phenomena and those contextual elements which furnish the possibility of their significance. It is fitting in this regard to refer to E. D. Hirsch and the distinction he makes between meaning and significance in *The Aims of Interpretation*. Hirsch states that whereas an element can have meaning or content in isolation, significance only arises when that element's use or function in relation to other elements is considered. Understanding the element in itself is possible, but explaining it requires going farther and viewing it relationally.[6]

Hirsch's distinction sheds light on the process of reading landscape both through the relational reading and by other methods. To be sure, in ordinary usage, "significance" and "meaning" can often be used interchangeably, but what is valuable in Hirsch's distinction is the recognition that something important and worthy of a distinctive terminology is involved when a relationship is discovered or established. Thus there is *significance* in landscape when a relation to something else is discovered. It then becomes apparent that more is at issue than *meaning*, that is, the denotative value of the words for plants, trees, rivers, mountains, and the other natural phenomena described.

But if other critical approaches to narrative landscape are similar to the relational reading in establishing connections, those other approaches typically do not highlight and promote the importance of specifically formal associations as does the relational reading. Therein lies its importance. And therein lies, moreover, the promise it offers of extending and enriching other readings, as a brief review of some other approaches to narrative landscape will reveal.

One common approach involves not only establishing relationships among such elements as the modalities of visual orientation or perspective within a single passage but also linking those elements to analogous elements in painting. That approach was discussed in chapter 1 as one of the positive features of a pictorial reading, as practiced in the *explication de texte* or other stylistic analyses. But even dealing with the modalities of point of view or pictorial features in a descriptive passage is not enough to account for the passage's significance in the novel as a whole. The pictorial reading's failure to account for landscape's significance for the larger context of the novel is tantamount to a failure to offer a thoroughgoing interpretation of it as a narrative phenomenon. In that reading, visual movements from one passage to another are as unconnected as the paintings in a museum. By providing a way to connect those passages, the relational reading can prove useful to a pictorial, stylistic type of reading.

The relational reading can similarly enhance a post-structuralist reading of narrative landscape, a type of reading that can be loosely grouped here with the pictorial reading because both eschew the search for a coherent attitude in the novel. What a reader does by looking for such an attitude, according to the post-structuralist position, is to impose a logic on texts that limits their literary diversity and creativity. Thus Jonathan Culler, for example, warns that "as a linguistic object the text is strange and ambiguous. We reduce its strangeness by reading it as the utterance of a particular narrator so that models of plausible human attitudes and of coherent possibilities can be made operative."[7]

Acknowledging "strangeness" can best be seen, however, as a beginning rather than an end in itself. Admittedly, not to assume coherence of expression is to steer clear of the pitfall of an unduly univalent, reductive interpretation. However, not to look for a plausible and coherent attitude in a novel—and instead to cast the narrative process in the exclusive mold of a modernist aesthetics of fragmentation and discontinuity—is tantamount to not interpreting the subgenre of the nineteenth-century novel at all. A more satisfactory and ultimately more enriching position, to my mind, is to read narrative landscape relationally, while at the same time making a place for such clearly crucial post-structuralist notions as strangeness and ambiguity. As the analysis of *Le Lys dans la vallée* has shown, a relational reading does not seek to dismiss ambiguity but rather to situate its workings within a meaningful literary context.

A second critical approach involves placing landscape in the context formed by individual and collective psychological forces, whether the context is drawn along Freudian, Jungian, or Lacanian lines. Although the psychological and psychoanalytic relations that are thereby established are undeniably illuminating for narrative analysis, most critics who consider the psychological type of relation confine their efforts to only that one formal, semantic feature, disregarding the other literary features of narrative texts. Indeed, psychological approaches perhaps have the most to gain from a reading such as the relational one because it highlights specifically literary and textual matters that are notably lacking in psychological readings.

I would add that psychological factors have been stressed on numerous occasions in this book; for indeed, psychological and social contexts are inextricably linked. For example, Starobinski was seen to show how the personal needs and drives of an author like Rousseau dovetail with the social and political issues of his times. And regarding *Paul et Virginie* it was discovered that psychological structures like Eliade's "space at the center of the world" similarly coincide with social structures. Between the structures of the individual and collective minds on the one hand and the structures of language and society on the other, there are surely important differences. Yet, while these differences are important, they are to my mind less important than the profound and inescapable similarities that join the psychological and the social at every turn. There is, in short, no theoretical incompatibility between a psychological reading and a relational reading but rather the promise of a fruitful cooperative endeavor.

A third approach involves landscape's relation to such elements as plot, character, or narrative structure. But although to link description to narrative elements is to practice a kind of formal approach, it is a kind that frequently relegates description to a position of inferiority and thus fails to integrate the description as an equal element into the text as a whole. As was seen in chapter 1, even in structuralist and semiotic writings until recently, description failed to assume the role of equal narrative partner that I have shown it can play. But in order for it to assume that role, its relation to narrative syntax has to be conceived of broadly to include not only such elements as plot or character but also other descriptions. And in fact, landscape's relation to other descriptive passages also turns out to be more important in many cases than its relation to other narrative elements. A relational reading can thus supplement and enrich structuralist and semiotic approaches through its valorization of description itself.

One issue that stands out as especially important with respect to the third approach, and which thus merits some elaboration, is that of symbolism. It is typical of a number of critical schools that can be loosely grouped together and associated with the third approach to deny or denigrate the validity and importance of the processes of symbolism. Thus, for example, American New Critics denounced the so-called "pathetic fallacy" whereby a writer attributes human sentiments to nature. And in a similar spirit, as I mentioned in the first chapter, French New Novelists like Ricardou and Robbe-Grillet adopted a prescriptive critical stance whereby the symbolic links between man and nature typically established in the nineteenth-century novel were found to be simplistic and démodé.

Precisely because it strives to give connotative processes such as symbolism their full measure of validity and importance, the relational reading has the potential for enriching and extending various New Critical, New Novel, or structuralist methods. A decisive example, which has substantially influenced and inspired the relational reading, has been set by Roland Barthes in *S/Z*. Especially noteworthy is Barthes's view that to refuse to read nineteenth-century novels connotatively is to eliminate the distinctive conventions according to which those novels were written and continue to this day to be most commonly read. Barthes points out that if semiotic critics tended initially to ignore connotation, it was largely due to their unwillingness to valorize an implied hierarchy between denotative and connotative meaning. But their refusal, he says, was counterproductive, blocking them as it did from all access to the fundamental system of meaning operative in the nineteenth-century text.

It is also worth mentioning in this context the special sense that Barthes gives to connotation in *S/Z*. Connotation, he states, is "a feature which has the power to relate itself to anterior, ulterior, or exterior mentions, to other sites of the text (or of another text)." Unlike the arbitrary and indeterminate process of association of ideas, which refers to "the system of a subject," connotation "is a correlation immanent in the text, in the texts; or again, one may say that it is an association made by the text-as-subject within its own system."[8] It is not subjective and intuitive because it is based on definable textual processes. Jonathan Culler explains that there can be agreement among readers as to what constitutes an acceptable symbolic interpretation. Restating Barthes's position in *Critique et vérité*, Culler observes that, just as certain sentences are acceptable according to the linguistic conventions of a language, so too certain symbolic interpretations are acceptable according to the poetic conventions of literature.

> Though there is no automatic procedure for determining what is acceptable, that does not matter, for one's proposals will be sufficiently tested by one's readers' acceptance or rejection of them. . . . The meaning of a poem within the institution of literature is not, one might say, the immediate and spontaneous reaction of individual readers but the meanings which they are willing to accept as both plausible and justifiable when they are explained.[9]

Connotation, as defined by Barthes, includes but is not limited to what is commonly designated as symbolism. His definition makes it possible to situate the human element more generally in the process of textuality itself. According to that definition, then, a fundamental part of recovering a text's connotative meaning involves relating descriptive passages to other passages in the novel—Barthes's "anterior, ulterior" mentions "to other sites of the text"—and thus integrating them into the novel as a whole. If they are not thus integrated they will be, as a Marxist might say, dehumanized, that is, disembodied and reified as isolated painterly "scenes" or literary "passages."

Another equally important part of the process of recovering a text's connotative meaning involves relating descriptive passages to other textual instances outside of the novel—Barthes's "exterior mentions" to sites "of another text"—and thus integrating them into the larger field of intertextuality. What must be emphasized, however, regarding both the textual and the intertextual moves is that they are both grounded in the formal bases of enunciation, syntax, and semantics. Because they are formal —because they involve an attention to the text rather than a movement away from it—they provide an enriched and complete reading. Because they are formal, they can avoid the pitfall that Susan Sontag warned against so compellingly in *Against Interpretation*, the danger of symbolic interpretations that prevent critics and readers from seeing the concrete and sensual reality of the text itself. What Sontag really warned against, then, was not interpretation per se but a certain constraining kind of interpretation, which the relational reading seeks to enhance and enrich.

A final critical approach that can be supplemented by the relational reading is the Marxist approach. It is also the approach with which the relational reading, in its fundamentally social and historical orientation, has the closest affinity. Indeed, the objections to Lukács's views voiced earlier should be seen as an indirect expression of that affinity and not as a rejection of it. Lukács and other Marxists have seriously and systematically explored the social significance of novels. That many have done so in too limiting a way, which leaves out important textual factors, attests to the need to enrich the Marxist approach, not to dismiss or depart from its fundamental premises.

As seen earlier, the chief limitation of Lukács's position centers in his dogged recourse to the author's attitudes. It is landscape's relation to the novel's point of view that most obviously and immediately explains how an attitude is expressed in the novel. The literary and political significance of the Republican point of view in *Les Chouans* discussed provides one illustrative example. Regarding point of view, the Marxist approach can also be extended and enriched by the relational reading's acknowledgment that point of view and focalization are not confined to matters of individual psychology and do not bypass the important collective issues expressed in literature. Individual and collective points of view are not incompatible in the literature of images. On the contrary, even when the point of view of a single character is adopted in a novel, that point of view typically embodies that of a larger social group. For example, Mâtho's point of view in *Salammbô* is representative of the social group of the mercenary soldiers and, by implication, of the masses in revolt in nineteenth-century France. The Marxist alternative of confining matters of attitude to the author and to the social and political views he is known to have held fails to shed light on narrative description itself as the relational reading succeeds in doing.

It must also be stressed that landscape's relation to other descriptive passages and to the social and political outlook of the novel are equally important for enhancing and enriching a Marxist criticism: for they extend a relational reading of landscape beyond such limited interpretive methods as examining the perspective in a single passage. By exploring these relations, the reader will look beyond isolated passages to other passages in which an attitude is also expressed, as for example in the opening and closing descriptions in *La Peau de chagrin*. The reader will also envision landscape as participating in the novel's larger system of values, as the description of mountains participates in the complex system of political values in *The Mysteries of Udolpho*.

What is urgently needed now for the novel generally, and for such subgenres as the literature of images specifically, is a Marxist poetics, a narrative theory and practice that is not only seriously and systematically social but also formal and textual. Already, the need has in part been met. As Fredric Jameson was earlier quoted as saying, Lévi-Strauss has set the decisive example of the necessity for proceeding "not by abandoning the formal level for something extrinsic to it—such as some inertly social 'content'—but rather immanently, by construing purely formal patterns as a symbolic enactment of the social within the formal and the aesthetic."[10] Jameson's own writings such as *The Political Unconscious* amply attest to the value and viability of such a method. Yet as I have illustrated in this book, it is necessary to take further steps. Notably, it is necessary to move beyond such obstacles to a completed formal reading as the Marxist bias against point of view or the structuralist bias against symbolism, by reading relationally. Only then will it be possible to grasp the full social and semiotic import of narrative landscape, a hitherto overlooked and undervalued component of the novel.

Notes

Chapter 1. Reading Landscape

1. Honoré de Balzac, *Lost Illusions*, trans. Kathleen Raine (New York: Modern Library, 1967), pp. 369–370.

2. Honoré de Balzac, *The Wild Ass's Skin*, trans. Herbert J. Hunt (Harmondsworth: Penguin, 1977), pp. 266–268. Quotations in English throughout my study are from this edition.

3. E. g., Gérard Genette, *Figures III* (Paris: Seuil, 1972), pp. 183–267; Mieke Bal, "Narration et focalisation: Pour une théorie des instances du récit," *Poétique* 29 (1977), 107-127; Susan Lanser, *The Narrative Act* (Princeton: Princeton University Press, 1981).

4. Fredric Jameson, *The Political Unconscious* (Ithaca: Cornell University Press, 1981), p. 63.

5. Jameson, *Political Unconscious*, p. 77.

6. For another reading that focuses on desire and explores the psycho-sexual connotations of nature description, see Samuel Weber, *Unwrapping Balzac* (Toronto: University of Toronto Press, 1979), pp. 138–149.

7. Jacques Derrida, *Of Grammatology*, trans. Gayatri Spivak (Baltimore: Johns Hopkins University Press, 1976), p. 66.

8. Claude Lévi-Strauss, *The Savage Mind* (Chicago: University of Chicago Press, 1966), p. 17.

9. Jean-Jacques Rousseau, *La Nouvelle Héloïse: Julie, or the New Eloise*, trans. Judith H. McDowell (University Park: The Pennsylvania State University Press, 1968), p. 335. Whenever possible, quotations throughout my study are from this edition (but cf. chap. 2, n. 6).

10. Ernst Robert Curtius, *European Literature and the Latin Middle Ages*, trans. Willard R. Trask (Princeton: Princeton University Press, 1953), p. 195.

11. Renato Poggioli, *The Oaten Flute* (Cambridge: Harvard University Press, 1975), p. 23.

12. Raymond Williams, *The Country and the City* (London: Chatto and Windus, 1973), pp. 48, 53.

13. Daniel Defoe, *Robinson Crusoe* (London: Oxford University Press, 1972), p. 99. Subsequent quotations are from this edition.

14. Northrop Frye, *The Secular Scripture* (Cambridge: Harvard University Press, 1976), p. 38; Henry Knight Miller, *Henry Fielding's Tom Jones and the Romance Tradition* (Victoria, B.C.: English Literary Studies, 1976), p. 11.

15. Henry Fielding, *Tom Jones* (New York: Norton, 1973), pp. 31–32.

16. Williams, *Country and City*, p. 125.

17. Samuel Richardson, *Sir Charles Grandison* (London: Oxford University Press, 1972), p. 273.

18. Samuel Richardson, *Pamela* (Boston: Houghton Mifflin, 1971), p. 405.

19. Philippe Hamon, *Introduction à l'analyse du descriptif* (Paris: Hachette, 1981), pp. 42–45; Michael Riffaterre, "Le poème comme représentation," *Poétique* 4 (1970), 404, 406.

20. Michael Riffaterre, "Système d'un genre descriptif," *Poétique* 9 (1972), 22.

21. Roland Barthes, "L'Effet du réel," *Communications* 11 (1968), 84–89; Hamon, *Introduction à l'analyse*, pp. 53, 55.

22. Michael Riffaterre, "Interpretation and Descriptive Poetry: A Reading of Wordsworth's 'Yew-Trees,'" *New Literary History* 4 no. 2 (1973), 230.

23. Christopher Hussey, *The Picturesque* (New York: Putnam, 1927), p. 12.

24. Barthes, *S/Z*, trans. Richard Miller (New York: Hill and Wang, 1974), pp. 54–56.

25. Alain Robbe-Grillet, *Pour un Nouveau Roman* (Paris: Minuit, 1963), pp. 59–66, 158–161; Jean Ricardou, *Problèmes du nouveau roman* (Paris: Seuil, 1964), pp. 198–205.

26. Gérard Genette, *Figures II* (Paris: Seuil, 1969), pp. 58–59, and Roland Barthes, "Introduction à l'analyse structurale des récits," *Communications* 8 (1966), 9. For a more thorough discussion of the oversimplification entailed in Genette's position, see my "Two Semiological Features of Four Functions of Description: The Example of Flaubert," *Romanic Review* 70 no. 3 (1979), 278–298.

Chapter 2. Conflicts in Nature: *La Nouvelle Héloïse*

1. Jean Starobinski, *Jean-Jacques Rousseau; la transparence et l'obstacle* (Paris: Gallimard, 1971), p. 14.

2. Manfred Kusch, "Landscape and Literary Form: Structural Parallels in *La Nouvelle Héloïse*," *L'Esprit créateur* 17 no. 4 (1977), 349–360.

3. Claude Lévi-Strauss, "The Story of Asdiwal," in *The Structural Study of Myth and Totemism*, ed. Edmund Leach (London: Tavistock, 1967), pp. 1–47.

4. Derrida, *Of Grammatology*, pp. 203, 145.

5. Derrida, *Of Grammatology*, pp. 308, 148.

6. Jean-Jacques Rousseau, *Oeuvres complètes*, II (Paris: Gallimard, Pléiade, 1964), 414. I have translated passages such as this which are not contained in the McDowell translation cited in chapter 1. Single page references after quotations in the text refer to the *Oeuvres complètes*; two page references in the text refer first to the McDowell translation and second to the *Oeuvres complètes*.

7. Jean-Louis Lecercle, *Rousseau et l'art du roman* (Paris: Armand Colin, 1969), p. 119.

8. For a different interpretation of the novel in terms of concentric circles, see Anne Srabian de Fabry, *Etudes autour de La Nouvelle Héloïse* (Sherbrooke: Naaman, 1977), pp. 76–77.

9. Starobinski, *Transparence et obstacle*, p. 105; my translation.

10. Tony Tanner, *Adultery in the Novel* (Baltimore: Johns Hopkins University Press, 1979), pp. 118–119.

11. Vivienne Mylne, *The Eighteenth-century French Novel* (Manchester: Manchester University Press, 1965), p. 183.

12. For a discussion of social equality or inequality in relation to Rousseau's gardens, see Peter V. Conroy, Jr., "Rousseau et le jardin polémique," *CAIEF* (1982), 91–105.

13. Michèle Duchet, "Clarens, 'le lac d'amour où l'on se noie,'" *Littérature* 21 (1976), 81.

14. Starobinski, *Transparence et obstacle*, p. 148.

15. Starobinski, *Transparence et obstacle*, pp. 34–35.

16. Manfred Kusch, "River and Garden: Basic Spatial Models in *Candide* and *La Nouvelle Héloise*," *Eighteenth-century Studies* 12 no. 1 (1978), 13–14.

Chapter 3. Exiled in Exotic Lands: *Paul et Virginie* and *Atala*

1. Jacques-Henri Bernardin de Saint-Pierre, *Paul et Virginie*, ed. Pierre Trahard (Paris: Garnier, 1964), p. xxx.

2. Jameson, *Political Unconscious*, chapter 5.

3. Jacques-Henri Bernardin de Saint-Pierre, *Paul and Virginia* (Cambridge: Riverside Press, 1875), p. 1; François-René de Chateaubriand, *Atala/René*, trans. Irving Putter (Berkeley: University of California Press, 1967), p. 17. Subsequent quotations are from these editions, unless otherwise noted.

4. Mylne, *Eighteenth-century French Novel*, p. 246.

5. Jameson, *Political Unconscious*, p. 210.

6. Albert Memmi, *The Colonizer and the Colonized*, trans. Howard Greenfeld (New York: Orion Press, 1965), pp. 38–39.

7. Memmi, *Colonizer and Colonized*, p. 10.

8. Jean-Paul Sartre, "Orphée noir," in *Anthologie de la nouvelle poésie nègre et malgache de langue française*, ed. Léopold Sédar Senghor (Paris: Presses Universitaires de France, 1948), p. ix.

9. Pierre Barbéris, *René de Chateaubriand* (Paris: Larousse, 1973), p. 43.

10. See Henri Coulet, *Le Roman jusqu'à la révolution* (Paris: Armand Colin, 1967), p. 462. Also, for an analysis of Bernardin's contribution in relation to the tradition of the pastoral novel, see Jean Fabre, *Lumières et romantisme* (Paris: Klincksieck, 1980), pp. 225–257.

11. Mylne, for example, maintains that the frame narrator plays no significant role in the novel and that the first major episode—Paul and Virginie's attempt to help the escaped slave—has no relevance to the main plot: *Eighteenth-century French Novel*, pp. 247, 253.

12. Memmi, *Colonizer and Colonized*, p. 68.

13. Mircea Eliade, *The Sacred and the Profane*, trans. Willard R. Trask (New York: Harcourt, Brace, 1959), p. 21.

14. Eliade, *Sacred and Profane*, p. 26.

15. Ibid.

16. *Paul et Virginie*, ed. Pierre Trahard (Paris: Editions Garnier, 1964), p. 209; my translation.

17. Quoted by Trahard in *Paul et Virginie*, p. 256.

18. Clifton Cherpack, "*Paul et Virginie* and the Myths of Death," *PMLA* 90 no. 2 (1975), 249.

19. Jean-Pierre Richard, *Paysage de Chateaubriand* (Paris: Seuil, 1967), pp. 29, 31.

20. Richard, *Paysage de Chateaubriand*, p. 103.

21. Michael Riffaterre, "Chateaubriand et le monument imaginaire," in *Chateaubriand Today*, ed. Richard Switzer (Madison: University of Wisconsin Press, 1970), pp. 63–81.

22. Dennis J. Spininger, "The Paradise Setting of Chateaubriand's *Atala*," *PMLA* 89 no. 4 (1974), 530–532. Spininger also notes the edenic reference to four rivers in paragraph two.

23. Ibid.

24. Thomas C. Walker, *Chateaubriand's Natural Scenery* (Baltimore: Johns Hopkins University Press, 1946), p. 141.

Chapter 4. Women and Nature:
The Mysteries of Udolpho and *Frankenstein*

1. Edward Malins, *English Landscaping and Literature 1660–1840* (London: Oxford University Press, 1966), chapter 4.

2. A. J. Greimas, "The Interaction of Semiotic Constraints," *Yale French Studies* 41 (1968), 86–105.

3. Jameson, *Political Unconscious*, p. 47.

4. For an application of this method to especially appropriate twentieth-century texts, see my "Meaning in *L'Immoraliste* and *La Symphonie pastorale*," *Kentucky Romance Quarterly* 32 no. 4 (1985), 383–391.

5. Jameson, *Political Unconscious*, p. 165.

6. Ibid.

7. Ann Radcliffe, *The Mysteries of Udolpho* (London: Oxford University Press, 1970), p. 227. All subsequent quotations are taken from this edition.

8. Thomas Middleton Raysor, ed., *Coleridge's Miscellaneous Criticism* (Cambridge: Harvard University Press, 1936), p. 357.

9. Mary Poovey, "Ideology and 'The Mysteries of Udolpho,'" *Criticism* 21 no. 4 (1979), 316–317.

10. Norman H. Holland and Leona F. Sherman, "Gothic Possibilities," *New Literary History* 8 (1977), 284–285.

11. Poovey, "Ideology," p. 326.

12. Daniel Cottom, *The Civilized Imagination* (Cambridge: Cambridge University Press, 1985), p. 37.

13. Coral Ann Howells, *Love, Mystery, and Misery: Feeling in Gothic Fiction* (London: Athlone Press, 1978), p. 48.

14. Holland and Sherman, "Gothic Possibilities," p. 286.

15. Mary Wollstonecraft Shelley, *Frankenstein* (New York: Bobbs-Merrill, 1974), p. 17. All quotations are taken from this edition.

16. Lee Sterrenburg, "Mary Shelley's Monster: Politics and Psyche in *Franken-*

stein," in *The Endurance of Frankenstein,* ed. George Levine and U. C. Knoepfl-macher (Berkeley: University of California Press, 1979), p. 157.

17. U. C. Knoepflmacher, "Thoughts on the Aggression of Daughters," in *The Endurance of Frankenstein,* p. 104.

18. Peter Dale Scott, "Vital Artifice: Mary, Percy, and the Psychopolitical In-tegrity," in *The Endurance of Frankenstein,* p. 174.

19. Daniel Cottom, "Frankenstein and the Monster of Representation," *Sub-stance* 28 (1980), 67.

20. Peter McInerney, "Frankenstein and the Godlike Science of Letters," *Genre* 13 no. 4 (1980), 472.

21. Knoepflmacher, "Thoughts," p. 107.

22. Mary Poovey, "My Hideous Progeny: Mary Shelley and the Feminization of Romanticism," *PMLA* 92 no. 2 (1980), 340.

Chapter 5. Politics and Landscape:
Les Chouans and *Le Lys dans la vallée*

1. Genette, *Figures III,* pp. 183–267; Bal, "Narration et focalisation," pp. 107–127; Lanser, *Narrative Act.*

2. Lanser, *Narrative Act,* p. 141.

3. Fredric Jameson, "The Ideology of Form: Partial Systems in *La Vieille Fille,*" *Sub-stance* 15 (1976), 40.

4. Honoré de Balzac, *The Chouans,* trans. Marion Ayton Crawford (Har-mondsworth: Penguin, 1972), pp. 41, 42. Subsequent quotations are taken from this edition.

5. Honoré de Balzac, *The Lily in the Valley,* trans. Lucienne Hill (London: Elek, 1957), pp. 8, 10. Unless otherwise indicated, subsequent quotations are taken from this edition. When necessary, I have followed the French edition pub-lished by Garnier (Paris, 1966).

6. Jameson, "Ideology of Form," p. 39.

7. Jameson, "Ideology of Form," p. 40.

8. Leo Bersani, *Balzac to Beckett* (New York: Oxford University Press, 1970), p. 27.

9. Reinhard Kuhn, "Collusion of Codes: Portentous Levity in Balzac's *Les Chouans,*" *French Review* 53 no. 2 (1980), 253.

10. Pierre Barbéris, *Balzac et le mal du siècle,* I (Paris: Gallimard, 1970), 778–798.

11. Barbéris, *Balzac,* p. 793.

12. Cited by Moise Le Yaouanc in the introduction to the Garnier edition of the novel, p. lxxxi.

13. O. N. Heathcote, "Time and Félix de Vandenesse: Notes on the Opening of *Le Lys dans la vallée,*" *Nineteenth Century French Studies* 8 (1979–1980), 50–51.

14. Heathcote, "Time," pp. 51, 52.

15. Bersani, *Balzac to Beckett,* p. 54.

16. Fernand Baldensperger, *Le Mouvement des idées dans l'émigration française* (New York: Burt Franklin, 1968), p. 305.

Chapter 6. Transcending History: *Salammbô* and *L'Education sentimentale*

1. For a discussion of these charges, see Anne Green, *Flaubert and the Historical Novel: "Salammbô" Reassessed* (New York: Cambridge University Press, 1981), p. 58.

2. R. J. Sherrington, *Three Novels by Flaubert* (Oxford: Oxford University Press, 1970), p. 125.

3. Jean Levaillant, "Flaubert et la matière," *Europe* 47 (1969), 203–204.

4. Georges Poulet, *Etudes sur le temps humain*, I (Paris: Plon, 1972), 346.

5. Jonathan Culler, *Flaubert: The Uses of Uncertainty* (Ithaca: Cornell University Press, 1974), p. 113.

6. Culler, *Flaubert*, 198–199.

7. Veronica Forrest-Thomson, "The Ritual of Reading *Salammbô*," *Modern Language Review* 67 (1972), 788.

8. Levaillant, "Flaubert et la matière," p. 206.

9. Quoted in Geneviève Bollème, *La Leçon de Flaubert* (Paris: Julliard, 1964), p. 136.

10. Jean Rousset, "Positions, distances, perspectives dans *Salammbô*," *Poétique* 6 (1971), 148.

11. Victor Brombert, *The Novels of Flaubert* (Princeton: Princeton University Press, 1966), p. 102.

12. Victor Brombert, "*L'Education sentimentale*: Articulations et polyvalence," in *La Production du sens chez Flaubert*, ed. Claudine Gothot-Mersch (Paris: U.G.E., 1975), p. 58.

13. Gustave Flaubert, *Correspondence*, V (Paris: Conard, 1929), p. 397.

14. Gustave Flaubert, *Sentimental Education*, trans. Dora Knowles Ranous (New York: New Directions, 1957), p. 20. Subsequent quotations are taken from this edition.

15. Gustave Flaubert, *Oeuvres complètes*, II (Paris: Seuil, 1964), p. 13.

16. Green, *Flaubert and Historical Novel*, pp. 27, 74.

17. Gustave Flaubert, *Salammbo*, trans. J. C. Chartres (London: Dent, 1969), p. 1. Subsequent quotations are taken from this edition.

18. Brombert, *Novels of Flaubert*, p. 115.

19. Sherrington, *Three Novels by Flaubert*, p. 157.

20. Jacques Neefs, "Le Parcours du zaïmph," in *La Production du sens chez Flaubert*, pp. 232–233.

21. Green, *Flaubert and Historical Novel*, p. 74.

22. Green, *Flaubert and Historical Novel*, p. 40.

23. *L'Education sentimentale*, ed. Alan Raitt (Paris: Imprimerie Nationale, 1979), p. 64.

24. Culler, *Flaubert*, p. 102; Brombert, *Novels of Flaubert*, p. 177.

25. Michael Danahy, "Flaubert Describes," *Kentucky Romance Quarterly* 26 no. 3 (1979), 365; and Victor Brombert, "Lieu de l'idylle et lieu du bouleversement dans *L'Education sentimentale*," *CAIEF* 23 (1971), 283.

26. Jean-Pierre Richard, *Littérature et sensation* (Paris: Seuil, 1954), pp. 191–192.

Chapter 7. The Woman's Eye and Voice: *Jane Eyre*

1. Charlotte Brontë, *Jane Eyre* (New York: Modern Library, 1933), p. 113. Subsequent quotations are taken from this edition.

2. See, for example, Rosemarie Bodenheimer, "Jane Eyre in Search of Her Story," *Papers in Literature and Language* 16 no. 4 (1980), 387–402; Janet H. Freeman, "Speech and Silence in *Jane Eyre*," *Studies in English Literature* 24 no. 4 (1984), 683–700; Mark M. Hennelly, Jr., "Jane Eyre's Reading Lesson," *English Literary History* 51 no. 4 (1984), 693–717.

3. Sandra M. Gilbert and Susan Gubar, *The Madwoman in the Attic* (New Haven: Yale University Press, 1979), pp. 49, 50.

4. Goran Hermeran, *Influence in Art and Literature* (Princeton: Princeton University Press, 1975), pp. 45–46.

5. Gilbert and Gubar, *Madwoman*, pp. 76, 69.

6. Bodenheimer, "Jane Eyre," pp. 395, 402.

7. Gilbert and Gubar, *Madwoman*, pp. 75, 82.

8. Sylvère Monod, "Charlotte Brontë and the Thirty 'Readers' of *Jane Eyre*," in *Jane Eyre*, ed. Richard J. Dunn (New York: Norton, 1971), p. 504.

9. Jerome Beaty, "Jane Eyre at Gateshead: Mixed Signals in the Text and Context," in *Victorian Literature and Society*, ed. James R. Kincaid and Albert J. Kuhn (Athens: Ohio University Press, 1984), pp. 183–185.

10. Gail B. Griffin, "The Humanization of Edward Rochester," *Women and Literature* 2 (1982), 125.

11. Jina Politi, "*Jane Eyre* Class-ified," *Literature and History* 8 no. 1 (1982), 65.

12. Cynthia A. Linder, *Romantic Imagery in the Novels of Charlotte Brontë* (New York: Barnes and Noble, 1978), p. 38.

13. Hennelly, "Jane Eyre's Reading Lesson," p. 703.

14. Politi, "*Jane Eyre* Class-ified," p. 65.

15. Igor Webb, *From Custom to Capital: The English Novel and the Industrial Revolution* (Ithaca: Cornell University Press, 1981), pp. 72–73.

16. Jane Millgate, "Narrative Distance in *Jane Eyre*: The Relevance of the Pictures," *Modern Language Review* 63 no. 2 (1968), 318.

17. Terry Eagleton, *Myths of Power: A Marxist Study of the Brontës* (New York: Barnes and Noble, 1975), p. 4.

18. Eagleton, *Myths of Power*, p. 29.

19. Politi, "*Jane Eyre* Class-ified," pp. 58–59.

Chapter 8. Conclusion

1. John Irving, "Guilt and Compassion," *New York Times Book Review* (26 June 1985), p. 25.

2. George Lukács, *Writer and Critic*, trans. A. D. Kahn (New York: Grosset and Dunlap, 1970), pp. 128–129.

3. Lukács, *Writer and Critic*, p. 130.

4. Lukás, *Writer and Critic*, p. 132.

5. Lukás, *Writer and Critic*, p. 133.

6. E. D. Hirsch, *Aims of Interpretation* (Chicago: University of Chicago Press, 1976), pp. 2–3.

7. Jonathan Culler, *Structuralist Poetics* (Ithaca: Cornell University Press, 1975), p. 146.

8. Barthes, *S/Z*, p. 8.

9. Culler, *Structuralist Poetics*, p. 124.

10. Jameson, *Political Unconscious*, p. 63.

Bibliography

Bal, Mieke. "Narration et focalisation: Pour une théorie des instances du récit." *Poétique* 29 (1977), 107–127.

Baldensperger, Fernand. *Le Mouvement des idées dans l'émigration française*. New York: Burt Franklin, 1968.

Balzac, Honoré de. *The Chouans*. Trans. Marion Ayton Crawford. Harmondsworth: Penguin, 1972.

———. *The Lily in the Valley*. Trans. Lucienne Hill. London: Elek, 1957.

———. *Lost Illusions*. Trans. Kathleen Raine. New York: Modern Library, 1967.

———. *The Wild Ass's Skin*. Trans. Herbert J. Hunt. Harmondsworth: Penguin, 1977.

Barbéris, Pierre. *Balzac et le mal du siècle*, I. Paris: Gallimard, 1970.

———. *René de Chateaubriand*. Paris: Larousse, 1973.

Bart, Benjamin F. "Descriptions of Nature in Chateaubriand." In *Chateaubriand Today*, ed. Richard Switzer. Madison: The University of Wisconsin Press, 1970. Pp. 83–93.

Barthes, Roland. "L'Effet du réel." *Communications* 11 (1968), 84–89.

———. "Introduction à l'analyse structurale des récits." *Communications* 8 (1966), 1–27.

———. *S/Z*. Trans. Richard Miller. New York: Hill and Wang, 1974.

Beaty, Jerome. "Jane Eyre at Gateshead: Mixed Signals in the Text and Context." In *Victorian Literature and Society*, ed. James R. Kincaid and Albert J. Kuhn. Athens: Ohio University Press, 1984.

Bernardin de Saint-Pierre, Jacques-Henri. *Paul et Virginie*. Ed. Paul Trahard. Paris: Garnier, 1964.

———. *Paul and Virginia*. Cambridge: Riverside Press, 1875.

Bersani, Leo. *Balzac to Beckett*. New York: Oxford University Press, 1970.

Bodenheimer, Rosemarie. "Jane Eyre in Search of Her Story." *Papers in Literature and Language* 16 no. 4 (1980), 387–402.

Bollème, Geneviève. *La Leçon de Flaubert*. Paris: Julliard, 1964.

Brombert, Victor. "*L'Education sentimentale*: Articulations et polyvalence." In *La Production du sens chez Flaubert*, ed. Claudine Gothot-Mersch. Paris: U.G.E., 1975.

———. "Lieu de l'idylle et lieu du bouleversement dans *L'Education sentimentale*." *CAIEF* 23 (1971), 277–284.

———. *The Novels of Flaubert*. Princeton: Princeton University Press, 1966.

Brontë, Charlotte. *Jane Eyre*. New York: Modern Library, 1933.

Chateaubriand, François-René de. *Atala/René*. Trans. Irving Putter. Berkeley: University of California Press, 1967.

201

Cherpack, Clifton. "*Paul et Virginie* and the Myths of Death." *PMLA* 90 no. 2 (1975), 247–255.

Conroy, Peter V., Jr. "Rousseau et le jardin polémique," *CAIEF* (1982), 91–105.

Cottom, Daniel. *The Civilized Imagination.* Cambridge: Cambridge University Press, 1985.

———. "Frankenstein and the Monster of Representation," *Sub-stance* 28 (1980), 60–71.

Coulet, Henri. *Le Roman jusqu'à la révolution.* Paris: Armand Colin, 1967.

Culler, Jonathan. *Flaubert: The Uses of Uncertainty.* Ithaca: Cornell University Press, 1974.

———. *Structuralist Poetics.* Ithaca: Cornell University Press, 1975.

Curtius, Ernst Robert. *European Literature and the Latin Middle Ages.* Trans. Willard R. Trask. Princeton: Princeton University Press, 1953.

Danahy, Michael. "Flaubert Describes." *Kentucky Romance Quarterly* 26 no. 3 (1979), 359–376.

Deane, C. V. *Aspects of Eighteenth-century Nature Poetry.* New York: Barnes and Noble, 1968.

Defoe, Daniel. *Robinson Crusoe.* London: Oxford University Press, 1972.

Derrida, Jacques. *Of Grammatology.* Trans. Gayatri Spivak. Baltimore: Johns Hopkins University Press, 1976.

Duchet, Michèle. "Clarens, 'le lac d'amour où l'on se noie.'" *Littérature* 21 (1976), 79–90.

Eagleton, Terry. *Myths of Power: A Marxist Study of the Brontës.* New York: Barnes and Noble, 1975.

Eliade, Mircea. *The Sacred and the Profane.* Trans. Willard R. Trask. New York: Harcourt, Brace, 1959.

Fabre, Jean. *Lumières et romantisme.* Paris: Klincksieck, 1980.

Fabry, Anne Srabian de. *Etudes autour de La Nouvelle Héloïse.* Sherbrooke: Naaman, 1977.

Fielding, Henry. *Tom Jones.* New York: Norton, 1973.

Flaubert, Gustave. *Correspondence*, V. Paris: Conard, 1929.

———. *L'Education sentimentale.* Ed. Alan Raitt. Paris: Imprimerie Nationale, 1979.

———. *Oeuvres complètes*, II. Paris: Seuil, 1964.

———. *Salammbo.* Trans. J. C. Chartres. London: Dent, 1969.

———. *Sentimental Education.* Trans. Dora Knowles Ranous. New York: New Directions, 1957.

Forrest-Thomson, Veronica. "The Ritual of Reading *Salammbô.*" *Modern Language Review* 67 (1972), 787–798.

Freeman, Janet H. "Speech and Silence in *Jane Eyre.*" *Studies in English Literature* 24 no. 4 (1984), 683–700.

Frye, Northrop. *The Secular Scripture.* Cambridge: Harvard University Press, 1976.

Genette, Gérard. *Figures II.* Paris: Seuil, 1969.

———. *Figures III.* Paris: Seuil, 1972.

Gilbert, Sandra M. and Susan Gubar. *The Madwoman in the Attic.* New Haven: Yale University Press, 1979.

Green, Anne. *Flaubert and the Historical Novel: "Salammbô" Reassessed.* New York: Cambridge University Press, 1981.

Greimas, A. J. "The Interaction of Semiotic Constraints." *Yale French Studies* 41 (1968), 86–105.

Griffin, Gail B. "The Humanization of Edward Rochester." *Women and Literature* 2 (1982), 118–129.

Guitton, E. *Jacques Delille (1783–1813) et le poème de la nature en France de 1750 à 1820.* Paris: Klincksieck, 1974.

Hamon, Philippe. *Introduction à l'analyse du descriptif.* Paris: Hachette, 1981.

Heathcote, O. N. "Time and Félix de Vandenesse: Notes on the Opening of *Le Lys dans la vallée.*" *Nineteenth Century French Studies* 8 (1979–1980), 47–52.

Hennelly, Mark M., Jr. "Jane Eyre's Reading Lesson." *English Literary History* 51 no. 4 (1984), 693–717.

Hermeran, Goran. *Influence in Art and Literature.* Princeton: Princeton University Press, 1975.

Hirsch, E. D. *Aims of Interpretation.* Chicago: University of Chicago Press, 1976.

Holland, Norman H. and Leona F. Sherman. "Gothic Possibilities." *New Literary History* 8 (1977), 278–294.

Howells, Coral Ann. *Love, Mystery, and Misery: Feeling in Gothic Fiction.* London: Athlone Press, 1978.

Hussey, Christopher. *The Picturesque.* New York: Putnam, 1927.

Irving, John. "Guilt and Compassion." *New York Times Book Review* (26 June 1985).

Jameson, Fredric. "The Ideology of Form: Partial Systems in *La Vieille Fille.*" *Sub-stance* 15 (1976), 29–49.

―――. *The Political Unconscious.* Ithaca: Cornell University Press, 1981.

Kadish, Doris Y. "Meaning in *L'Immoraliste* and *La Symphonie pastorale.*" *Kentucky Romance Quarterly* 32 no. 4 (1985), 383–391.

―――. "Two Semiological Features of Four Functions of Description: The Example of Flaubert." *Romanic Review* 70 no. 3 (1979), 278–298.

Kuhn, Reinhard. "Collusion of Codes: Portentous Levity in Balzac's *Les Chouans.*" *French Review* 53 no. 2 (1980), 248–256.

Kusch, Manfred. "Landscape and Literary Form: Structural Parallels in *La Nouvelle Héloïse.*" *L'Esprit créateur* 17 no. 4 (1977), 349–360.

―――. "River and Garden: Basic Spatial Models in *Candide* and *La Nouvelle Héloïse.*" *Eighteenth-century Studies* 12 no. 1 (1978), 1–15.

Lanser, Susan. *The Narrative Act.* Princeton: Princeton University Press, 1981.

Lecercle, Jean-Louis. *Rousseau et l'art du roman.* Paris: Armand Colin, 1969.

Levaillant, Jean. "Flaubert et la matière." *Europe* 47 (1969), 202–209.

Levine, George and U. C. Knoepflmacher, eds. *The Endurance of Frankenstein.* Berkeley: University of California Press, 1979.

Lévi-Strauss, Claude. *The Savage Mind.* Chicago: University of Chicago Press, 1966.

―――. "The Story of Asdiwal." In *The Structural Study of Myth and To-* ed. Edmund Leach. London: Tavistock, 1967. Pp. 1–47.

Linder, Cynthia A. *Romantic Imagery in the Novels of Charlotte Brontë*. New York: Barnes and Noble, 1978.

Lukács, George. *Writer and Critic*. Trans. A. D. Kahn. New York: Grosset and Dunlap, 1970.

Malins, Edward. *English Landscaping and Literature 1660–1840*. London: Oxford University Press, 1966.

McInerney, Peter. "Frankenstein and the Godlike Science of Letters." *Genre* 13 no. 4 (1980), 455–475.

Memmi, Albert. *The Colonizer and the Colonized*. Trans. Howard Greenfeld. New York: Orion Press, 1965.

Miller, Henry Knight. *Henry Fielding's Tom Jones and the Romance Tradition*. Victoria, B.C.: English Literary Studies, 1976.

Millgate, Jane. "Narrative Distance in *Jane Eyre*: The Relevance of the Pictures." *Modern Language Review* 63 no. 2 (1968), 315–319.

Monod, Sylvère. "Charlotte Brontë and the Thirty 'Readers' of *Jane Eyre*." In *Jane Eyre*, ed. Richard J. Dunn. New York: Norton, 1971. Pp. 496–507.

Mornet, Daniel. *Le Sentiment de la nature en France de Jean-Jacques Rousseau à Bernardin de Saint-Pierre*. New York: Burt Franklin, 1971.

Mylne, Vivienne. *The Eighteenth-century French Novel*. Manchester: Manchester University Press, 1965.

Neefs, Jacques. "Le Parcours du zaïmph." In *La Production du sens chez Flaubert*, ed. Claudine Gothot-Mersch. Paris: U.G.E., 1975. Pp. 227–241.

Poggioli, Renato. *The Oaten Flute*. Cambridge: Harvard University Press, 1975.

Politi, Jina. "*Jane Eyre* Class-ified." *Literature and History* 8 no. 1 (1982), 56–66.

Poovey, Mary. "Ideology and *The Mysteries of Udolpho*." *Criticism* 21 no. 4 (1979), 307–330.

———. "My Hideous Progeny: Mary Shelley and the Feminization of Romanticism." *PMLA* 92 no. 2 (1980), 332–347.

Poulet, Georges. *Etudes sur le temps humain*, I. Paris: Plon, 1972.

Radcliffe, Ann. *The Mysteries of Udolpho*. London: Oxford University Press, 1970.

Raysor, Thomas Middleton, ed. *Coleridge's Miscellaneous Criticism*. Cambridge: Harvard University Press, 1936.

Ricardou, Jean. *Problèmes du nouveau roman*. Paris: Seuil, 1964.

Richard, Jean-Pierre. *Littérature et sensation*. Paris: Seuil, 1954.

———. *Paysage de Chateaubriand*. Paris: Seuil, 1967.

Richardson, Samuel. *Pamela*. Boston: Houghton Mifflin, 1971.

———. *Sir Charles Grandison*. London: Oxford University Press, 1972.

Riffaterre, Michael. "Chateaubriand et le monument imaginaire." In *Chateaubriand Today*, ed. Richard Switzer. Madison: University of Wisconsin Press, 1970. Pp. 63–81.

———. "Interpretation and Descriptive Poetry: A Reading of Wordsworth's 'Yew-Trees.'" *New Literary History* 4 no. 2 (1973), 229–256.

———. "Le poème comme représentation." *Poétique* 4 (1970), 401–418.

———. "Système d'un genre descriptif." *Poétique* 9 (1972), 15–30.

Robbe-Grillet, Alain. *Pour un Nouveau Roman.* Paris: Minuit, 1963.

Rousseau, Jean-Jacques. *La Nouvelle Héloïse: Julie, or the New Eloise.* Trans. Judith H. McDowell. University Park: The Pennsylvania State University Press, 1968.

———. *Oeuvres complètes*, II. Paris: Gallimard, Pléiade, 1964.

Rousset, Jean. "Positions, distances, perspectives dans *Salammbô*." *Poétique* 6 (1971), 145–154.

Sartre, Jean-Paul. "Orphée noir." In *Anthologie de la nouvelle poésie nègre et malgache de langue française*, ed. Léopold Sédar Senghor. Paris: Presses Universitaires de France, 1948.

Scholes, Robert and Robert Kellogg. *The Nature of Narrative.* London: Oxford University Press, 1966.

Shelley, Mary Wollstonecraft. *Frankenstein.* New York: Bobbs-Merrill, 1974.

Sherrington, R. J. *Three Novels by Flaubert.* Oxford: Oxford University Press, 1970.

Spininger, Dennis J. "The Paradise Setting of Chateaubriand's *Atala*." *PMLA* 89 no. 4 (1974), 530–536.

Starobinski, Jean. *Jean-Jacques Rousseau; la transparence et l'obstacle.* Paris: Gallimard, 1971.

Tanner, Tony. *Adultery in the Novel.* Baltimore: Johns Hopkins University Press, 1979.

Texte, Joseph. *Jean-Jacques Rousseau and the Cosmopolitan Spirit in Literature.* Trans. J. W. Matthews. New York: Steckert, 1929.

Walker, Thomas C. *Chateaubriand's Natural Scenery.* Baltimore: Johns Hopkins University Press, 1946.

Webb, Igor. *From Custom to Capital: The English Novel and the Industrial Revolution.* Ithaca: Cornell University Press, 1981.

Weber, Samuel. *Unwrapping Balzac.* Toronto: University of Toronto Press, 1979.

Williams, Raymond. *The Country and the City.* London: Chatto and Windus, 1973.

Index